P9-DEI-996

ON THE ORIGINS OF SPORTS

ON THE ORIGINS OF SPORTS

The Early History and Original Rules of Everybody's Favorite Games

GARY BELSKY & NEIL FINE

NEW YORK

Library of Congress Cataloging-in-Publication Data
Names: Belsky, Gary.
Title: On the origins of sports / Gary Belsky and Neil Fine.
Description: New York : Artisan, [2016] | Includes bibliographical references and index.
Identifiers: LCCN 2015034241 | ISBN 9781579656843
Subjects: LCSH: Sports—History.
Classification: LCC GV576 .B375 2016 | DDC 796--dc23 LC record available at
http://lccn.loc.gov/2015034241

Design by Jacob Covey

Published by Artisan
A division of Workman Publishing Company, Inc.
225 Varick Street
New York, NY 10014-4381
artisanbooks.com

Published simultaneously in Canada by Thomas Allen & Son, Limited

Printed in China

First printing, March 2016

10 9 8 7 6 5 4 3 2 1

For my great-nephews and -nieces—
Noa, Yani, Zay, Ayla, Elijah, Liam, and Riley—
a book about whom would be called
On the Origins of Joy.

—G. B.

For Sharlene, because she keeps my game
from tumbling into chaos.

—N. F.

CONTENTS

INTRODUCTION

BECAUSE EVERYTHING HAS TO START SOMEWHERE

IN THE BEGINNING WAS THE BALL . . . OR PIG'S BLADDER . . . or lump of peat . . . or pie tin. But then what?

The sports world roils with thousands of questions: Who is the greatest quarterback of all time? Why does a curveball curve? Why isn't the United States very good at cricket? But the one question seldom asked is the most basic of all: How did we get here?

And, frankly, that's more than a little bewildering when one considers the importance of sport in modern society. Wars have been started over it, cities set aflame because of it. Treasuries have been emptied, marriages ended, murders committed. Today few of us are shocked—or even upset—when governments vie maniacally (not to mention underhandedly) for the rights to host money-losing mega-events like the Olympics or the World Cup.

This passion, of course, is completely understandable: it is established fact that self-worth is directly related to one's favorite team's winning percentage. (Or maybe that's just us.) More to the point, the outsize attention humans in all cultures devote to sports makes sense on a primal level. We are tribal by nature—genetically programmed to define "us" by "them"—and few things make that task easier than team jerseys. Sports have long been a source of identity and pride among our species, the gauntlet through which so many of us bond with others, test our abilities, and prove our loyalty. But who can truly claim to be a fan of a game if they don't understand its provenance?

To paraphrase Santayana: those who ignore history are doomed to repeat that silly story about Abner Doubleday inventing baseball.

Helping true fans avoid such faux pas is the purpose of this book, in which we get to the bottom of it all. For the first time, the kick-starting rules of the world's most popular sports are identified and collected in a single volume, along with the story of how those dictates came to be, and how the playing of these games has changed over decades or centuries. What caused the split between soccer and rugby (then rugby and football)? How did we get from a shepherds' cure for boredom to golf's British Open? Who thought to include dribbling in basketball? Knowing the history and lore of our favorite sports can only enhance our experience of watching or competing in them. Maybe, too, understanding the journeys from ancient amusements to modern spectacles will even help us to connect with the fan in the jersey next to us. Unless he's wearing a different one than we are. Then screw that guy.

AUTHORS' NOTE

We took great care assembling the rules and histories in this book, doing our best to cover the world's most popular spectator and participatory sports. That said, a sport is included only if we were able to identify a set of rules that people with more of a vested interest than us—historians, sport founders, and other experts—recognize as the operating system for the primary version played today. (Wrestling is our exception that proves the rule; the rules we chose have a unique genesis.) Some well-attended sports like thoroughbred racing and Formula One were left out because, try as we might, we couldn't pin down the set of rules that launched them.

We annotated the rules for clarity, and also to log the most important changes and interesting developments that have transpired since their inception. Nonetheless, observant readers will notice that most of the original rules don't even bother to explain the purpose of the game. Back in the day, rule makers were usually writing for people who already knew how to play. Their purpose was to standardize procedures and conduct to avoid fights that often arose when athletes from different schools or towns got together to kick around or swat at a ball (or one another, for that matter).

For nearly every sport, we transcribed the rules in their entirety. Thank the British for the fact that the original rules of most modern sports are laid out in English (and see page 63 to learn why). Of course, many of the source documents date from 100 to 250 years ago, so the language may seem odd to a modern reader. Still, we generally left words and punctuation as we found them, although we fixed typesetting and spelling errors. We made a similar judgment call when identifying which version of a sport—the NBA's for basketball, say, or rugby union over rugby league—should guide our commentary.

Finally, in condensing centuries of history into short, informative, and (we hope) entertaining tales, we undoubtedly omitted notable individuals, important events, and crucial dates. For these and any other transgressions, we beg forgiveness. Rules are made to be broken, but we did try to toe the line.

BASEBALL

BOYS AND GIRLS—NOT TO MENTION MEN AND WOMEN—have been hitting balls with sticks for millennia, either for fun or as part of a religious ritual. Images on ancient temple walls show the Egyptians playing a stick-and-ball game called *seker-hemat* as early as 2400 BC. It's worth remembering this as we consider the long-fought intellectual battles over the beginnings of baseball, which on New World shores is deemed to be a uniquely American creation.

In reality, one of the earliest known references to "base-ball" appears in a 1744 English publication, *A Little Pretty Pocket-Book*. Yes, thirty-two years before the signing of the Declaration of Independence, a British poem titled "Base-Ball" featured the lines: "The *Ball* once struck off / Away flies the *Boy* / To the next destin'd post / And then Home with Joy." An accompanying engraving shows three youths engaged in what appears to be "stoolball," a similar game from southern England that dates to at least the eleventh century and is thought to have been created by milkmaids who used overturned stools as wickets, the precursors to bases. The British developed lots of stick-and-ball games over the centuries, including cricket and rounders.

So why do so many people continue to believe that a Union general named Abner Doubleday invented baseball? It's a convoluted story, one to which Doubleday himself never made claim. The West Point graduate and Civil War hero was declared baseball's prime mover by the Mills

Commission, a group of "experts" convened by the sporting goods magnate Albert Spalding in 1905 to establish the game's American provenance. Even at the time, the notion of Doubleday as the sport's creator was absurd. A pair of letters—written by another Abner, surnamed Graves—supported the Doubleday creation myth, which went like this: One day around 1840 Doubleday sketched a diamond in the dirt of a Cooperstown, New York, street, marked player positions, coined the term "baseball," and established all the rules. Never mind that Graves was six years old in 1840, spent time in an insane asylum, and never produced conclusive evidence to support his claim. Americans love a patriotic legend. Thus Cooperstown was ensconced as baseball's birthplace, home to Doubleday Field and the National Baseball Hall of Fame (into which, tellingly, the man himself has not been inducted).

The true origins of the "American" game, then: The United States has always been a country of immigrants, and many of them brought their own recreations here. We now know that forms of baseball were played on farms in New England in the 1700s. By the 1800s, as cities like New York, Philadelphia, and Boston prospered, a professional class emerged that had the opportunity for leisure. Those citizens formed social clubs that often centered on their old-country games.

Not surprisingly, the unwritten rules for these games differed from club to club and region to region, which made playing one another difficult. (Anyone who thinks the Red Sox–Yankees rivalry is fierce never tried to get New Yorkers to play the "Massachusetts game.") People also gambled on this erstwhile kids' game, which made it decidedly interesting for adults and hastened the need for uniformity. In 1845 Alexander Cartwright, a founder of New York's Knickerbocker Base Ball Club, put on paper the rules his club followed. Whether these are the first rules of baseball or simply the earliest recorded is hard to say. Then again, whether baseball is an all-American game or some kind of international hybrid is beside the point. Today there are more than 120 national governing bodies in the International Baseball Federation. All of them, more or less, play a game that hews to the Knickerbocker rules.

"RULES AND REGULATIONS OF THE KNICKERBOCKER BASE BALL CLUB" (1845)

RULES	NOTES
1st **Members must strictly observe the time agreed upon for exercise, and be punctual[1] in their attendance.**	*1. Members of the Knickerbocker Base Ball Club often had to decamp to New Jersey to find a suitable field of play. They didn't want to boat across the Hudson River only to discover that there weren't enough players to field two teams.*
2nd **When assembled for exercise, the President, or in his absence the Vice-President, shall appoint an Umpire,[2] who shall keep the game in a book provided for that purpose,[3] and note all violations of the By-Laws and Rules during the time of exercise.**	*2. Umpiring was an amateur gig until 1876 (when the National League instituted a per-game rate of $5, payable by the home team) and a one-man operation until the turn of the century (when a second umpire was added). A four-man crew was introduced at the 1909 World Series, but only for the postseason; regular-season quartets didn't hit the diamond until 1952.* *3. The box score as modern fans know it was invented in 1859 by the sportswriter Henry Chadwick, who was himself sometimes called the "father of baseball." (Chadwick never warmed to the honor, arguing, "Baseball never had no 'fadder'; it jest growed.")*
3rd **The presiding officer shall designate two members as Captains, who shall retire and make the match to be played, observing at the same time that the players put opposite to each other should be as nearly equal as possible, the choice of sides to be then tossed for,[4] and the *first in hand*[5] to be decided in like manner.**	*4. A coin was tossed.* *5. "First in hand" means the first team up to bat, "hands" being innings. Not until the late 1880s did it become common practice for the visiting team to bat first.*

RULES	NOTES
∞ *4th* ∞ **The bases shall be from "home"[6] to second base, forty-two paces;[7] from first to third base, forty-two paces, equidistant.**	*6. Back in the day, home was round—hence home plate—before morphing into first a diamond and then, around the turn of the twentieth century, the five-cornered beauty it is today.* *7. A "pace" in 1845 was the vague measure of a man's step, or roughly 3 feet. That put the distance across the diamond at 126 feet, give or take, and the distance between consecutive bases at a tad over 89 feet—very close to 90 feet, which has been the standard since the 1850s.*
∞ *5th* ∞ **No stump match[8] shall be played on a regular day of exercise.**	*8. An unofficial or truncated version of the game. Basically, the rule makers didn't want players to get hurt in a game that didn't count.*
∞ *6th* ∞ **If there should not be a sufficient number of members[9] of the Club present at the time agreed upon to commence exercise, gentlemen not members may be chosen in to make up the match, which *shall not be broken up* to take in members that may afterward appear; but, in all cases, members shall have the preference, when present, at the making of the match.**	*9. That number wasn't nine until 1857, when rules were formalized at a convention in New York. In fact, there was an early intraclub rebellion among Knickerbockers about appropriate squad size. Those pushing for eighteen-man teams left the club when the faction pushing for a lower number prevailed.*
∞ *7th* ∞ **If members appear after the game is commenced, they may be chosen in if mutually agreed upon.**	

RULES | NOTES

∞ 8th ∞

The game [is] to consist of twenty-one counts, or aces;[10] but at the conclusion an equal number of hands[11] must be played.

10. In other words, the first to score twenty-one wins! Aces—probably a card-playing reference, like twenty-one—was eventually changed to the cricket term of "runs."

11. Games were standardized at nine innings in 1857.

∞ 9th ∞

The ball must be pitched, and not thrown,[12] for the bat.

12. A distinction is being made here between overhand and underhand tosses. The point of the pitch was to serve the ball to the batter, making it as easy as possible to hit, thereby leaving his fate to the fielders. Pitches transformed into overhand defensive weapons in 1884. In the Knickerbocker game, anyway. In the Massachusetts game—which disappeared as the New York game spread and evolved—pitchers delivered overhand from the start.

∞ 10th ∞

A ball knocked out [of] the field,[13] or outside the range of the first or third base, is foul.

13. That's right, what is now a home run was at first a foul. The reason is purely situational: the regular playing area—Elysian Fields, located in Hoboken, New Jersey—abutted the Hudson River. When balls were hit out of bounds, they landed in the water. Balls were expensive, so irretrievable shots were discouraged.

∞ 11th ∞

Three balls being struck at and missed[14] and the last one caught, is a hand out;[15] if not caught is considered fair, and the striker bound to run.

14. It wasn't until 1858 that a batter (the striker) could be called out on a hittable pitch—a rule instituted as a punishment for batters who refused to swing at anything—but only after a warning from the ump.

15. Here and elsewhere in these rules, "hand out" refers to an out of any kind.

RULES	NOTES
∞ *12th* ∞ **If a ball be struck, or tipped, and caught, either flying or on the first bound,[16] it is a hand out.**	*16. Until 1864, anyway, for balls in play. Foul balls caught on a bounce continued to be outs until 1883.*
∞ *13th* ∞ **A player running the bases shall be out, if the ball is in the hands of an adversary on the base, or the runner is touched with it before he makes base; it being understood, however, that in no instance is a ball to be thrown at him.[17]**	*17. This admonishment seems obvious—they don't call it hardball for nothing—but in rounders and other stick-and-ball games (not least the Massachusetts game), fielders were allowed to throw at runners to get them out.*
∞ *14th* ∞ **A player running who shall prevent an adversary from catching or getting the ball before making his base, is a hand out.**	
∞ *15th* ∞ **Three hands out, all out.**	
∞ *16th* ∞ **Players must take their strike[18] in regular turn.**	*18. An at bat in this case, but as with "hand," "strike" had multiple meanings in the early days. In these rules, it could also mean a hit ball. In the 1850s the term began to take on its current meanings, i.e., a swing and a miss; a foul ball; or a pitch the batter lets pass that the umpire deems to have been in a hittable zone.*

RULES | NOTES

∞ *17th* ∞

All disputes and differences relative to the game, to be decided by the Umpire,[19] from which there is no appeal.

19. "Umpire" descends from the Middle English "noumpere," which in turn descends from the Old French "nonper," or "not equal." This etymology likely has less to do with umpires being a class above than with their task of acting as mediators of disputes. Indeed, "noumpere" denoted an arbitrator.

∞ *18th* ∞

No ace or base can be made on a foul strike.[20]

20. Today a runner may, after tagging up, advance and score on a caught foul pop.

∞ *19th* ∞

A runner cannot be put out in making one base, when a balk is made by the pitcher.

∞ *20th* ∞

But one base allowed when a ball bounds out of the field when struck.[21]

21. The modern ground rule calls for two bases.

CATCH THIS
EVOLUTION OF THE BASEBALL GLOVE

The need for hand protection when fielding a very hard flying or bouncing ball may seem self-evident to players and fans today, but it was not so obvious to the pioneers of America's first true national game.

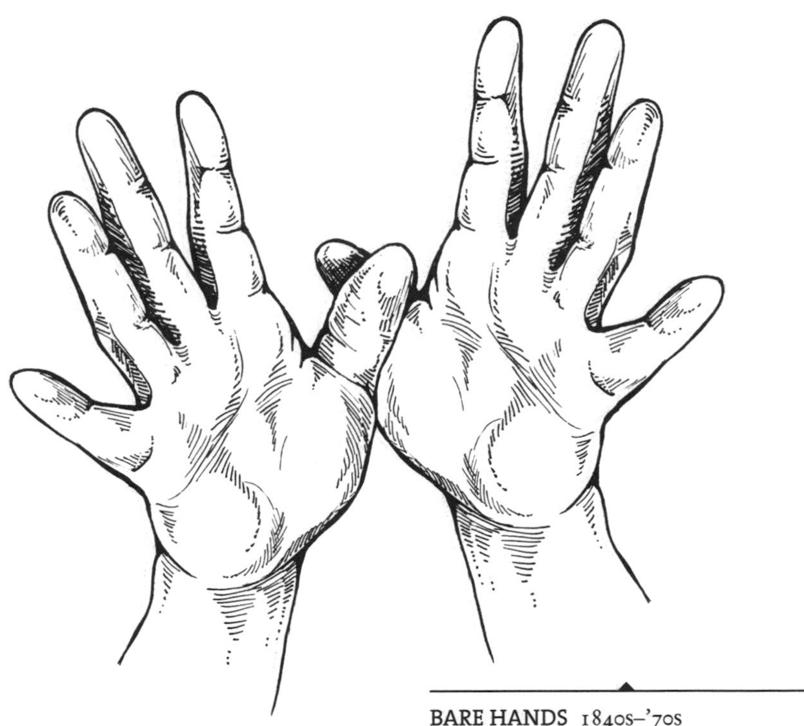

BARE HANDS 1840s–'70s
Early on, baseball was played barehanded. The implementation of glove use was slow, because no one had invented gloves for the purpose of playing baseball, and it was thought that tough guys didn't need them.

For the first seventy-five years of the modern game's history, most players left their gloves in the field at their position when their side came in to bat. For many reasons—not least because opposing players could trip on the left-behind equipment—Major League Baseball banned the practice in 1954.

FINGERLESS GLOVE 1870s

Cincinnati Red Stockings catcher Doug Allison was likely the first professional to use a glove, in 1870, as protection for an injured hand. It started no trend, however. When St. Louis Brown Stockings first baseman Charles Waitt donned a fingerless leather pair (to maintain dexterity) in 1875, he was mocked. Gloves began to catch on only when the highly regarded Chicago White Stockings first baseman (and future sporting goods magnate) Albert Spalding copied Waitt two years later. By the end of the nineteenth century, all pros wore them.

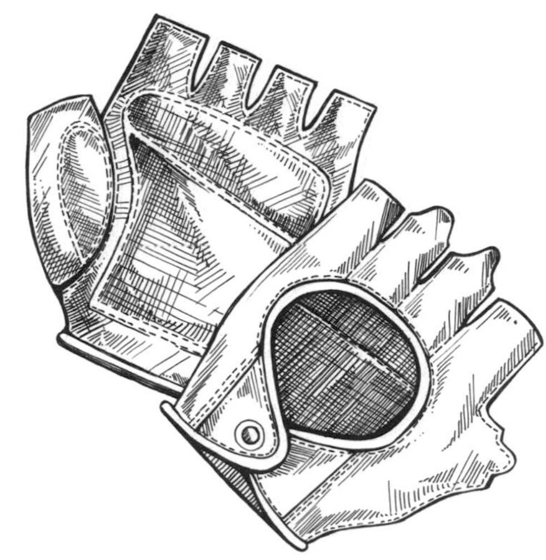

PADDED GLOVE WITH FINGERS 1880s

In 1883 the New Hampshire glove maker Draper and Maynard developed the first padded glove, which had full fingers. It took nearly seventy more years for players and manufacturers alike to abandon the idea that baseball gloves should resemble hands.

FIRST BASEMAN'S GLOVE 1910s

Although most baseball players (like most people) are right-handed, many first basemen are left-handed, because they can throw to other fielders without having to make a full turn and it is easier for them to field to their right, where most fair balls will be hit.

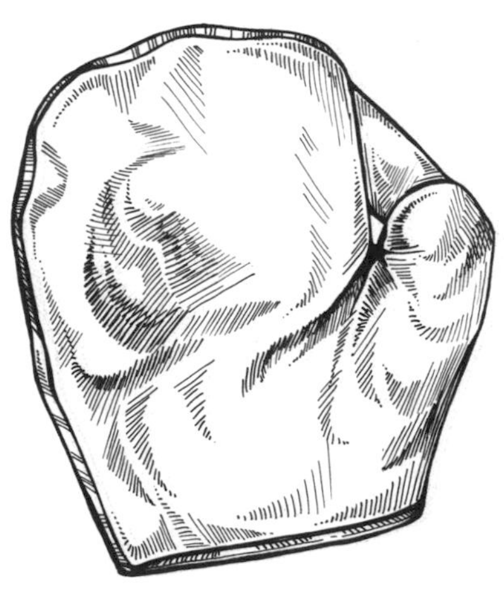

BILL DOAK MODEL 1920s

Bill Doak, a St. Louis Cardinals pitcher, is generally credited as the father of the modern baseball glove. In 1919 he suggested to sporting-goods maker Rawlings that flexible braided webbing be created between the thumb and first finger, elongating the natural catching "pocket."

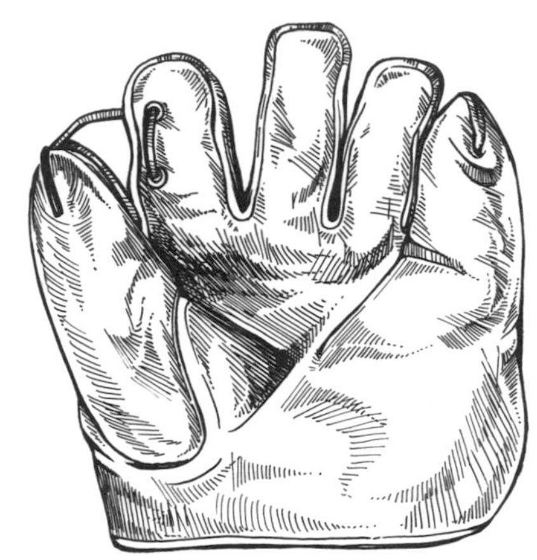

WILSON A2000 1950s

The Wilson A2000, which debuted in 1957, was the first glove to feature a hinge (of sorts) through the palm, which allowed it to close easily around the ball. Just as crucial as the technological innovation was the success of this model; its wide adoption finally liberated manufacturers and players from the idea that the basic glove should be modeled to look like a padded hand.

Most baseball gloves are made of cowhide, but the skins of pigs, deer, elk, buffalo, and even kangaroo are sometimes used. And while most mitts are brown or black, many colors have come into and gone out of fashion, including green, red, and blue. Major League Baseball forbids the use of white and gray gloves, or any other color deemed to be distracting by an umpire.

Modern Glove Varieties

Major League Baseball players are technically not obligated to wear a glove when playing the field, but all do. Here are the five basic types of specialized gloves.

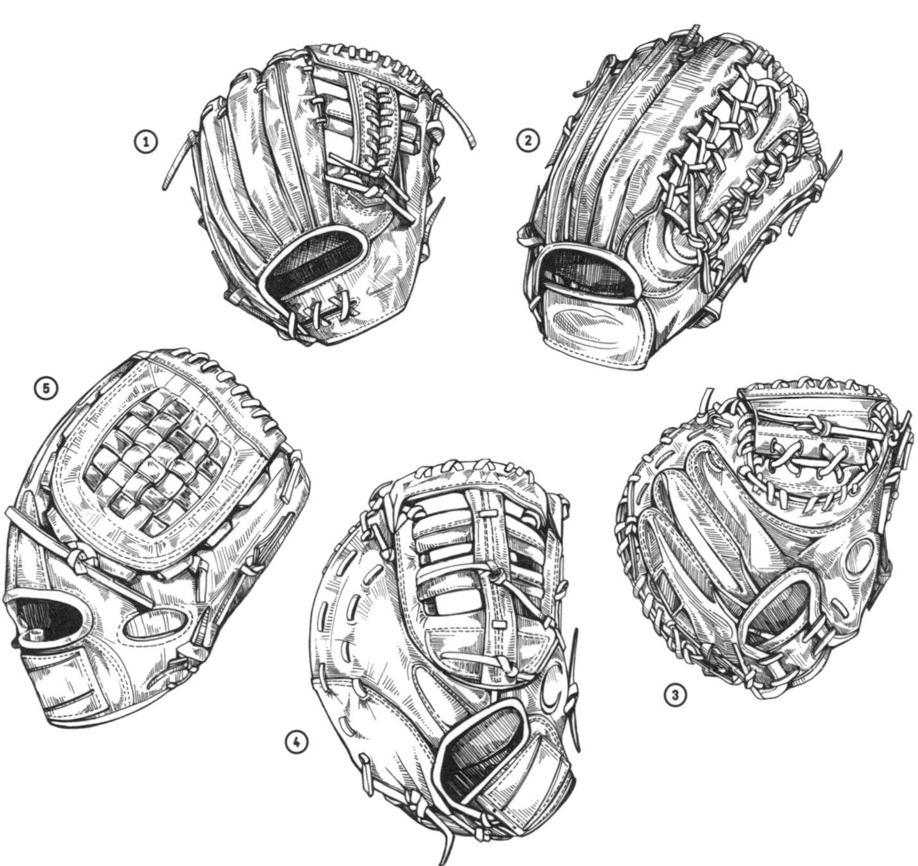

① **INFIELDER'S GLOVE** Features a shallow pocket to allow for quick retrieval of fielded balls. ② **OUTFIELDER'S GLOVE** Longer than an infielder's glove, with deep pockets that make it easier to catch and hold on to balls while running or diving. ③ **CATCHER'S MITT** Least flexible glove, owing to the extra padding necessary to protect the hand from 100-mph pitches. ④ **FIRST BASEMAN'S MITT** Lacks individual finger slots and is typically longer and wider than other infielders' gloves, making it easier to scoop low throws. ⑤ **PITCHER'S GLOVE** Typically features tight webbing that helps conceal from batters the grip that determines the type of pitch about to be thrown.

BASKETBALL

MOST SPORTS BEGIN AS A CASUAL MARRIAGE OF TOO MUCH time on some kids' hands and an available implement or two. These games are played flexibly, motivated only by the twin goals of fun and distraction, making the answer to "How do you play?" almost always a function of where, when, and by whom the question is asked (if an adult, a response that omits the dangerous parts; if a child, some version of "Leave now before you get hurt!"). The rules of any of these protosports tend to evolve organically—through years or even centuries—until they are finally codified by people who have been playing a particular version of the game for most of their lives.

That is the origin story for 99 percent of organized sports in the world, especially the most familiar ones. But there is a notable exception: basketball, today one of the most popular international sports, was pretty much created in a couple of weeks, born whole from the mind of a single man.

In December 1891 the director of physical education at the YMCA International Training School in Springfield, Massachusetts, charged one of his employees, a thirty-year-old Canadian named James Naismith, with the task of coming up with an indoor "athletic distraction" that was "not too rough" to occupy students through the fast-descending New England winter. Naismith pondered existing game options but appropriated from virtually none of them. Instead, after thinking it over for a few days, he typed up a set of instructions on two sheets of paper that he affixed to a wall at the Y. The title at the top of the first page read "Basket Ball."

Naismith considered wrestling and gymnastics to be superior forms of physical education to his invention, but his game offered less hazardous contact than the former and more of a workout than the latter. His game, the object of which was to throw a ball into one of two peach baskets nailed to an elevated track 10 feet above the hardwood gym floor, was an instant hit, in spite of one obvious nuisance: after each point was scored, the balls (generally of the soccer variety) had to be retrieved from the baskets, either by ladder or by someone on the track above. That inefficiency was soon rectified; a hole was cut in the basket bottoms so the balls could be knocked out with a stick. (Eventually the whole bottom went.)

Springfield could not contain the game. YMCAs were spreading across the United States and taking basketball with them. Colleges and high schools also embraced the sport—for men and women—not least because it was weatherproof. Within a decade, basketball was one word and being played everywhere. By 1904 the Summer Olympics in St. Louis featured it as a demonstration sport.

Soon after his breakthrough, Naismith moved to Denver, where he earned a degree in medicine. But he couldn't escape the reach of what he had wrought. In 1898 the good doctor relocated to Lawrence, Kansas, to be the chapel director and physical education instructor at the local university. His reputation having preceded him, he was asked to start a school team, which he ran through 1907. The Kansas Jayhawks grew into a perennial college power; Naismith, in fact, is the only coach in the team's storied history with a losing record. No matter; a legacy had already been forged. In 1959 he led the inaugural class into the Basketball Hall of Fame—the Naismith Memorial Basketball Hall of Fame, to be exact.

JAMES NAISMITH'S RULES FOR "BASKET BALL" (1891)

RULES	NOTES
The ball to be an ordinary Association foot ball.[1]	*1. A soccer ball.*
∞ 1st ∞ The ball may be thrown in any direction with one or both hands.	
∞ 2nd ∞ The ball may be batted in any direction with one or both hands (never with the fist).	
∞ 3rd ∞ A player cannot run with the ball.[2] The player must throw it from the spot on which he catches it, allowance to be made for a man who catches the ball when running at a good speed if he tries to stop.	*2. The first team credited with advancing the ball using dribbling played at Yale in 1897. They interpreted the passing rule to include a bounce pass to the player himself. More official changes allowing the dribble—just one per possession initially—were adopted four years later.*
∞ 4th ∞ The ball must be held in or between the hands; the arms or body must not be used for holding it.	
∞ 5th ∞ No shouldering, holding, pushing, tripping, or striking in any way the person of an opponent shall be allowed.[3] The first infringement of this rule by any person shall count as a foul; the second shall disqualify him until the next goal is made or, if	*3. Such offenses were not recorded as personal fouls until 1910, with the advent of a rule disqualifying a player for committing four of them. That total was raised to five in 1946 by the inaugural rules of the Basketball Association of America (the original name of the National Basketball Association), and to six the next year.*

RULES	NOTES
there was evident intent to injure the person, for the whole of the game, no substitute shall be allowed.[4]	*4. Nowhere in these rules is the number of competitors delineated. That's because Naismith wanted a game adaptable enough to include whoever wanted to play.*
6th **A foul is striking at the ball with the fist, violations of Rules 3 and 4,[5] and such as described in Rule 5.**	*5. Running with the ball—traveling—stopped being lumped in with "contact" fouls in 1921. It remained a loss-of-ball violation, however.*
7th **If either side makes three consecutive fouls, it shall count a goal[6] for the opponents (consecutive means without the opponents in the meantime making a foul).**	*6. This rule disappeared in 1895 with the introduction of the free throw line, the first iteration of which was 21 feet from the hoop. Almost immediately, it was moved to its current spot, 15 feet away. For a year, goals—today's field goals or baskets—and free throws each counted as one point. After that, field goals were worth two. The upstart American Basketball Association's long-distance three-pointer was coopted by the NBA in 1979.*
8th **A goal shall be made when the ball is thrown or batted from the grounds into the basket and stays there,[7] providing those defending the goal do not touch or disturb the goal. If the ball rests on the edge and the opponent moves the basket, it shall count as a goal.[8]**	*7. Relevant until 1913, when open-ended nets replaced closed woven cast-iron rims (which had replaced the peach baskets in the mid-1890s).* *8. This kind of defensive meddling sounds like goaltending, but that violation as it is now defined—interfering with a shot after it has begun its downward trajectory to the rim—was specifically made illegal only in 1944. That rule was a direct response to an influx of players finally tall enough to impact virtually any shot around the rim.*
9th **When the ball goes out of bounds, it shall be thrown into the field, and played by the person first touching it.[9]**	*9. This is one wrinkle Naismith didn't quite think through. Scrambles to be first to touch out-of-play balls resulted in downright injurious*

RULES	NOTES
In case of a dispute, the umpire shall throw it straight into the field.[10] The thrower-in is allowed five seconds. If he holds it longer, it shall go to the opponent. If any side persists in delaying the game, the umpire shall call a foul on that side.	*confrontations before the rule was modernized in 1913, giving the ball to whichever team was not the last to touch it.* *10. Today unclear possession is settled by a jump ball, a facet of the game that began in 1937 as a tool to restart play after every basket. Now it is used only at the beginning of games and overtimes.*
∞ *10th* ∞ **The umpire shall be judge of the men and shall note the fouls, and notify the referee when three consecutive fouls have been made. He shall have the power to disqualify men according to Rule 5.**	
∞ *11th* ∞ **The referee shall be the judge of the ball and shall decide when the ball is in play, in bounds, to which side it belongs, and shall keep the time.[11] He shall decide when a goal has been made, and keep account of the goals with any other duties that are usually performed by a referee.**	*11. To be fair, there wasn't all that much time to keep: the 24-second shot clock wasn't instituted until 1954, to combat stalling tactics NBA teams had begun to employ.*
∞ *12th* ∞ **The time shall be two fifteen-minute halves with five minutes' rest between.[12]**	*12. When the BAA was formed in 1946, two halves were rejiggered as four quarters of twelve minutes each to give fans more ball for their buck.*
∞ *13th* ∞ **The side making the most goals in that time shall be declared the winner. In case of a draw, the game may, by agreement of the captains, be continued until another goal is made.[13]**	*13. It wasn't until the 1960s that this sudden death gave way to five-minute overtime periods.*

STYLE POINTS

BASKETBALL UNIFORMS OVER TIME

Fashion in every sport has evolved, but this garb may have changed the most.

1890s In the early days of basketball, men's uniforms featured everything from trouser-style pants with belts to tracksuits. (Women mostly wore dresses or long skirts with slippers.) The first hoops-specific uniforms debuted in Spalding's 1901 catalog: pants of varying lengths and shirts of differing styles were offered.

1910s Shorts grew more popular because they allowed for increased mobility. Uniforms also began to represent the organization behind the players, from colleges to professional clubs. This coincided with Converse Rubber Shoe Company's 1917 release of the Chuck Taylor, a shoe named after the company's All Star, who traveled the United States teaching the game to children. His footwear featured high tops and rubber soles that offered better support and traction.

1920s–'30s By the 1920s, wool shorts and sleeveless jerseys were ubiquitous. Women more often wore knee pads, but otherwise their uniforms started to match what men were wearing. The invention of nylon in the 1930s offered a much better and lighter alternative to wool.

1940s–'50s As the quality and pace of play increased, wool was scrapped altogether for varying combinations of cotton, polyester, and nylon. Custom numbering and lettering became the norm, and the elastic waistband replaced the belt.

1960s Imitating American fashion in the 1960s, basketball uniforms became tighter and more colorful. In conjunction with the rise of less conservative clothing, sleeveless women's basketball jerseys began to appear as well.

1970s–'80s Following broader fashion trends, striped tube socks became a popular staple of NBA uniforms in the 1970s. Shorts were exceptionally snug, with an inseam as small as 3 inches—or roughly that of men's underwear. They stayed that way through most of the 1980s, until Michael Jordan requested that his Chicago Bulls get longer shorts so he wouldn't have to tug on them so hard when he bent over to rest his hands on his sweaty knees.

1990s Shorts continued to get longer and baggier in the 1990s, in sync with the absorption of hip-hop culture into American sports. In college basketball, the University of Michigan's star-studded 1991 recruiting class (aka the Fab Five) popularized the look. Meanwhile in the NBA, players followed Jordan's lead, and by the end of the decade, the baggy look was the only look.

2000–2010s Since the turn of the twenty-first century, basketball uniforms have been tailored to focus as much on function as on fashion. Shorts and jerseys have remained baggy for maximum maneuverability, while shoes have become lighter even as they offer better floor grip and stronger ankle and arch support.

BOXING

IT'S PROBABLY SAFE TO SAY THAT HUMANS HAVE ENGAGED in hand-to-hand combat since they walked upright; some of the earliest cave paintings depict primitive versions of fisticuffs. The first reference to pugilism in recorded history can be found on a Sumerian wall relief that dates to the third millennium BC. The earliest depictions of fistfighting with hand coverings—gloves, more or less—are in frescoes painted in Crete circa 1500 BC.

But boxing as organized sport rather than self-protective strategy or anger-fueled mayhem developed later. "Organized" is a relative concept, however. If it includes one-off battles between fighters backed by bosses, chiefs, or other grandees looking for entertainment and financial gain from successful bets, then, yes, organized fighting occurred in many early civilizations. But boxing was thought to be enough of a skill, not to mention a measure of manhood, to earn a spot in the ancient Olympics in the seventh century BC. Similarly, fighting for prizes—typically freedom—by slaves, servants, and criminals was a popular spectator sport in ancient Rome. Held on estates or in marketplaces and amphitheaters, these contests were often fought to the death; leather thongs wrapped around boxers' knuckles were sometimes studded with metal. The sport was so deadly that it was abolished in AD 393.

Although men doubtless continued to punch each other for fun and bragging rights, the sport as such didn't formally resurface until the late seventeenth century, in Great Britain. The first account of a boxing match there appeared in 1681, detailing a bout between a nobleman's butler and butcher. Soon enough, prizefights were regular newspaper fodder, and "boxing" the term of choice, most likely because fighters competed in a square. By 1719 England had its first bare-knuckle champion, James Figg. What it did not have was written rules for this increasingly popular sport (not to mention weight divisions, round limits, or a referee).

Such basic codification emerged a couple of decades down the road, established by someone who had intimate knowledge of what he was legislating. As a young man, Jack Broughton was a ferryman working at the Port of London. But in the 1730s he also fought, and fought well, earning a reputation to match his impressive physique: he was 6 feet tall and a muscular 195 pounds at a time when the average man was several inches shorter and many pounds lighter. Trading on his status, and with help from backers, Broughton opened a fighting venue of his own in 1743, after his retirement. There, he staged boxing matches for the paying public, for which he drew up seven rules, the primary purpose of which was to protect contestants. Broughton's set remained definitive for almost a hundred years, until the publication of the London Prize Ring Rules in 1838, which expanded on it. In the next three decades, those rules were updated a couple more times, the last version at the behest of John Sholto Douglas. If the name doesn't ring a bell, maybe that's because he was better known as the ninth Marquess of Queensberry, an avid sportsman who sponsored the publication of a revised set of boxing rules compiled by his associate John Chambers.

Chambers's name faded into history, while Queensberry's remains associated with the rules that continue to govern boxing. But it was Broughton who first formalized the sport. That he still doesn't get the credit he deserves should come as no surprise. Recognition has always come slowly to the big man. Following his death in 1789, Broughton was buried at Westminster Abbey. For centuries, his headstone bore no epitaph, the fault for which lies with the dean of the abbey, who disapproved of the one Broughton had requested. But in 1988, the pugilist's wish was granted when the words "Champion of England" were engraved at his final resting place.

JACK BROUGHTON'S RULES OF BOXING (1743)

RULES TO BE OBSERVED IN ALL BATTLES ON THE STAGE

RULES	NOTES
1st **That a square of a Yard be chalked in the middle of the Stage;[1] and on every fresh set-to after a fall,[2] or being parted from the rails, each Second is to bring his Man[3] to the side of the square, and place him opposite to the other, and until they are fairly set to at the Lines, it shall not be lawful for one to strike the other.**	*1. The roped-off ring was instituted in 1838. Two ropes marked off a 24-foot square, a size that more or less lives on today. And why is that square called a ring? Because fights in the street and school yard always seemed to draw circles of spectators.* *2. The determination of a fighter's ability to continue was his willingness to stand within a yard of his opponent—a reasonable punching range.* *3. Early boxers were allowed to benefit from a fair amount of physical help from their corner. When the London Prize Ring Rules superseded Broughton's in 1838, such boosts were prohibited.*
2nd **That in order to prevent any Disputes, the time a Man lies after a fall, if the Second does not bring his Man to the side of the square, within the space of half a minute,[4] he shall be deemed a beaten Man.**	*4. Half a minute? That seems awfully coddling. (To be fair, even back then anyone staying down for so long, especially when the reason seemed to be rest more than recovery, was considered unmanly.) The ten count has been the presiding principle since 1867, with the introduction of the Marquess of Queensberry's rules that ushered in boxing's modern era.*
3rd **That in every main Battle, no person whatever shall be upon the Stage, except the Principals and their Seconds, the same rule to be observed in bye-battles,[5] except that in the latter, Mr. Broughton is allowed to be upon the stage to keep decorum,**	*5. The bouts that preceded the main event, otherwise known as the undercard.*

RULES | NOTES

and to assist Gentlemen in getting to their places, provided always that he does not interfere in the Battle; and whoever pretends to infringe these Rules to be turned immediately out of the house. Everybody is to quit the Stage as soon as the Champions are stripped,[6] before set-to.

6. Then as now, boxers fought bare-chested. Male boxers, anyway.

∞ *4th* ∞

That no Champion be deemed beaten, unless he fails coming up to the line in the limited time,[7] or that his own Second declares him beaten. No Second is to be allowed to ask his man's Adversary any questions, or advise him to give out.

7. With thirty seconds to regain one's senses, and with entourage members permitted to lend a hand, these early matches didn't always end quickly. The longest lasted six hours and fifteen minutes. In fact, even when the Marquess of Queensberry instituted three-minute rounds (before then rounds ended whenever a fighter went down), he refrained from putting a cap on the number of them. In 1893 Jack Burke and Andy Bowen fought 111—and it would have been more, but the fighters were too drained to continue.

∞ *5th* ∞

That in bye-battles, the winning man to have two-thirds of the Money given, which shall be publicly divided upon the Stage, notwithstanding any private agreements to the contrary.

∞ *6th* ∞

That to prevent Disputes, in every main Battle the Principals shall, on coming on the Stage, choose from among the gentlemen present two Umpires, who shall absolutely decide all Disputes that may arise about the

RULES	NOTES
Battle; and if the two Umpires cannot agree, the said Umpires to choose a third, who is to determine it.[8]	*8. All modern title fights are three-judge affairs.*

7th

That no person is to hit his Adversary when he is down, or seize him by the ham, the breeches,[9] or any part below the waist,[10] a man on his knees to be reckoned down.

9. Yes, this was the bare-knuckles era, but Broughton attempted to elevate the sport above its brawling origins. Toward that end, he encouraged boxers to wear "mufflers," a glove precursor of his own invention, during exhibitions and sparring sessions. Ironically, the standardization of glove boxing with the Queensberry rules increased ring injuries. With their fists protected, boxers were more likely to attack an opponent's hard head, rather than focus on softer parts of his body.

10. A fair amount of above-the-waist grappling was okay, though.

CLOCK WATCH
TIME UNITS IN SPORTS

At three minutes, the traditional boxing round is a relatively short period of athletic activity. This makes sense because, generally, time frames get longer as the number of competitors increases.

0:01-1:00
Steer wrestling (clock stops when steer is roped)

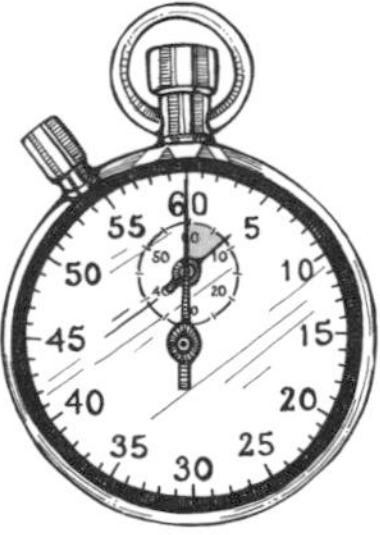

0:08
Bull/steer riding, rough stock rodeo

0:50
Modern pentathlon, shooting portion: interval to hit target five times

2:00
College wrestling, second and third rounds

2:50
Figure skating, short program

3:00
Boxing round; college wrestling, first round

4:00
Figure skating, long program (ladies); ice dancing, free dance

4:30
Figure skating, long program (men's)

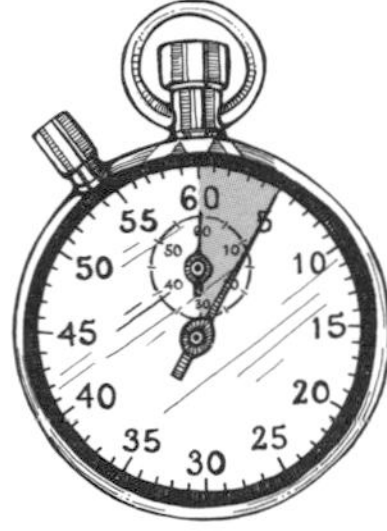

5:00
Mixed martial arts round

7:00
Polo chukker; water polo quarter

7:30
Bicycle polo quarter

10:00
WNBA basketball quarter; international basketball period

12:00
NBA basketball quarter; roller hockey quarter

15:00
Lacrosse quarter; professional football quarter; college football quarter; netball quarter

20:00
College basketball half; Australian rules football quarter; ice hockey period

30:00
Team handball half; korfball half

35:00
Field hockey half

40:00
Rugby half (union and league)

45:00
Soccer half; bandy half

CRICKET

NEARLY ALL U.S. SPORTS NUTS, NO MATTER HOW PAROCHIAL, know that soccer is the world's most popular spectator sport, but even the most cosmopolitan American fans might be surprised to learn that cricket is runner-up on that list. (It helps to be the favorite sport in India, the world's second-most populous country.) There is irony in this ignorance, given that cricket is very much a forerunner of baseball: a player on one team delivers a ball to bat-wielding players on the other, who attempt to hit said orb between fielders and advance from base to base in pursuit of runs.

Yet cricket, not to mention baseball, would not hold such an exalted place in the global sports firmament were it not for the simultaneous rise a few centuries back of another border-neutral pastime: gambling. (Another irony, since both sports have experienced more than their fair share of betting-related scandals.) The upper crust of pre-Victorian England loved their cricket, but they loved their gambling even more, and by the mid-1700s the more ambitious among them had taken to running private cricket clubs to improve their odds of succeeding at both. In fact, the earliest rule books connected to the sport were concerned almost entirely with adjudicating betting disputes.

Exactly *when* grown men began to take seriously what was little more than rural child's play isn't quite clear. The first references to cricket appear in the mid-1500s, but most historians believe the game developed well before that, around the twelfth century, among the Norman and Saxon tribes in southeast England. Children sent into the fields to tend livestock passed the long days whacking around rocks (or possibly hardened balls of wool) with a herding staff, aka crook (*crycc* in Old English). Almost assuredly inspired by another medieval game called bowls (essentially bowling on grass), players eventually started to use their staffs to protect a target—say, a tree stump—from thrown balls. There were no set rules, so people in different parts of the country played different versions. And in at least one of them, balls were aimed at a particular target: the gates, or wickets, of the livestock pens.

Until the mid-seventeenth century, cricket players remained almost exclusively preteen children. Back then, most working-class adults—an age cohort that included teenagers—had little time for games, especially ones that took a while and tired them out. (They spent their "spare time"—the few hours a day when they weren't straining to earn a coin or two—eating and sleeping.)

But in the wake of the English Civil War, commoners got their first real taste of individual liberties and, just as important, a chance to have some fun. Cricket became an afternoon amusement for residents of rival parishes, and these competitions soon doubled as a high-stakes showdown backed by wealthy local landowners. Once the press became less regulated in the late seventeenth century, newspapers began to write about these matches, giving everyone access to the results of even faraway contests. Early accounts focused almost entirely on amounts wagered—sums that would surpass $20,000 today. Little if any ink was devoted to the particulars of the sport itself. Not surprisingly, with so many people paying attention and so much money riding on each game, a consensus soon developed among players, spectators, and bettors: a uniform version of cricket was necessary. A committee in London made up of representatives of various local clubs laid down the first official rules in 1744. By the turn of the next century, the same form of cricket had taken hold throughout the British Commonwealth, otherwise known as all over the world.

"THE GAME OF CRICKET,[1] AS SETTLED BY YE CRICKET CLUB AT YE STAR AND GARTER IN PALL MALL" (1744)

RULES

The pitching of ye first Wicket is to be determined by ye cast of a piece of Money[2] when ye first Wicket is pitched and ye popping Crease[3] Cut which must be exactly 3 Foot 10 Inches from ye Wicket. Ye Other Wicket is to be pitched directly opposite at 22 yards distance[4] and ye other popping crease cut 3 Foot 10 Inches before it. The Bowling Creases[5] must be cut in a direct line from each Stump. The Stumps must be 22 Inches long and ye Bail 6 Inches.[6] The Ball must weigh between 5 and 6 Ounces. When ye Wickets are both pitched and all ye Creases Cut the Party that wins the toss up may order which side shall go in first at his Option.

1. *The first mention of cricket by name—*creckett, *to be exact—appears in 1598, in a record of a land dispute in Surrey, England. By 1700 that name was recognized throughout the country. Those who codified the sport in London certainly figured it was well enough known that their rules didn't need to state either the game's purpose—to score the most runs (or notches, as they were then called)—or that a match was composed of two innings, with each team running through its eleven-man lineup twice.*
2. *The pregame coin flip remains a staple, with the winning captain earning the chance to choose whether his side bats or bowls (pitches, to U.S. fans) first. Although no longer the case, he once got to pick which 22-yard stretch of a bigger expanse would be marked as the bowling and running area—aka the playing pitch, or field. Choosing the pitch offered an advantage, as particular attributes (flat or bumpy, grassy or sandy) could benefit the skill sets of one of the teams. Beginning in the late 1770s, the toss was sidelined for a few decades, and visiting teams were given the task of selecting the pitch and who batted first.*
3. *The dimensions of the pitch remain essentially the same, although the popping crease is now 2 inches longer. The popping crease is the "home" or "safe" zone at either end of the strip where the two batsmen run after one of them has hit the ball. It is so named because early on a player had to "pop" his bat in a hole to register a notch, or run. Touching the zone with a bat suffices today.*

4. Though the size of the entire playing area wasn't originally delineated, current rules mandate side boundaries must be at least 65 yards from the center and 70 yards from the ends, while being no longer than 90 yards in any direction. The typical playing area is circular or oval.

5. Why is "bowling" the common term rather than "throwing" or "pitching"? Because the action is performed with an unbending elbow and thus a straight arm, making it much different from a baseball pitcher's motion. Bowlers are not allowed to throw, or "chuck," the ball.

6. Stumps—the vertical stakes that together with a horizontal "bail" make up the wicket, aka the bowler's target—are now 28 inches. They were lengthened in 1931 to give bowlers a bigger target.

LAWS FOR YE BOWLERS 4 BALLS[7] AND OVER

7. The number of pitched balls in an over—a bowler's turn—has varied through the years. The four-ball over was common until 1889, when it became five, then six in 1900. Some places, notably Australia, played eight-ball overs for a while, but six balls have been the global standard since 1979.

Ye Bowler must deliver ye Ball with one foot behind[8] ye Crease even with ye Wicket, and When he has Bowled one Ball or more shall Bowl to ye number 4 before he changes Wickets, and he shall change but once in ye same Innings.[9] He may order ye Player that is in at his Wicket to stand on which side of it he pleases at a reasonable distance.[10] If he delivers ye Ball with his hinder foot over ye bowling Crease, ye Umpire shall call No Ball, though she be struck, or ye Player bowled out, which he shall do without being asked, and no Person shall have any right to ask him.

8. It remains true today that if a bowler's back foot is outside the crease when he bowls, his offering does not count. But it's not quite that simple: the no-ball rule now contains sixteen clauses, some containing up to four subclauses, which in some cases contain up to three sub-subclauses.

9. Four or five bowlers are used in an inning now, in part because current rules state that no bowler can bowl two consecutive overs but also because the choice of bowler depends on which batter is hitting and which side he is hitting from.

10. Still the case in practice, as the bowler tells the umpire on which side of the stumps he will make his run-up, and the batsman at the bowling end stands out of the way to leave the bowler an unobstructed run. The length of the run-up depends on the bowler's personal style. Some run just a few meters before delivering the ball; faster bowlers run a greater distance to build speed before the release.

LAWS FOR YE STRIKERS, OR THOSE THAT ARE IN

If ye Wicket is Bowled down, it's Out.[11] If he strikes, or treads down, or falls himself upon ye Wicket in striking, but not in over running, it's out. A stroke or nip over or under his Batt, or upon his hands, but not arms, if ye Ball be held before she touches ye ground, though she be hugged to the body, it's Out. If in striking both his feet are over ye popping Crease and his Wicket put down, except his Batt is down within, it's Out. If he runs out of his Ground to hinder a Catch, it's Out. If a ball is nipp'd up and he strikes her again, willfully, before she comes to ye Wicket, it's Out. If ye Players have cross'd each other, he that runs for ye Wicket that is put down is Out. If they are not cross'd[12] he that returns is Out.

---

11. *Strikers, or batsmen, are "out" for the same reasons today: a bowled ball knocks the bail off the stumps; bails are knocked off by another means (for instance, the batsman accidentally knocks it off himself or a fielder throws the ball at the bail and knocks it over before a runner reaches the safe zone); or a fielder catches a batted ball in the air.*
12. *"Crossed" is used here to identify the point at which the two runners have passed each other on their runs. To score a run, both batsmen have to safely reach the "zone."*

BATT FOOT OR HAND OVER YE CREASE

If in running a notch[13] ye Wicket is struck down by a Throw, before his foot hand or Batt is over ye popping Crease, or a stump hit by ye Ball though ye Bail was down, it's Out. But if ye Bail is down before, he that catches ye Ball must strike a Stump out of ye ground, Ball in hand, then it's Out. If ye Striker touches or takes up ye Ball before she is lain quite still unless asked by ye Bowler or Wicket-keeper, it's Out. When ye Ball has been in hand by one of ye Keepers or Stoppers,[14] and ye Player has been at home, He may go where he pleases till ye next ball is bowled. If either of ye Strikers is cross'd in his running ground designedly, which design must be determined by the Umpires,[15] N.B. The Umpire(s) may order that Notch to be scored. When ye Ball is hit up, either of ye Strikers may hinder ye catch in his running ground,

or if she's hit directly across ye Wickets, ye other Player may place his body anywhere within ye swing of his Batt, so as to hinder ye Bowler from catching her,[16] but he must neither strike at her nor touch her with his hands. If a Striker nips a ball up just before him, he may fall before his Wicket, or pop down his Batt before she comes to it, to save it. Ye Bail hanging on one Stump, though ye Ball hit ye Wicket, it's Not Out.

---

13. *Yes, a physical notch, carved into wood by a designated scorer to keep track of each run. It is unclear when pencil and paper prevailed.*
14. *The wicketkeeper is the only position with a dedicated spot on the pitch: behind the stumps, there to catch or stop (or at least attempt to) all balls that sail past the batsmen unhit. Where the other fielders, or stoppers, are positioned is a matter of intricate strategy.*
15. *Although it is mostly a clear-cut observation, on occasion the fate of a run is a marginal call. Specifically, it may not be obvious which runner is farther across the 22 yards when the bails are off. The umpire is the ultimate arbiter of which batsman should have gotten to which safe zone if there is any confusion.*
16. *At the time, a batsman was allowed to obstruct a catch as long as he was attempting a run. The batsman wasn't allowed to use his hands in the attempt, but a little shoulder nudge was allowed. (Those were the days.)*

LAWS FOR WICKET KEEPERS

Ye Wicket Keepers shall stand at a reasonable distance behind ye Wicket, and shall not move till ye Ball is out of ye Bowler's Hands and shall not by any noise incommode[17] ye Striker, and if his hands knees foot or head be over or before ye Wicket, though ye Ball hit it, it shall not be Out.

---

17. *The wicketkeeper is still forbidden to make noises that might unsettle a batsman, but gentlemen cricketers of yesteryear would be shocked at how often such etiquette is ignored. "Sledging"—or verbally rattling an opponent during play—by wicketkeepers and stoppers alike is so common that the rudest and crudest put-downs have become lore.*

To allow 2 Minutes for each Man to come in when one is out, and 10 minutes between each Hand.[18] To mark ye Ball that it may not be changed.[19] They are sole judges of all Outs and Ins, of all fair and unfair Play, of frivolous delays, of all hurts, whether real or pretended, and are discretionally to allow what time they think proper before ye Game goes on again.[20] In case of a real hurt to a Striker, they are to allow another to come in and ye Person hurt to come in again, but are not to allow a fresh Man to play, on either Side, on any Account. They are sole judges of all hindrances, crossing ye Players in running, and standing unfair to strike, and in case of hindrance may order a Notch to be scored. They are not to order any Man out unless appealed to by one of ye Players.[21] (These Laws are to ye Umpires Jointly.) Each Umpire is sole judge of all Nips and Catches, Ins and Outs, good or bad Runs, at his own Wicket, and his determination shall be absolute, and he shall not be changed for another Umpire without ye consent of both Sides. When ye 4 Balls are bowled, he is to call Over. (These Laws are Separately.) When both Umpires shall call Play, 3 Times, 'tis at ye peril of giving ye Game from them that refuse to Play.

---

18. *Although "hand" seems to be another word for "inning," the term is no longer in use.*
19. *Keeping tabs on the game ball isn't as crucial as it once was. New balls can now be introduced; the rules that govern such a substitution depend on the version of the game being played or the venue.*
20. *The ultimate authority of the umpire was enshrined in these first laws. It was his responsibility to make calls on a batsman "standing unfair to strike"—obstructing his own wicket so the bowler can't fairly attempt to hit it, an early version of today's illegal leg before wicket (lbw). The idea that Hawk-Eye or another computer-based decision-review system might one day help to make the right calls would have been as far-fetched as the fact that India, not England, plays host to the world's richest tournament (the IPL), which doesn't even play the classic version of cricket but rather Twenty20, a truncated form created in 2003.*
21. *Batsmen who are clearly out walk off on their own all the time, but it is true to this day that a fielder must ask the umpire to declare an out to make it so.*

SIZE MATTERS
TEAM-SIDE COUNTS ACROSS SPORTS

Cricket's field may look crowded, but with "only" eleven players to a side, it isn't the most populated of games.

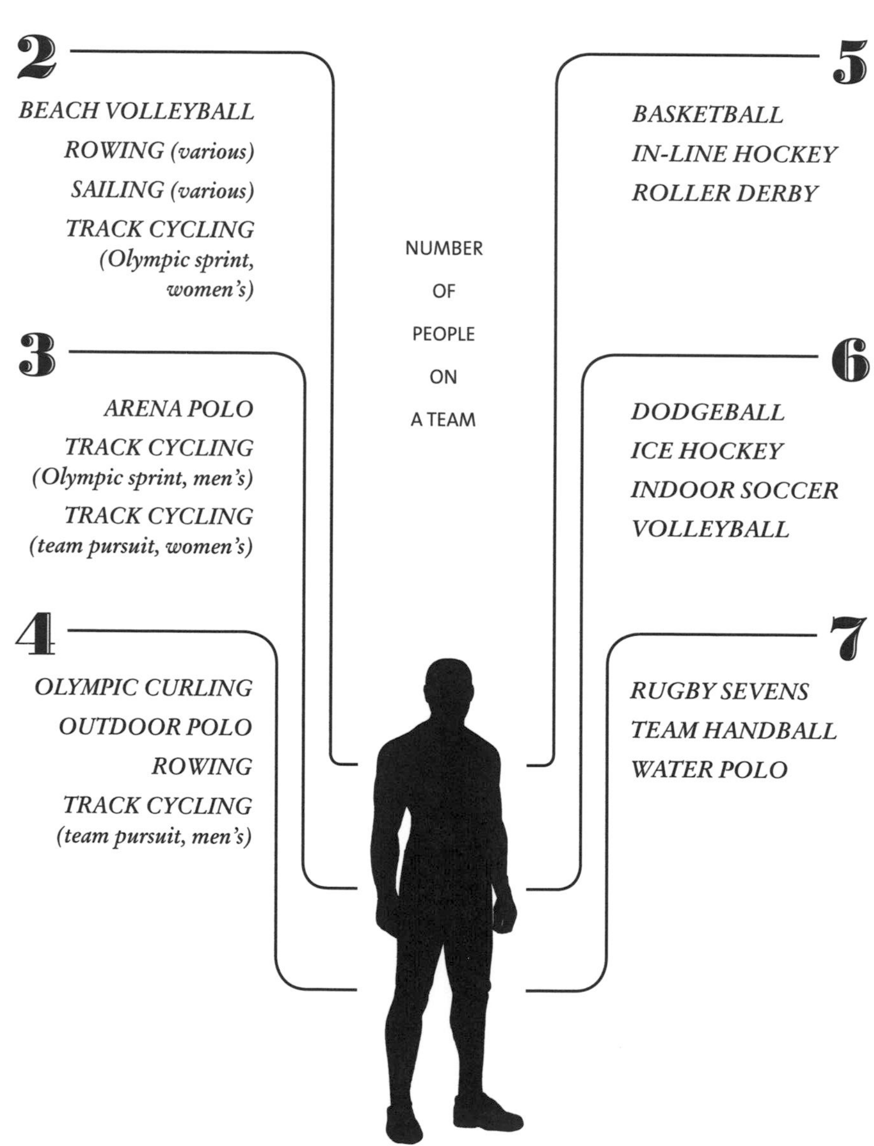

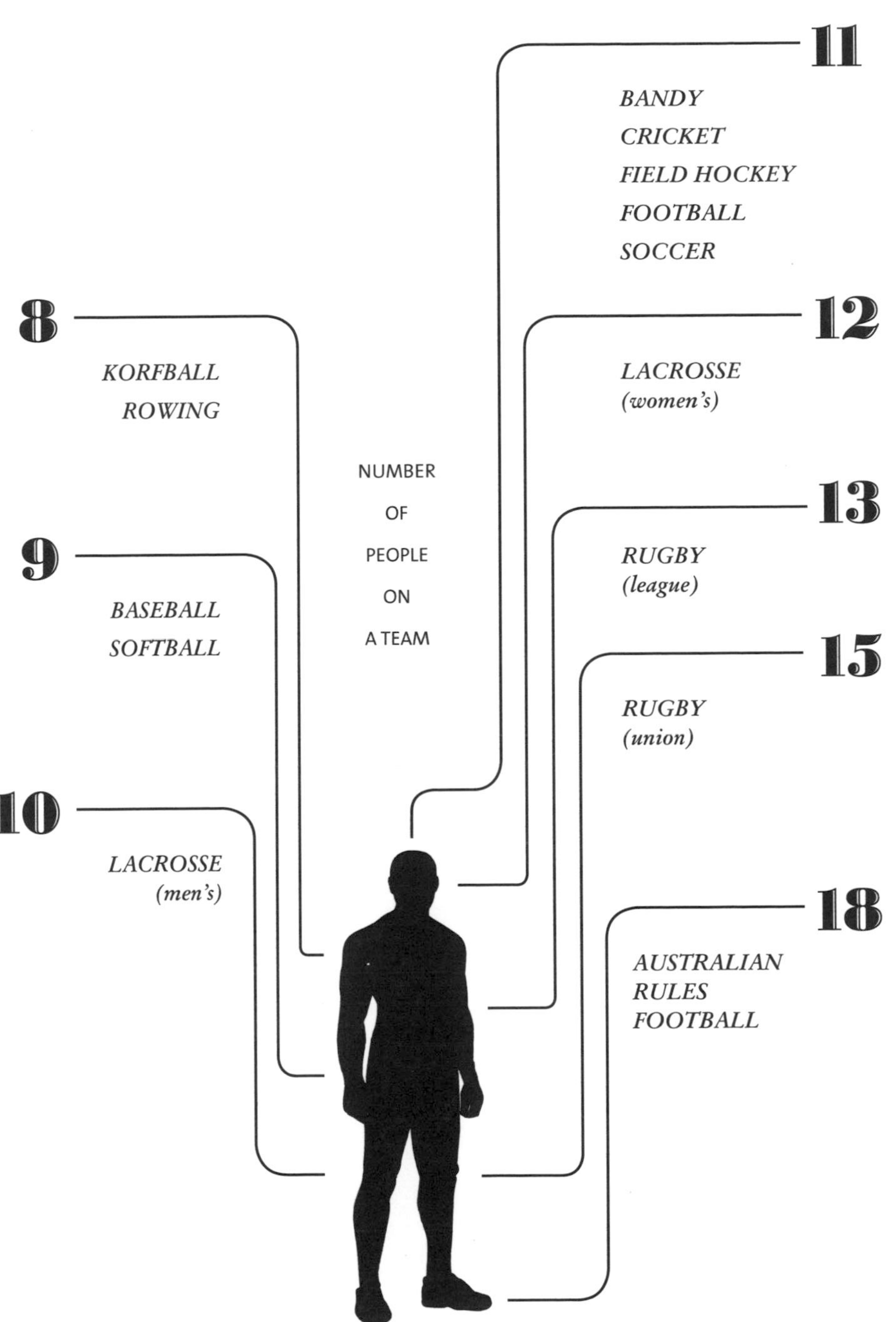
11
BANDY
CRICKET
FIELD HOCKEY
FOOTBALL
SOCCER
8
KORFBALL
ROWING
12
LACROSSE
(women's)
NUMBER
OF
PEOPLE
ON
A TEAM
13
RUGBY
(league)
9
BASEBALL
SOFTBALL
15
RUGBY
(union)
10
LACROSSE
(men's)
18
AUSTRALIAN
RULES
FOOTBALL

Cricket

FANTASY FOOTBALL

THE AMERICAN FOOTBALL LEAGUE'S OAKLAND RAIDERS lost their first thirteen games in 1962, after going 2–12 the year before. If a line can be reasonably drawn from the devastation of post–World War II England to the euphoric release of the Beatles, then a similar connection can be made between the Raiders' ineptitude that season and one of the sports world's greatest revolutions. Holed up in a New York City hotel in the midst of his team's three-game East Coast swing, Oakland minority owner Bill "Wink" Winkenbach, along with team PR man Bill Tunnell and *Oakland Tribune* sportswriter Scott Stirling, crafted the rules for a game they actually had a chance to win: fantasy football.

Ever since Henry Chadwick designed the modern baseball box score in 1859, Americans have defined athletes by the numbers they produced. Before TV and the Internet, a newspaper's daily stat lines brought the games to life for all those fans unable to snag a seat at the park. It was only a matter of time—a century, give or take—before the game itself became an afterthought. Fantasy sports are, in essence, proxy sports, whereby the performance of athletes on their fields/courts/rinks of play is harnessed by fans to create a statistical facsimile with which they compete.

The most popular fantasy sports today involve team games: football, baseball, basketball, and soccer. Participants draft or bid for players from various teams to create their own rosters. But Winkenbach had actually first tried to build a proxy game around an individual sport—golf—in the 1950s: competitors chose a group of golfers before a tournament; the winner's "team" had the lowest stroke total when it was over. Similar games were built around baseball performance statistics in the 1960s. In National Baseball Seminar, which was invented by the sociology professor William Gamson, participants chose teams of MLB players and were awarded points based on end-of-season stats. Gamson, who devised National Baseball Seminar while on the faculty at Harvard, brought his game with him when he was hired to teach at the University of Michigan. In 1980 a Michigan alumnus named Dan Okrent invented Rotisserie baseball, which is rightfully credited as starting the fantasy sports era/craze/movement. (It didn't hurt that Okrent and most of his fellow Rotisserie founders were in the media business.) But the first true fantasy sports game and league as we recognize them now emerged from that New York hotel room in 1962. From just three bits of data available in any football box score—who scored, how, and the distance covered by the scoring play—the Greater Oakland Professional Pigskin Prediction League (GOPPPL) was born.

And so it was that shortly before the commencement of the 1963 football season, eight team "owners" gathered in Winkenbach's rumpus room in Oakland to launch the GOPPPL. Everything a fantasy player today would recognize was present: good humor, bountiful refreshments, obsessive fans, copious rules, and, of course, shoddy drafting. The first pick in fantasy football history was Raiders quarterback George Blanda, drafted by Stirling and his "coach," bar manager Andy Mousalimas. The pair passed over legendary Cleveland Browns running back Jim Brown, who scored fifteen touchdowns that season and carried the fantasy team that drafted him to a championship; Stirling and Mousalimas finished last.

"OFFICIAL RULES & REGULATIONS OF GOPPPL" (1963)

The Greater Oakland Professional [Pigskin] Prediction[1] League, hereafter also known as the GOPPPL, is hereby created. It shall be composed of eight (8) clubs, each club to have an owner and one or two coaches.

To be eligible for club ownership, one of the three following qualifications must be met:

1. Affiliation with an AFL professional football team in an administrative capacity.

2. A direct relationship to professional football in a journalistic capacity.

3. Either have purchased or have sold ten (10) season tickets for the Oakland Raiders for 1963.[2]

The club owners of the GOPPPL are:

1. Bob Blum.................... Raider Radio Announcer
2. Phil Carmona .... Season Ticket Seller
3. Ralph Casebolt.............. Season Ticket Seller
4. George Glace[3] .... Raider Ticket Manager
5. George Ross .... Oakland Tribune Sports Editor
6. Scotty Stirling.............. Oakland Tribune Beat Writer
7. Bill Tunnell .... Raider Public Relations Man
8. Bill Winkenbach .... Season Ticket Seller

---

1. The third P *in GOPPPL, which didn't even earn a mention in the origin document, is often mistakenly thought to stand for Prognosticators.*

2. If the criteria for ownership seem arbitrary and limiting, please note the list of original owners that follows them.

3. Glace comanaged his team with a young scout named Ron Wolf, who later won an actual Super Bowl as the real-life general manager of the Green Bay Packers.

PURPOSE OF LEAGUE

The purpose of this league is to bring together some of Oakland's finest Saturday morning[4] gridiron forecasters to pit their respective brains (and cash)[5] against each other. Inasmuch as this league is formed only with owners having a deep interest and affection for the Oakland Raiders Professional Football Team,[6] it is felt that this tournament will automatically increase closer coverage of daily happenings in professional football.[7]

Inasmuch as this test of skill and knowledge of the players in the AFL and NFL Leagues will be backed with coin of the realm, it behooves each club owner to study carefully, prior to draft, all available statistics,[8] schedules, weather conditions, player habits and other factors, so as to preserve one's prestige and finances.

Lack of skill or study will also afford the heaviest loser the yearly trophy, symbolic of the loser's ineptness in this grueling contest.[9] This award will be presented by the League Commissioner at the Annual GOPPPL Banquet, held in late January for club owners, coaches and wives.[10]

---

4. *Although professional football is now recognized as a predominantly Sunday pastime, Saturday games were common in the 1960s.*
5. *The game was scored differently then, with players' stats translating into money earned (as delineated in the Payoff section of these rules). Today points are awarded or deducted for individual statistical milestones—for instance, yards gained or fumbles lost—and those points yield a team total that is matched against the total of a weekly challenger. Through the course of a season, weekly wins and losses are kept as part of running league standings.*
6. *If only the Raiders were so loyal to their fan base. The team split Oakland for a better stadium deal in Los Angeles in 1982, where they stayed until the end of the 1994 season. They've been back in Oakland since, although they constantly threaten to pick up and leave again.*
7. *On average, fantasy players devote almost nine hours a week to their teams.*
8. *In pre-Internet days, the sports editor of a major metropolitan newspaper would seem to have a distinct advantage. Guess who won?*
9. *Specifically, a wooden face in the shape of a football with a dunce cap on top.*
10. *Women weren't welcome in the game's infancy; today they make up 20 percent of fantasy football players.*

LEAGUE OFFICIALS

The GOPPPL will have two officials—a Commissioner and a Secretary. The Commissioner will preside at all meetings, handle all arbitration[11] and appoint all committees. The Secretary will keep league records and scoring data[12] and be responsible for the collection and distribution of all monies at the end of the season. These two officials will be selected at the Draft Dinner.

---

11. For $15 FantasyJudgment.com will resolve a dispute within twenty-four hours; $100 buys unlimited dispute resolution for an entire season.

12. League secretaries the world over celebrated the day the Internet made automated scoring a reality.

RULES OF DRAFTING

Prior to the opening of the professional football season, at an evening dinner meeting, club owners will draft 20 players[13] from either league. However, no more than 8 imports can be drafted from the NFL. In event of injury, which depletes a position, owner shall apply to Commissioner for approval to activate a temporary replacement[14] from undrafted players.

---

13. Twenty rounds is a bit excessive. Standard drafts today go sixteen rounds, tops.

14. Current leagues run weekly add/drop periods, in which owners can substitute unclaimed players for those on their roster. In the GOPPPL's defense, computers have made this task much easier.

METHOD OF DRAFTING

At the first draft, cards will be cut for first choice, second choice, etc. The last choice, or eighth choice, will also get ninth choice going back up the ladder.[15] Thus, the first choice will get sixteenth and seventeenth choice. After all cuts have been made, each owner will declare in what position he wants to draft. The following year, first choice goes to the heaviest loser of the preceding year, and so forth.

---

15. Aka snake drafting.

PLAYER DRAFT

DRAFT	PLAY
1. 4 Offensive Ends[16]	2 Offensive Ends
2. 4 Halfbacks	2 Halfbacks
3. 2 Fullbacks	1 Fullback
4. 2 Quarterbacks	1 Quarterback
5. 2 Kickoff or Punt Returners	1 Kickoff or Punt Returner
6. 2 Field Goal Kickers	1 Field Goal Kicker
7. 2 Defensive Backs or Linebackers	2 Defensive Backs or Linebackers
8. 2 Defensive Linemen	1 Defensive Lineman[17]

Field Goals and Conversions can only be credited to player so specified.[18] Lineup has to be posted with League Secretary prior to 12:00 o'clock Friday Morning.[19] If no lineup is posted the preceding week's lineup will be in effect.

16. Offensive ends are wide receivers and tight ends.

17. In current standard fantasy leagues, teams commonly play one quarterback, two running backs, two wide receivers, one tight end, one flex player (running back, wide receiver, or tight end), one kicker, and one team defense.

18. In the early days of football, kickers weren't one-job specialists like their modern counterparts. For example, Gino Cappelletti was also a receiver for the Boston Patriots and Paul Hornung was a running back for the Packers. The field goals and extra points they made would count only if they had been designated by their owners as the fantasy kicker.

19. Today fantasy owners can wait until a minute before a player's team kicks off before deciding whether to insert him into their lineup.

PAYOFF

The following method for payoffs[20] for scoring will prevail:

1. **Fifty cents for rushing touchdown by any player.**
2. **Twenty-five cents for any player receiving pass for touchdown.[21]**
3. **Twenty-five cents for any player throwing touchdown pass.**
4. **Double the above for any score from more than 75 yards out.**
5. **Twenty-five cents for each field goal.[22]**

6. Two dollars and fifty cents for kickoff or punt return for touchdown.[23]

7. Two dollars and fifty cents for touchdown by defensive back or linebacker on pass interception.

8. Five dollars for touchdown by defensive lineman.[24]

BLOW THE WHISTLE[25]

---

20. This method of reward has, for the most part, given way to a one-time, end-of-season distribution of a league-wide price-of-entry pool of cash.

21. Why are rushing TDs worth twice as much as passing TDs? For every rushing touchdown in the pass-happy AFL of 1963 there were 1.6 receiving, and ten receivers scored at least ten touchdowns, while only two running backs did.

22. Through a modern lens it seems ridiculous that a field goal should be as valuable as a touchdown. A fantasy field goal (at least those of 39 yards or fewer) is now worth exactly what it is on the field—three points, or half of a touchdown's six. But field goals were fairly uncommon in 1963: fewer than one a game was kicked per team versus 2.7 touchdowns. (In 2014 teams averaged 1.6 field goals and 2.5 touchdowns.)

23. In 1963, there were sixteen kickoff and punt-return TDs.

24. Number of defensive linemen recording a touchdown that year: zero.

25. A reference to the ref's pre-kickoff signal, and just the kind of goofy closing exhortation you'd expect from this bunch.

DREAM TIME
A LINEAR HISTORY OF FANTASY SPORTS

The idea of using the accomplishments of actual athletes to power a virtual game is much older than most fantasy fans realize. And more wide-ranging: the list of sports today with meaningful fantasy participation includes auto racing (multiple circuits), baseball, basketball, bass fishing, cricket, field hockey, football (American and Australian Rules), golf, hockey, rugby, soccer, and wrestling.

1951
The first sports simulation game, American Professional Baseball Association, debuts. Chance, in the form of rolled dice, determined the outcomes of real-life players (represented by cards) in specific situations.

1960
William Gamson creates National Baseball Seminar, a proto-fantasy game that counts only four stats: runs batted in, batting average, earned run average, and wins.

1961
Strat-O-Matic debuts. This dice-based tabletop game simulates results based on statistical research. It came in three versions: baseball, football, and hockey.

1963
The world's first fantasy league, the Greater Oakland Professional Pigskin Prediction League, holds its inaugural draft. About a dozen Americans now play fantasy sports.

1974
The GOPPPL Ladies' Division, thought to be the earliest women's fantasy sports group, is launched at Kings X Sports Bar in Oakland.

1980
Rotisserie baseball is founded. The name of the league credited with making fantasy sports go viral is derived from La Rotisserie Française, a French restaurant in Manhattan frequented by founder Dan Okrent and his fellow "owners." Each "spends" $250 on twenty-two players; the next season they add a pitcher to rosters and hike the salary cap to $260, which remains the standard for "Roto" leagues today.

1981
Neil Smith, a scout for the New York Islanders, and a friend invent fantasy hockey. The Off-Ice Hockey League features ten "owners" but only counts goals scored.

1984
Bantam Books publishes the first edition of *Rotisserie League Baseball*. Soon after, *The New York Times* prints an article on a self-published book, *The 1984 Fantasy Football Digest*, written by Minnesota fans Tom Kane Jr. and Cliff Charpentier. Fantasy football goes national.

1992
An article in the Cleveland *Plain Dealer,* written by Dennis LePore, introduces the idea of fantasy basketball to help fill the void that is baseball's off-season.

1995
ESPN launches an online fantasy football platform and charges $29.95 to use it.

1998
SI.com, FoxSports.com, and others enter the fantasy business, all charging fans to play.

1999
Responding to congressional scrutiny of online gambling, several organizations unite to form the Fantasy Sports Trade Association. Meanwhile, Yahoo.com launches the first free fantasy football website.

2002
English Premier League fantasy soccer debuts.

2003
More than 15 million Americans and Canadians, twelve and older, now play fantasy sports.

2006
Congress passes the Unlawful Internet Gambling Enforcement Act of 2006 but exempts fantasy sports as a game of skill rather than chance.

2007
Aided by the favorable congressional ruling, Fantasy Sports Live launches a daily fantasy game. A slew of others, including eventual market leader FanDuel.com, ready their wares.

2008
Nearly 30 million Americans and Canadians, twelve and older, now play fantasy sports.

2010
The Toyota Hall of Fame—an online shrine to fantasy participants—debuts.

2014
More than 41 million Americans and Canadians, twelve and older, now play fantasy sports.

2015
Daily fantasy sites come under siege. After a scandal in which employees allegedly benefitted from inside information, government agencies set about trying to shutter the sites, deeming them gambling and not games of skill.

FIELD HOCKEY

MANY OF THE SPORTS DEALT WITH HEREIN MIGRATED FROM England in the middle of the nineteenth century. Field hockey is one of them. The game's specific origins are difficult to pin down, but its rapid international spread—from the earliest codification of its rules in 1875 to its inclusion in the Summer Olympics in 1908—is a direct result of the unmatched reach of the British Empire.

After routing Napoléon's France in 1815, Great Britain stood as the world's sole superpower. Its outposts, colonies, territories, and protectorates incorporated some 10 million square miles and roughly 400 million subjects—at the time, one quarter of the global population. For the next one hundred years, it was said, the sun never set on the empire. And across all of it, Britain disseminated not only its technological and industrial know-how but also its sporting pursuits.

Thousands of Englishmen—soldiers, bureaucrats, and business types alike—needed something to do when they weren't writing laws, collecting taxes, trading goods, or otherwise modernizing/exploiting their conquered lands. So they would play their favorite games and sports, usually in social clubs staffed by locals. Those waiters, butlers, cooks, and handymen experimented with (and more often than not mastered) "English" sports—rugby, soccer, cricket, and field hockey—which is why they are played pretty much everywhere today.

But long before England's imperial spread, different kinds of field hockey were already played in far-flung geographic patches. The earliest archetypes date to classical Greece. Forms of the game also appear to have been played in India as far back as 1270 BC—well ahead of the British moving in. And sixteenth-century European explorers reported on a sport played in Chile called *chueca*, which meant "twisted one," an apparent reference to the curved sticks used in the game. The European version of field hockey seems to have begun in England in the fourteenth century, only to be quickly banned by royal decree—along with almost every other sport that was thought by the crown to be too distracting (from work or military duties).

Field hockey was revived in the 1840s by English public school students in the market for an alternative to association football (aka soccer). Several clubs sprouted in and around London, all adapting the rules of soccer to accommodate the use of sticks. Some clubs favored a rougher version played with a rubber cube—yes, really—but the more sensible rendition was backed by members of the Teddington Hockey Club, the patriarchs of modern field hockey. (The Teddington players honed their game in the outfield of an unused cricket pitch, favoring the ball of that sport because its movement was more predictable than a cube's.) The rules they formulated circa 1875 included a prohibition against raising the stick above the shoulders and a requirement that shots be taken only from within the circle, or "D," in front of the goal. Most experts consider the Teddington rules to be the spark of the modern game, but reconciling the mismatched versions of the various clubs wasn't possible until a stable governing body, the Hockey Association, was convened in London in 1886. Only then did the game become truly exportable.

In the end, bequeathed British games did not begin to eradicate the resentment the imperialists faced away from home; in fact, they may have provided a way to channel them. Field hockey, for example, was played by just a handful of nations in its first appearance at the Olympics. By 1928 the number of participants had tripled, and English dominance of the sport was on the wane. India, the often-restive colony, took that year's Olympics final (defeating the Netherlands), then proceeded to secure gold in each subsequent Summer Games for the next twenty-eight years.

THE TEDDINGTON HOCKEY CLUB'S FIELD HOCKEY RULES (1875)

RULES	NOTES
∞ 1st ∞ **The maximum length of the ground shall be 150 yards and the minimum 100 yards;[1] the maximum breadth shall be 80 yards and the minimum 50 yards. The length and breadth shall be marked with flags and the goals shall be upright posts 6 yards apart, with a tape across them 7 feet from the ground.[2]**	*1. The playing grounds, or pitch, have been downsized over time, to dimensions not unlike a soccer field's: 100 yards by 60 yards.* *2. Today's goalmouths are smaller, too, at 4 yards wide. The height, though, remains at 7 feet, though a crossbar has taken the place of that fragile tape.*
∞ 2nd ∞ **The sticks used shall be curved ones approved by the committee of the association.[3] The ball shall be an ordinary sized cricket ball.[4]**	*3. The Hockey Association has given way to the International Hockey Federation (referred to by the acronym FIH, following the French order of the words), which was founded in 1924. The FIH oversees all the sticks and balls used in international play, including the switch to composite sticks—made of tough but lightweight materials like Kevlar and fiberglass—from wooden ones in 1994.* *4. Oh no it shan't. Balls are made of hard dimpled plastic, and are about 9 inches in circumference.*
∞ 3rd ∞ **The game shall be commenced and renewed by a bully in the centre of the ground.[5] Goals shall be changed at half time only.[6]**	*5. The bully, or face-off, has been replaced by a coin toss. Bullies are used only to restart play after a stoppage. They consist of two opponents tapping sticks together once above a stationary ball, before trying to hit it.* *6. Each half is thirty-five minutes long.*

RULES	NOTES
4th	
When the ball shall be hit behind the goal-line by the attacking side, it shall be brought out straight 15 yards and started again by a bully;[7] but if hit behind by one of the side whose goal-line it is, a player of the opposite side shall hit it from within one yard of the nearest corner flag post and no player shall be allowed within 20 yards of the ball until hit out.	*7. In the early iterations of many games, the ball was returned to the team that knocked it out of bounds. Eventually, wisdom held that teams should lose control of the ball for, well, losing control of the ball. The 15-yard rule (now the 15-meter rule) described here is invoked these days only when the defensive team knocks the ball past the end line (likely in a last-ditch effort to thwart a scoring chance) within 15 meters of its own goal. The result is a free hit for the offense.*
5th	
When a ball is in touch,[8] a player of the opposite side to that which hit it out shall roll it out from the point on the boundary line where it left the ground, in a direction at right angles[9] with the boundary line at least 10 yards,[10] and it shall not be in play until it has touched the ground, and the player rolling it shall not play it until it has been played by another player, every player being then behind the ball.	*8. Out of bounds.* *9. Still true—minus the right angle. And it's no longer a "roll-in," which actually was done with hands, but a "hit-in" or "push-in" with a stick.* *10. As field hockey is today a predominantly international game, all dimensions are commonly rendered in metric measurements, although imperial units are still used in the United States.*
6th	
When a player hits the ball any one of the same side who at the moment of hitting is nearer to the opponent's goal-line is out of play, and may not touch the ball himself nor in any way whatsoever prevent any other player from doing so, until the ball has been played, unless there are at least three of his opponents nearer their own goal-line;[11] but no player is out of play when the ball is hit from the goal-line.	*11. The FIH scrapped this offside rule in 1998 to boost scoring chances.*

RULES	NOTES
7th **The ball may be stopped,[12] but not carried or knocked on by any part of the body. No player shall raise his stick above his shoulder. The ball shall be played from right to left, and no left or back-handed play,[13] charging, tripping, collaring, kicking or shinning shall be allowed.**	*12. Except players can't use their feet on purpose to stop the ball.* *13. A field hockey stick (see page 230) is flat on only one side of its face, and the ball can be played only with that side, which makes the game a tricky proposition for naturally lefty swingers (left-hand-oriented sticks are illegal). Backhanded play requires some clever twisting of the stick, but it is possible (and allowed today).*
8th **To obtain a goal a player must hit the ball between the posts and under the tape.**	
9th **No goal shall be allowed if the ball be hit from a distance of more than 15 yards from the nearest goal posts.[14]**	*14. All shots on goal must be taken from within the scoring circle, or the "D," an arc that surrounds the goal area. The penalty stroke, or flick, however, is taken from a line just 7 yards (6.4 meters) from the goal.*
10th **In all cases of a bully every player shall be behind the ball.[15]**	*15. Not exactly; players just need to stand no closer than 5 yards away.*
11th **On the infringement of any of the above rules[16] the ball shall be brought back and a bully shall take place.**	*16. Today some infractions are governed by a card system, similar to the one used in soccer. Referees issue a green card for a warning. Yellow demands temporary removal from the field (a minimum of five minutes). And red means ejection.*
12th **The ordinary number of players shall be 11 a side.**	

TO THE POINT

SCORING SIGNALS AND THE PEOPLE WHO MAKE THEM

By whatever name we call the men and women who maintain order in sports—referee, official, umpire, linesman, back judge—a primary responsibility of most of them is to decide whether a side has scored and to communicate that fact. Here is a sampling of those confirming gestures.

(Note: In some sports there are multiple ways to score; not all are included here.)

AUSTRALIAN RULES FOOTBALL
(Goal)
The signal depends on how the score has occurred. The goal umpire—one of four on-field officials—points forward with his hands at elbow height if it's a goal (between the two closer, taller uprights). He makes the same signal, but with one hand, not two, if it's a behind (between a taller and a shorter upright, or hitting any of the four uprights).

BASEBALL *(Run)*
There's some disagreement about the use of this unofficial signal—a straight-arm point at the plate—which is how some home plate umpires (one of a crew of four, each stationed at a base, during a regular season game) indicate a run has scored when a safe call is not needed. The problem is that failing to point could suggest that a player did not touch home. That miscue is in any case the obligation of the opposing team's manager to note and report.

BASKETBALL *(Three-Point Field Goal)*
There are three referees on the court in an NBA game, all of whom had been male until 1997, when Violet Palmer and Dee Kantner became the first female officials in any major professional U.S. sport. When a three-point shot is attempted, a referee will raise one arm; if that shot is successful, a second arm is raised.

CRICKET *(Six)*
Cricket sixes are signaled by an umpire raising both hands overhead. There are two on-field umpires in most matches today, situated behind the creases at each end of the pitch.

FIELD HOCKEY *(Goal)*
A referee crouches and points to the middle of the field to signal a goal. There are two referees in every game.

FOOTBALL *(Touchdown, Field Goal, Extra Point)*
There are seven officials on a football field—referee, umpire, back judge, field judge, side judge, line judge, and head linesman. Each has specific responsibilities, but any of them may signal a score by raising both arms.

ICE HOCKEY *(Goal)*
In the NHL, either of the two referees (but neither of the two linesmen) decides whether a player has scored, extending one arm to his side for a goal.

LACROSSE *(Goal)*
Major League Lacrosse (MLL) employs a trio of on-field officials, any of whom can signal a goal by raising his arms as for a touchdown before extending them forward.

RUGBY LEAGUE *(Try)*
There are three officials on the field: one referee, two assistants. A try is signaled with a straight-arm point to the ground.

RUGBY UNION *(Try)*
Three officials patrol the field. A try is signaled with one arm straight in the air.

SOCCER *(Goal)*
One referee and two assistant referees (formerly known as linesmen) preside over the field. While there's no official referee signal for a goal, many will confirm a score using a straight-arm point toward the center line of the field, where play will resume.

FOOTBALL

A NATION'S SPORTING PASSIONS REVEAL MUCH ABOUT ITS character. Exhibit B in support of this contention is the version of soccer played in Brazil, a beautiful display of flowing movement and creative passing that mirrors the artistic and celebratory soul of that country. But Exhibit A is without doubt the symbiosis of sport and society that is American football.

As played in the United States, football is foremost a game of territorial acquisition, fitting for a sport born in the century that saw Manifest Destiny emerge as the national credo. The incremental, often-obtuse rule changes that have redefined the game for each succeeding generation of players and fans echo the complexities of the U.S. legal system. And, finally, the rough-and-tumble nature of the sport appeals to the darker side of the American psyche.

Of all the varieties of "football" that emerged in the latter half of the nineteenth century, America's version was unquestionably the most violent. It began in the late 1860s as an amalgam of rugby and soccer: teams of mostly college players—as many as twenty-five on a side—tried to kick or punch the ball across a goal line but didn't carry or pass it. As the Victorian philosophy of Muscular Christianity took root in this country, football began to morph into a more physical, ball-carrying game. (Muscular Christianity, which stressed piety and masculinity, was also a reason for the emphasis on sports at America's YMCAs, where basketball and volleyball were invented.) Teams tended to rely on "mass momentum," essentially ramming full speed into the opposition in hopes of moving the ball up the field.

American football, like other emerging sports of the time, wasn't played the same way everywhere and would likely have faded into history without a set of mutually agreed upon rules. Fittingly for a country fond of the "Great Man" theory of history, there was an American with the singular vision and force of will to forge a viable game on the gridiron. Walter Camp, widely considered to be the father of American football, was an accomplished player and coach at Yale. His first game changer was the introduction of the line of scrimmage, which he revealed at a rules conference in 1880. Arguably the single most distinguishing feature of the game, the line clearly established possession, eliminating the need for the restart free-for-all, or scrum, that follows a tackle in rugby. Its implementation quickly led to the evolution of many of the offensive positions that still define the game. But football continued to lack style and substance, being both incredibly dangerous (from head-on collisions) and exceedingly boring (thanks to rules interpretations that allowed for lengthy stall tactics). At rules conventions through the years, Camp continued to push for his vision of football, by creating downs, the scoring system, the center snap, and the safety, as well as instigating many fundamental strategies.

Despite Camp's innovations, football remained notably unsafe. Mass momentum was still employed by most teams, and players risked serious injury on virtually every play. In 1905 nineteen students were killed playing college football, and there were widespread calls for the game to be banned. But many powerful forces, including President Theodore Roosevelt, were vocal advocates of football, and they didn't want to see it disappear. Roosevelt convened the heads of several major colleges (in what led to the creation of what we now know as the National Collegiate Athletic Association) and instructed them to devise rules to enhance player safety. A committee, headed by Walter Camp, was delegated the task of reform.

Yes, more than a quarter century after he first began to refine football, Camp was still at it. This time around, the sport finally took flight, literally: in *Spalding's Official Foot Ball Guide for 1906*, advocates of the forward pass—long ridiculed as a quasi-legal trick play—finally won the day. As Spalding trumpeted on its cover, "The New Rules" were edited by Walter Camp, and they included a toe-dip into the waters of passing. That autumn witnessed the birth of modern American football.

WALTER CAMP'S "OFFICIAL FOOT BALL RULES 1906"

FIELD, EQUIPMENT, PLAYERS, OFFICIALS, ETC.

RULE 1.

(*a*) The game shall be played upon a rectangular field, 330 feet in length and 160 feet in width,[1] enclosed by heavy white lines marked in lime[2] upon the ground. The lines at the two ends shall be termed "goal lines." Those on the two sides shall be termed "side lines" and shall be considered to extend beyond their points of intersection with the goal lines.

The field shall be marked off at intervals of 5 yards with white lines parallel to the *goal lines*, and also at intervals of 5 yards with white lines parallel to the *side lines*.[3]

The goal shall be placed in the middle of each goal line, and shall consist of two upright posts exceeding 20 feet in height[4] and placed 18 feet 6 inches apart, with horizontal cross-bar 10 feet from the ground.

(*b*) The foot ball used shall be of leather, enclosing an inflated rubber bladder. The ball shall have the shape of a prolate spheroid.

(*c*) The game shall be played by two teams of eleven men each.

---

1. *The field today is 360 feet long, including the 10 yards of end zone on either end. The end zone was introduced in 1912 to offer teams room to complete goal line passes; previously, passes (which were only instituted with this set of rules—see Rule 14) had to be completed on the "in bounds" side of the goal line and the ball run over for a touchdown.*
2. *Something in the chalky calcium carbonate family, anyway—or white paint.*
3. *Camp annotated his rules with Notes and Exceptions throughout. For instance, here he explained that lines parallel to the goal line would prove useful in gauging distance gained, while lines parallel to the sidelines delineated a space within which a ball could not be thrown. Camp also recommended, in a separate note, using two poles connected by 10 yards of chain or rope to confirm first-down yardage, which was changed to 10 yards from 5. The "chains" remain a tool of the trade today.*
4. *Stronger kickers called for taller uprights—45 feet tall, to be exact. The posts were moved to the back of the end zone in the 1920s, but they were returned to the goal line less than a decade later. It wasn't until 1974 that the much less intrusive spot was made their permanent home.*

(*d*) A player may be substituted for another at any time. In such a case the substitute must go directly to the Referee and report himself before engaging in play. A player who has been replaced by a substitute may not return to further participation in the game.[5]

(*e*) No player having projecting nails or iron plates on his shoes or any projecting metallic or hard substance on his person shall be allowed to play in a match. If head protectors are worn, no sole leather, papier-mâché,[6] or other hard or unyielding material shall be used in their construction, and all other devices for protectors must be so arranged and padded as, in the judgment of the umpire, to be without danger to other players. Leather cleats upon the shoes shall be allowed as heretofore.

(*f*) The officials of the game shall be a Referee, two Umpires and a Linesman.[7]

---

5. *Players removed from the game were first allowed to return in 1941, a change that opened the door to today's offense/defense platoon system. Until then, team members played on both sides of scrimmage.*
6. *Helmets have come a long way (see "Top Story," page 92). And yet evidence suggests that football players are still not protected well enough, as more of them experience serious symptoms of brain trauma long after they retire. Some experts argue that all the advances in helmet technology have actually increased the chance of injury, because it makes players more reckless.*
7. *Today there are seven, including a side judge who makes sure players stay in bounds, a back judge who patrols the action downfield, and a line judge who keeps his eye on the line of scrimmage.*

RULE 2.

(*a*) The length of the game shall be 60 minutes, divided into two halves of 30 minutes each,[8] exclusive of time taken out. There shall be ten minutes intermission between the two halves.

(*b*) Whenever the commencement of a game is so late that in the opinion of the Referee, there is any likelihood of the game being interfered with by darkness,[9] he shall, before play begins, arbitrarily shorten the two halves to such length as shall insure two equal halves being completed, and shall notify both captains of the exact time thus set. Either side refusing to abide by the opinion of the Referee on this point shall forfeit the game.

8. Make that four quarters of fifteen minutes each.

9. The first National Football League game played under the lights was in 1929.

RULE 3.

The game shall be decided by the final score at the end of the two halves. The following shall be the value of plays in scoring:

Touchdown, 5 points.[10]

Goal from touchdown, 1 point.[11]

Goal from the field, 4 points.[12]

Safety by opponents, 2 points.

10. In 1912 a touchdown became worth the six points it is today.

11. Aka the extra point, although it existed in a slightly different form until 1922.

12. Aka field goal. Within three years it was downgraded by a point.

RULE 4.

METHODS OF KICKING THE BALL.

(*a*) A *Place-kick* is made by kicking the ball after it has been placed on the ground.[13]

(*b*) A *Kick-off* is a place-kick from the center of the field of play. A kick-off cannot score a goal. (Rule 7.)

(*c*) A *Punt* is made by dropping the ball from the hands and kicking it before it touches the ground.

(*d*) A *Punt-out* is a punt made by a player of the side which has made a touchdown to another of his own side for a fair catch. (Rule 21, *c*.)

(*e*) A *Drop-kick* is made by dropping the ball from the hands and kicking it the instant it rises from the ground.[14]

(*f*) A *Kick-out* is a drop-kick, place-kick or punt made by a player of the side which has made a safety or a touchback.[15]

(*g*) A *Free-kick* is a term used to designate any kick when the opponents are restrained by rule from advancing beyond a certain point before the ball is put in play.

13. Ever try to kick a football that's lying flat on the ground? That's why a teammate is tasked with holding it upright.

14. A drop-kick is no more accurate than it was back in the day, and thus is a rarely employed tactic. The last successful NFL attempt was in 2006.

15. After a touchdown, no; after a safety, yes, where it has effectively been replaced by the free kick.

RULE 5.

DEFINITION OF TERMS.

(*a*) The "*Field of Play,*" as technically termed in these rules, is the rectangular space bounded by the goal lines and the side lines.

(*b*) A *Scrimmage* takes place when the holder of the ball places it flat upon the ground, with its long axis at right angles to the line of scrimmage, and puts it in play by kicking it forward or snapping it back.

1. The scrimmage does not end until the ball is again declared dead.

2. The ball is always put in play from a scrimmage, except in cases where other specific provision is made.

(*c*) The *Line of Scrimmage* for each side is an imaginary line parallel to the goal line and passing through that point of the ball nearest the side's own goal line.

(*d*) A *Fair Catch* consists in catching the ball after it has been kicked by one of the opponents and before it touches the ground, or in similarly catching a "punt-out" by another of the catcher's own side, provided the player while advancing toward the ball signals his intention of making a fair catch by raising his hand *clearly* above his head and takes not more than two steps after making the catch.

(1) The mark of the catch shall be the spot at which the ball is actually caught, and in case the catcher advances within his lawful limit after the catch, the ball shall be brought back to the mark.

(2) It is not a fair catch if the ball, after the kick, was touched by another of a player's side before the catch. Opponents who are off-side shall not in any way interfere with a player who has an opportunity for making a fair catch; nor shall a player be thrown to the ground after he has made such catch.

(3) If a side thus obtains a fair catch the ball may be put in play by a punt, drop-kick, place-kick, or scrimmage. If the ball is put in play by a kick, the opponents may not come within 10 yards of the spot on which the fair catch was made; and the ball must be kicked

from some point directly behind the spot where the catch was made, on a line parallel to the side line.[16]

(*e*) A *Down* occurs when the Referee blows his whistle or declares the ball dead. The Referee shall blow his whistle or declare the ball dead: (1) When a player having the ball cries "Down";[17] (2) When any portion of his person, except his hands or feet, touches the ground while he is in the grasp of an opponent; (3) When he goes out of bounds; or, (4) Whenever he is so held that his forward progress has been stopped; (5) When, on a forward pass, the ball, after being passed forward, touches the ground before being touched by a player of either side; (6) When, on a forward pass, the ball, after being passed forward, crosses the goal line without touching a player of either side; (7) When a kicked ball (except a kick-off or free-kick) strikes inside the field of play and then rolls over the goal line before being touched by a player of either side.

(*f*) A *Touchdown* is made when the ball lawfully in possession of a player is declared dead by the Referee, any part of it being on, above or behind the opponent's goal line.

(*g*) A *Touchback* is made when the ball in possession of a player guarding his own goal is declared dead by the Referee, any part of it being on, above or behind the goal line, provided the impetus which sent it to or across the line was given by an opponent. The referee shall declare the ball dead behind the goal line just as if it were on the field of play.

(*h*) A *Safety* is made when the ball in the possession of a player guarding his own goal is declared dead by the Referee, any part of it being on, above or behind the goal line, provided the impetus which sent it to or across the line was given by the side defending the goal. Such impetus could come: (1) From a kick, pass, snap-back or fumble by one of the player's own side; (2) From a kick which bounded back from an opponent; (3) In case a player carrying the ball is forced back, provided the ball was not declared dead by the Referee before the line was reached or crossed.

---

16. *Clearly, there was once much more of an emphasis on kicking—for field position, ball movement, and scoring. As passing opened up the game, many of these fairly arcane instructions involving kicks became irrelevant.*

17. *Sounds a little like crying "Uncle!" Needless to say, it's no longer an option.*

A safety is also made when a player of the side in possession of the ball commits a foul which would give the ball to the opponents behind the offender's goal line; also when the ball, kicked by a man behind his goal line, crosses the extended portion of either side line.

(*i*) A *Goal from Touchdown* is made by a place-kick direct, or a place-kick preceded by a punt-out.

(*j*) A *Goal from the Field* is made by kicking the ball from the field of play over the cross-bar of the opponents' goal in any way except by a punt or a kick-off.

(*k*) A *Foul* is a violation of any rule.

(*l*) The ball is *Out of Bounds* when either the ball or any part of a player who holds it touches the ground on or outside the side line or side line extended.

(*m*) A player trips another when he obstructs below the knee, with that part of his leg that is below the knee.

(*n*) *Hurdling* in the open is jumping over or attempting to jump over an opponent who is still on his feet. Hurdling in the line is jumping over, or attempting to jump over, a player on the line of scrimmage, with the feet or knees foremost, within the distance of 5 yards on either side of the point where the ball was put in play.

RULE 6.

The ball is *Dead:*

(*a*) When the Referee blows his whistle or declares that a down, touchdown, touchback, safety or goal has been made.

(*b*) When a fair catch has been made.

(*c*) When any portion of the person (except the hands or feet) of the player carrying the ball touches the ground, when the player is in the grasp of an opponent.

(*d*) When the ball goes out of bounds after a kick, before touching a player who is on-side or is otherwise entitled to it.

(*e*) When a player carrying the ball goes out of bounds.

RULE 7.

(*a*) The captains of the opposing teams shall toss up a coin before the game, the winner of the toss to have his choice of goal or kick-off. If the winner of the toss selects the goal, the loser must take the kick-off. The teams shall change goals after every try-at-goal following a touchdown,

and after every goal from the field, and the side just scored upon shall have the option of kicking off or of having their opponents kick off.[18] At the beginning of the second half the teams shall take opposite goals from those assumed at the beginning of the first half, and the kick-off shall be made by the side which did not first kick off at the beginning of the game.

(*b*) At kick-off, if the ball goes out of bounds before it is touched by an opponent, it shall be brought back and be kicked off again. If it is kicked out of bounds a second time it shall go as a kick-off to the opponents. If either side thus forfeits the ball twice, it shall go to the opponents, who shall put it in play by a scrimmage at the center of the field.[19]

(*c*) At kick-off, if the ball is kicked across the goal line and is there declared dead when in the possession of one of the side defending the goal, it is a touchback. If the ball is not declared dead, the side defending the goal may run with it or kick it exactly as if it had not crossed the goal line. If it is declared dead in possession of the attacking side, provided that the man was on-side, it is a touchdown.

(*d*) At kick-off and on a punt, drop-kick, or place-kick from a fair catch, the opposite side must stand at least 10 yards in front of the ball until it is kicked.

---

18. *Why would a team that has been scored upon opt to kick the ball back to its opponent? Moving the ball was quite difficult, so a team just scored upon might kick off, hoping to force a punt from deep in its opponent's territory, then return* that *kick for a better field position than they might have gained in a conventional offensive drive.*
19. *Teams today get one shot at kicking off. If the ball goes out of bounds, the opponent takes over at the 35-yard line.*

RULE 8.

(*a*) Time shall be taken out whenever the game is necessarily delayed or while the ball is being brought out for a try-at-goal, kick-out, or kick-off, after a fair catch has been made, or when play is for any reason suspended by the Referee. Time shall begin again when the ball is actually put in play.[20]

(*b*) Either captain[21] may ask that time be called three times during each half without penalty. If thereafter, however, time is taken out at

the request of a captain, his side shall be penalized by a loss of two yards for each time (unless a player be removed from the game), the number of the down and the *distance* to be gained remaining the same as they were before the request was made. The Referee, however, may suspend play at any time at his own discretion without penalty to either side.

(*c*) Time shall not be called for the end of a half until the ball is dead, and in case of a touchdown, the try-at-goal shall be allowed.

(*d*) No delay arising from any cause whatsoever shall continue more than two minutes.[22]

---

20. *True, but if the clock hasn't been stopped, teams cannot lollygag. There are forty seconds between when one play ends and the next must begin.*

21. *Actually, the head coach or any player on the field can call a time-out.*

22. *The two-minute rule was instituted to prevent stalling tactics, which are no longer an issue. But it would be nice if today's replay officials abided by it.*

RULE 9.

(*a*) The snapper-back shall be entitled to full and undisturbed possession of the ball. The opponents must not interfere in any way whatever with the snapper-back, nor touch him or the ball until it is actually put in play.

(*b*) When snapping the ball back, the snapper-back must be on-side, except for his head, and the hand or foot[23] **used in snapping the ball.**

(*c*) If, after the snapper-back has taken the position, he voluntarily moves the ball as if to snap it, whether he withholds it altogether or only momentarily, it shall be considered as in play, and the scrimmage as begun.

(*d*) The snapper-back and the player opposite him in the scrimmage may not afterward touch the ball until it has touched some player other than these two.

(*e*) If the snapper-back in a scrimmage kicks the ball forward, no player of his side of the ball may touch it until it has been touched by an opponent or until it has gone 10 yards into the opponents' territory.

(*f*) If a player other than the snapper-back of the side in possession of the ball makes a deliberate attempt,[24] **by a false start or otherwise, to draw the opponents off-side, the ball, if snapped, shall not be regarded as in play or the scrimmage as begun.**

23. Again with the feet. It has been quite a while since a center thought it prudent to heel the ball back to his quarterback to begin a play.

24. This would be news to today's quarterbacks, many of whom are adept at drawing a defense offside with changes in their signal-calling cadences.

RULE 10.

The player who first receives the ball when it is snapped back shall not carry the ball forward beyond the line of scrimmage unless he shall have regained it after having delivered it wholly out of his possession to another player, or unless he shall have crossed the line of scrimmage at least 5 yards outside of the point where the ball was snapped.[25]

25. Today, once the ball is snapped, whoever receives the snap is free to move the ball forward on his own regardless of where he is relative to the center—and thus is the quarterback sneak allowed.

RULE 11.

(*a*) Before the ball is put in play no player shall lay his hands upon, or by the use of his hands or arms, interfere with an opponent in such a way as to delay putting the ball in play. Any such interference shall be regarded as delay of game.
(*b*) At the moment when the ball is put in play in a scrimmage, no player of the side which has the ball shall be in motion.[26]
(*c*) When the ball is put in play at least six players of the side holding the ball must be on the line of scrimmage. If only six players are on the line of scrimmage, one player of those not on the line of scrimmage must stand with both feet outside the outside foot of the player on the end of the line.

1. No player of those ordinarily occupying the position of center, guard, or tackle—that is, the five middle players of the line—may drop back from the line of scrimmage on the offense unless he is at least 5 yards back of the line of scrimmage when the ball is put in play, and another player of those ordinarily behind the line of scrimmage takes his place on the line of scrimmage.

26. While the reason behind this prohibition—to prevent offenses from making it impossible for defenses to follow what is going on—is still a guiding principle of the rule book, one member of the offense can be moving laterally along the line of scrimmage when the ball is snapped.

RULE 12.

(*a*) After the ball is put in play, the players of the side in possession may obstruct the opponents with the body only,[27] except the player running with the ball, who may ward off opponents with his hands and arms.
(*b*) After the ball is put in play, the players of the side not in possession may use their hands and arms, but only to get their opponents out of the way in order to reach the ball or stop the player carrying it.

27. *Through the years, offensive linemen have been allowed, to varying degrees, to use arms and at times hands to fend off onrushing defenders. These days, grabbing and holding are illegal, but pushing with open hands is not, as long as it is done without fully extending the arms.*

RULE 13.

If the ball goes out of bounds, whether it bounced back or not, a player of the side which secures it must bring it to the spot where the ball crossed the side line, and there, after declaring how far he intends walking, walk out with it,[28] in company with the Referee, at right angles to the side line, any distance not less than 5 nor more than 15 yards, and at a point indicated by the Referee put it down for a scrimmage.

28. *Placement of the ball is the job of the referee alone. Nor is there any question about where the ball goes: football fields are marked with hashes both to the right and to the left of center, for ball-spotting.*

RULE 14.

(*a*) A player may throw, pass, or bat the ball in any direction except toward his opponent's goal.
EXCEPTION—(1) One forward pass shall be allowed to each scrimmage,[29] provided such pass may be made by a player who was behind the line of scrimmage when the ball was put in play, and provided the ball, after being passed forward, does not touch the ground before being touched by a player of either side.[30]
EXCEPTION—(2) The pass may not be touched by a player who was on the line of scrimmage when the ball is put in play—except by either of the two men playing on the ends of the line.

EXCEPTION—(3) A forward pass over the line of scrimmage within the space of 5 yards on each side of the center shall be unlawful.[31]
EXCEPTION—(4) A forward pass by the side which does not put the ball in play in a scrimmage shall be unlawful.
EXCEPTION—(5) A forward pass which crosses the goal line on the fly or bound without touching a player of either side shall be declared a touchback for the defenders of the goal.[32]

---

29. *And thus the game was forever changed. Well, set upon a path to changing, anyway. It would be twenty-eight years before the offense could pass more than one time per series of downs.*
30. *One reason it took a while for passing to gain traction was that Camp punished an untouched incompletion with this change of possession wherever the ball hit the ground.*
31. *The intention was to make the game a little less dangerous by opening up the center of the field—with passes so thrown resulting in loss of possession.*
32. *This extreme sanction was dropped with the introduction of end zones. It was almost as if Camp devised his exceptions in an attempt to lessen the very effects he was hoping the forward pass would create. He was fighting a losing battle: today NFL teams average about thirty-five passes a game, and the sport has never been more popular.*

RULE 15.

(*a*) If in three consecutive downs (unless the ball shall have crossed the goal line), a team, having constantly had the ball in its possession, shall not have advanced the ball 10 yards, it shall go to the opponents on the spot of the fourth down.[33]
(*b*) When a distance penalty is given, the ensuing down shall be counted as first down if the offense was committed by the side *not in possession* of the ball. In case the side *in possession* of the ball was the offender, the number of the down and *point* to be gained for first down shall remain the same as they were at the beginning of the scrimmage during which the foul occurred.

---

33. *Within a couple of years, a fourth down was added to get the requisite 10 yards.*

RULE 16.

(*a*) In a scrimmage, no part of any player shall be ahead of his line of scrimmage.
(*b*) A player is put off-side if the ball in play has been touched by one of his own side behind him.[34] No player, when off-side, shall touch the ball except on a fumble or a muff, nor shall he interrupt or obstruct any opponent with his hands or arms until again on-side. (This shall not be so interpreted as to prevent a player who is running down the field under a kick from using his hands or arms to push opponents out of the way in order to get at the ball or the player catching it.) No player may, however, be called off-side behind his own goal line.
(*c*) If a kicked ball, before it touches the ground or the person of an opponent is touched when inside the opponents' 10-yard line by a player who is off-side, it is a foul, and a touchback shall be declared for the defenders of the goal.

34. As Rules 16 and 17 indicate, offside violations were a major consideration of the early game, which held close to the rudiments of soccer and rugby.

RULE 17.

(*a*) A player being off-side is put on-side only when the ball has touched an opponent, or when a kicked ball touches the ground, in the field of play.

(1) The player who, standing back of his own line of scrimmage, receives the ball from one of his own side and then kicks it beyond the line of scrimmage, may not himself get the ball until after it has touched a player of the opposing side.

RULE 18.

(*a*) The side which has a free-kick must be behind the ball when it is kicked, except in case of a punt-out.
(*b*) In the case of a kick-off, kick-out, kick from the fair catch, the ball must be kicked from a distance of at least 10 yards toward the opponents' goal line[35] from the line restraining the player making the kick, unless it is touched by an opponent; otherwise the ball is not in play.

35. An onside kick in modern idiom.

RULE 19.

(*a*) A side which has made a touchback or a safety must kick out from some point inside the kicker's 25-yard line.[36] The kicker's side must be behind the ball when it is kicked and the opponents must be on the 25-yard line or nearer their own goal.

36. Today the kick is made only after a safety, and from the 20-yard line.

RULE 20.

(*a*) Starting forward beyond the restraining line is lawful, in case of a punt-out or kick-off, as soon as the ball is kicked; but the opponents must not so start until the ball is kicked.

(*b*) Starting forward beyond the restraining line is lawful in case of any other free-kick, viz., a kick-out, kick from a fair-catch and place-kick for goal after a touchdown: (1) When the player of the side having the free-kick advances beyond his restraining line or mark with the ball in his possession; (2) If he allows the ball to touch the ground by accident or otherwise.

RULE 21.

(*a*) A side which has made a touchdown may try at goal only by a place-kick direct, or by a place-kick preceded by a punt-out.

(*b*) If the try be by a place-kick direct, a player of the side which has made the touchdown shall hold the ball for a kick by another of his side at some point outside the goal on a line parallel to the side line passing through the point where the touchdown was declared.[37] The kicker may touch or adjust the ball in the hands of the holder so long as the ball does not touch the ground. The opponents must remain behind their goal line until the Referee signals with his hand that the ball has been placed upon the ground.

(*c*) If the try-at-goal is to be preceded by a punt-out, the punter shall kick the ball from the point at which the line parallel to the side line, and passing through the spot of the touchdown, intersects the goal line. The players of his side must stand in the field of play not less than 5 yards from the goal line.

(1) The opponents may line up anywhere on the goal line except within the space of 15 feet on each side of the punter's mark, but

they shall not interfere with the punter. If a fair catch is made from a punt-out, the mark shall serve to determine the positions as the mark of any fair catch, and the try-at-goal shall then be made by a place-kick from the spot, or any point directly behind it. If a fair catch is not made on the first attempt, the ball shall go as a kick-off at the center of the field.

(*d*) The holder of the ball and no other player in a place-kick after a fair catch or touchdown may be off-side or out of bounds without invalidating the kick.

(*e*) After the try-at-goal, whether the goal be made or missed, the ball shall be kicked off at the center of the field as provided in Rule 7.

---

37. As of the 2015 season, point-after attempts in the NFL are kicked from the 15-yard line, in response to the almost-guaranteed success (and lack of drama) of kicks from the previous official line of scrimmage, the 2-yard line. Two-point conversion attempts continue to be attempted from the 2-yard line.

RULE 22.

PROHIBITIONS.

(*a*) There shall be no coaching, either by substitutes or by any other persons not participating in the game. In case of accident to a player, one representative of the player's team may, if he has first obtained the consent of the umpire, come upon the field of play to attend to the injured player. This representative need not always be the same person. No person other than the players, the officials, the representatives above mentioned or an incoming substitute shall at any time come upon the field of play. Only five men shall be allowed to walk up and down on each side of the field. The rest, including substitutes, water carriers, and all who are admitted within the enclosure, must be seated throughout the game.[38]

(*b*) There shall be no striking with the fist or elbows, kneeing, kicking, meeting with the knee, nor striking with the locked hands by line men, when they are breaking through; nor shall a player on defense strike in the face with a heel of the hand, the opponent who is carrying the ball.

(*c*) There shall be no piling up on the player after the Referee has declared the ball dead. There shall be no tripping, tackling the

runner when clearly out of bounds, hurdling,[39] or any other acts of unnecessary roughness.

(*d*) There shall be no unsportsmanlike conduct on the part of the players. This shall include the use of abusive or insulting language to opponents or officials.

(*e*) There shall be no tackling below the knees, except by the men on the line of scrimmage on the defense, and of these, the two men occupying the positions on the ends of the line of scrimmage may not tackle below the knees.[40]

---

38. Camp's attempt to keep the sideline orderly and uncrowded is admirable, but it was a fool's errand. Today's sidelines teem with close to a hundred people—players, coaches, support staff, and random hangers-on.

39. Although sometimes flagged, hurdling is just as often allowed—and praised on postgame highlight shows.

40. All members of the defense can tackle below the knees today, but they may get yelled at if they do. The most-taught, "fundamental" technique is shoulder-to-rib-cage contact followed by a strong-arm wrap-up of the torso.

TOP STORY

FOOTBALL HEADGEAR OVER TIME

An argument can be made that the helmet is the single most important piece of equipment in sports for the job it is designed to do. But despite a march of innovation, the evidence suggests that further improvements will be coming.

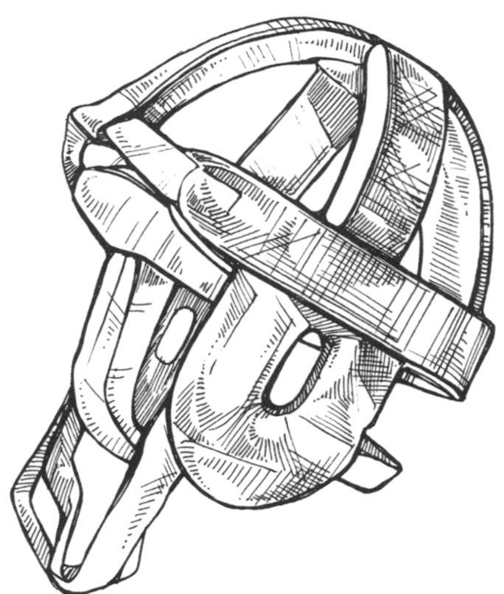

SOFT LEATHER SKULLCAP AND HARNESS 1890s–1909
There is much debate about who developed the first helmet and why. Some say it was a shoemaker trying to protect a player who'd been kicked in the head once too often; others believe the helmet was developed to avoid cauliflower ear, an unsightly condition more common today in wrestling than in football.

SOFT LEATHER 1920s
The addition of padding increased shock absorption. Helmets also got slightly bigger (to encompass the entire head) and earflap holes were standardized (so players could hear what was going on).

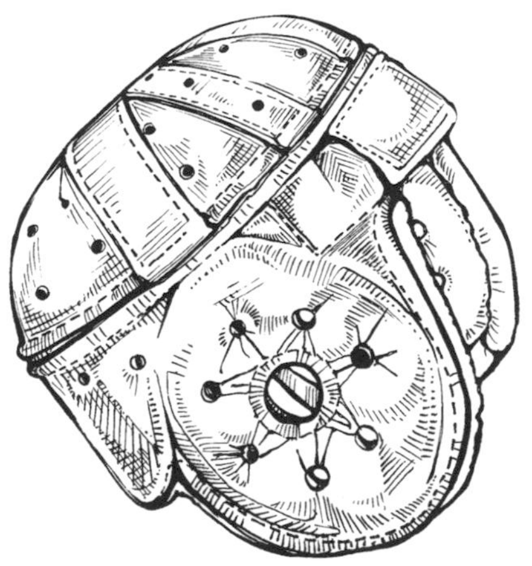

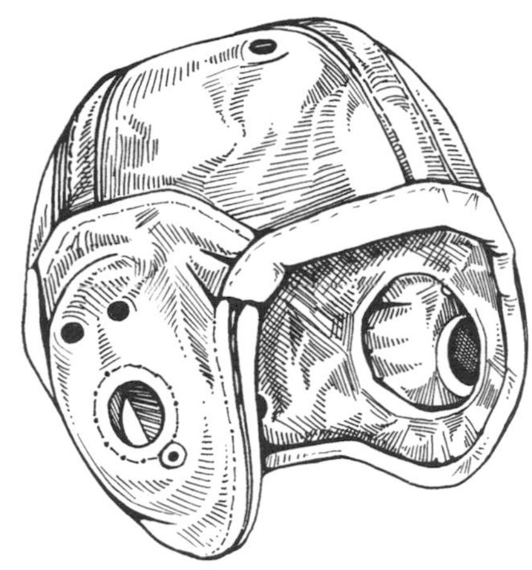

HARD LEATHER WITH INTERNAL COTTON PADDING 1930s
This further upgrade in safety features coincided with the growth of the game.

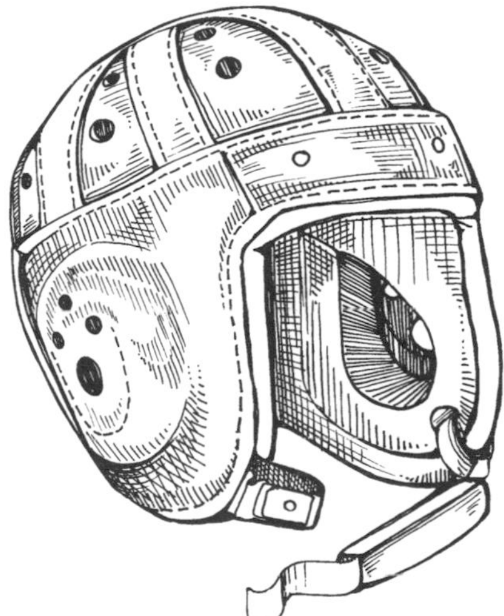

HARD LEATHER WITH SUSPENSION PADDING AND CHIN STRAP 1940s
Most serious players were already voluntarily wearing helmets by the time their use was finally mandated by the NFL in 1943 (three years after the chin strap was added). At the end of the decade, the league adopted plastic lids manufactured and patented by the John T. Riddell Company (which makes NFL helmets to this day).

HARD PLASTIC WITH SINGLE-BAR FACE MASK 1950s
The face mask began to gain traction in 1953. One story has it that the tipping-point incident was Cleveland Browns quarterback Otto Graham being knocked out of a game following an elbow to the face. The team's trainer attached a single bar to Graham's helmet that ran across his mouth, protecting it from further harm. In 1955 the bar was added to all helmets.

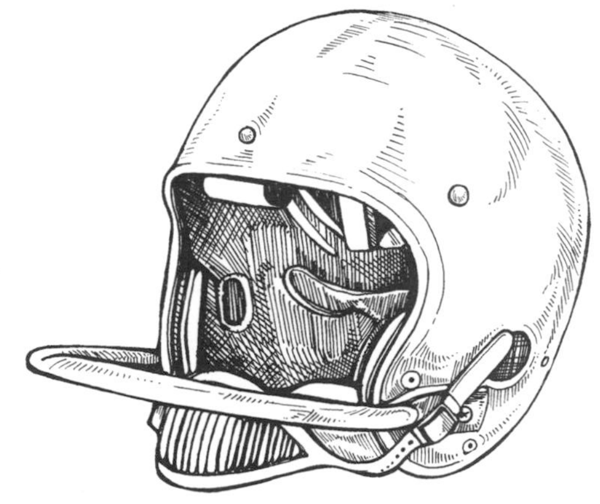

DOUBLE-BAR FACE MASK 1960s
By the early part of the decade, every player in the NFL wore a face mask, and some began to customize their own, opting for two bars across or a bar down the middle (between the eyes).

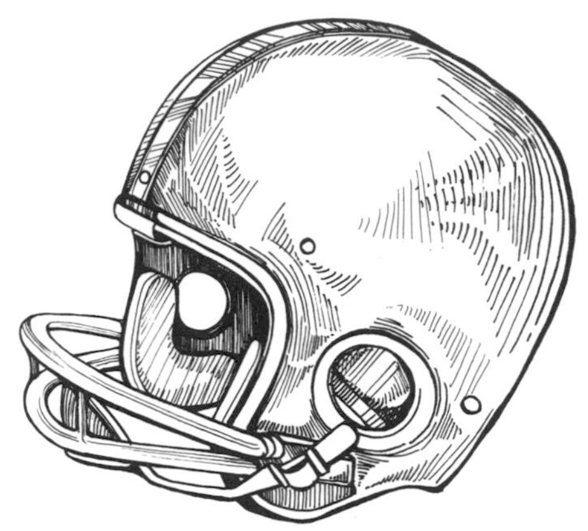

FULL FACE MASK AND AIR-BLADDER PADDING 1970s
The "full" face mask debuted in the 1970s and featured several bars, both vertical and horizontal. Riddell continued to innovate, creating an energy-absorbing helmet with "air bladders," interior pads that could be inflated to soften the impact of collisions and custom-fit the helmet to a player's head size.

EYE VISORS 1980s
In the middle of the decade the NFL switched from run-of-the-mill plastic to stronger, lighter polycarbonate, and more players—most notably the star running back Eric Dickerson—started to wear protective visors over their eyes.

IMPACT-ABSORBING FOAM PADDING 2000–2009
More than two decades after the previous major helmet change, Riddell's Revolution Speed model became the NFL standard. It features impact-absorbing foam padding and a more spherical design, all with an eye toward improved safety. The NFL also banned single-bar face masks in 2004.

CONTOURED SKULL WITH SLITS, SHOCK-DETECTING SENSORS 2015
In response to magnified concerns about player risk, the NFL continues to push helmet technology. The latest examples include shock-detecting sensors on chin straps—to indicate the possibility of a concussion—and a contoured, more flexible shape with slits that reduce the amount of energy transferred to the skull upon collision.

GOLF

FOR A SPORT EXEMPLIFIED BY PRISTINE TRACTS OF PRIME real estate owned and operated by exclusive clubs, golf has a rather humble ancestry. The wide swaths of sand and grass that make up much of Scotland's eastern coast weren't suitable for farming or much of anything else except grazing sheep and cattle. The shepherds who tended to these herds in the first few centuries of the second millennium (and surely much earlier) were often lonely and bored, so they were on the lookout for an activity to help them pass the hours.

One that engaged them was a form of target practice: hitting rocks or frozen sheep dung at stumps, boulders, and possibly holes in the ground dug by furrowing animals. It's a virtual certainty that shepherds in other parts of the world developed similar time-wasting habits, which explains some disagreement around the origins of the game. But golf as we know it today indisputably originated in Scotland.

For reasons quite beyond the average weekend duffer's grasp—aside from a dearth of things to do in rural Scotland six hundred years before the invention of smartphones—this shepherd's pastime caught on among the broader Scottish population. Eventually, golf grew so prevalent that King James II had to ban it in 1457 as a matter of national security: all that swinging at dung and rocks was keeping the citizenry from important archery practice. Indeed, his edict is recognized as the first written reference to golf (a name thought to be derived from a word meaning "club").

The king's decree did little to dull golf's appeal. The game remained illegal well into the sixteenth century, but it continued to spread surreptitiously throughout the British Isles as an ad hoc leisure activity governed primarily by local geographic peculiarities. Players in some regions toiled on courses with as few as five holes, others on courses with twenty-two. Today's total of eighteen is simply the result of circumstance. The course that eventually became the Royal and Ancient Golf Club of St. Andrews—the R&A, golf's most hallowed ground—initially had eleven holes. Golfers walked the eleven "out" (away from the clubhouse) before turning around to walk the same eleven "in" (hence a "round" of golf). After a time, the wise and watchful keepers of St. Andrews deemed the first four holes too easy, and they combined them into two, leaving nine.

St. Andrews helped define the game in other ways, too. The legendary course was originally a rabbit farm, and the critters were apt to build their warrens in the lushest areas of the coastline—or "linksland," from a Scottish word for "rising ground." Over time, areas surrounding those warrens were worn down by the rabbits' feet into flat patches that became early versions of putting greens. Golf's sand traps were also the result of instinctive animal behavior. Sheep burrowed into the dunes to take shelter from howling Scottish gales. Deep depressions were left behind when they ambled away. (What was good for the sheep was not good for the golfer.)

Even though golf had been played in and around the town of St. Andrews for centuries, it wasn't until 1754 that a group of professors, landowners, and other prominent citizens formed the Society of St. Andrews Golfers, the precursor to the R&A. By that time, the oldest surviving rules of the game had been written down by the Gentlemen Golfers of Leith (sometimes known as the Gentlemen Golfers of Edinburgh) for a tournament in April 1744. Today the two primary sets of modern golf regulations (those of the R&A and the United States Golf Association) fill small books and are the subject of fierce parsing and debate. But at their core, they prescribe the same game as those written nearly three hundred years ago.

THE GENTLEMEN GOLFERS OF LEITH'S "ARTICLES & LAWS IN PLAYING AT GOLF" (1744)

RULES	NOTES
1st **You must Tee your Ball within a Club's length of the Hole.[1]**	*1. That's right, just off the green. A golfer putted out at one hole, walked a few steps, then teed up the next drive. Tee boxes, the designated areas from which golfers now hit their drives, became regular course features in the late nineteenth century.*
2nd **Your Tee[2] must be upon the Ground.[3]**	*2. "Tee" comes from the Scottish Gaelic* tigh, *meaning "house."* *3. Golfers once hit their first shot at each hole off a mound of sand. America's first portable tee, patented in 1890, was a small rubber slab that rested flat on the ground; three vertical rubber prongs held the ball aloft. Two years later, the Perfectum, a rubber circle with a metal spike, was the first that penetrated the ground. The first commercial tee—the Reddy Tee, a version of which is still used today—was invented in 1921 by an American dentist, William Lowell. Building a tee from sand or turf is still legal.*
3rd **You are not to change the Ball which you Strike off the Tee.[4]**	*4. So a player can't switch midhole to a ball with properties more advantageous to a particular situation. But there was an ancillary benefit: thrift. The standard ball, the featherie, wasn't cheap, made as it was of leather and stuffed with "the down of unfledged birds." It's even pricier today. Old Tom Morris, a golf pioneer who lived and died in St. Andrews, made featheries. One of them commands thousands of dollars at auction.*

RULES	NOTES
∞ *4th* ∞ **You are not to remove Stones, Bones or any Break Club, for the sake of playing your Ball, Except upon the fair Green and that only within a Club's length of your Ball.[5]**	*5. In other words, "Play it as it lays."*
∞ *5th* ∞ **If your Ball comes among watter, or any wattery filth, you are at liberty to take out your Ball & bringing it behind the hazard and Teeing it, you may play it with any Club and allow your Adversary a Stroke for so getting out your Ball.[6]**	*6. Still true, but only if it's a tee shot that hits the drink. A dunked shot from elsewhere on the course gets dropped on a line extending directly back to the point from where the shot was hit. In either case, though, it costs a stroke.*
∞ *6th* ∞ **If your Balls be found any where touching one another, You are to lift the first Ball, till you play the last.**	
∞ *7th* ∞ **At Holling,[7] you are to play your Ball honestly for the Hole, and not to play upon your Adversary's Ball, not lying in your way to the Hole.[8]**	*7. That is, putting.* *8. Balls in the way these days are replaced by a ball marker, a small coin or similar object set immediately behind the ball before it is picked up. If the ball marker looks like it might interfere with the shot of another player, it is placed a club-head length or so to the side. Before this rule was instituted in the 1950s, golfers had to hit around, or chip over, an opponent's obstructing ball.*
∞ *8th* ∞ **If you should lose your Ball, by its being taken up, or any other way, you are to go back to the Spot, where you struck last & drop another Ball, and allow your adversary a Stroke for the misfortune.[9]**	*9. The first reference to a phrase every amateur golfer hears just about every time he plays: "stroke and distance." The concept of out of bounds was a nineteenth-century addition, and time limits governing the search for lost balls were instituted in the mid-twentieth century.*

RULES	NOTES
9th **No man at Holling his Ball, is to be allowed, to mark his way to the Hole with his Club or, anything else.**	
10th **If a Ball be stopp'd by any Person, Horse, Dog or anything else,[10] the Ball so stop'd must be play'd where it lyes.**	*10. As the first golf courses were laid down on fields and pastures, all kinds of fauna were among the original hazards.*
11th **If you draw your Club in Order to Strike, & proceed so far in the Stroke as to be bringing down your Club; If then, your Club shall break,[11] in any way, it is to be Accounted a Stroke.**	*11. Wooden shafts are brittle and subject to shattering. That's why early golfers routinely carried as many as two dozen of them. Today everyone uses metal shafts, although wood is still legal, and the official club limit is fourteen.*
12th **He whose Ball lyes farthest from the Hole is obliged to play first.[12]**	*12. Or as golfers phrase it today, "Who's away?"*
13th **Neither Trench, Ditch or Dyke, made for the prescrvation of the Links, nor the Scholar's Holes or the Soldier's Lines,[13] shall be accounted a Hazard; But the Ball is to be taken out/Teed/ and play'd with any Iron Club.[14]**	*13. "Scholar's holes" were trampled areas on the edge of the St. Andrews course where students from the local university congregated in fair weather to read (and maybe talk a little golf). "Soldier's lines" were the military marching ground that ringed St. Andrews.* *14. Today this is known as "relief without penalty," a free drop in the fairway.*

FORESEEABLE
GOLF BALLS OVER TIME

Early hackers made due with hardened sheep dung or hairies, leather-covered clumps of fur that were borrowed from other stick-and-ball games. Then things got more involved.

WOOD 1300s–1500s
These carved balls were most likely appropriated from other games that were popular at the time.

FEATHERIE 1600s–1850s
Made of boiled (chicken or goose) feathers stuffed inside a leather pouch, a single ball cost the equivalent of $10 to $20 today. The expense, plus the fact that featheries rarely flirted with true roundness—which resulted in unpredictable flight patterns—hindered widespread use.

GUTTY 1850s–1900
Made from tree gum called gutta-percha, this version was cheaper than featheries to produce, which contributed to golf's rise in popularity among the masses. Soon players realized that scratched and grooved gutties were easier to manipulate than untarnished balls, allowing for controlled fades (shots moving away from the ball striker) and draws (shots moving across the line of the ball striker's body). By century's end, intentionally grooved gutties—in effect balls covered in small pimples—were the standard around the world.

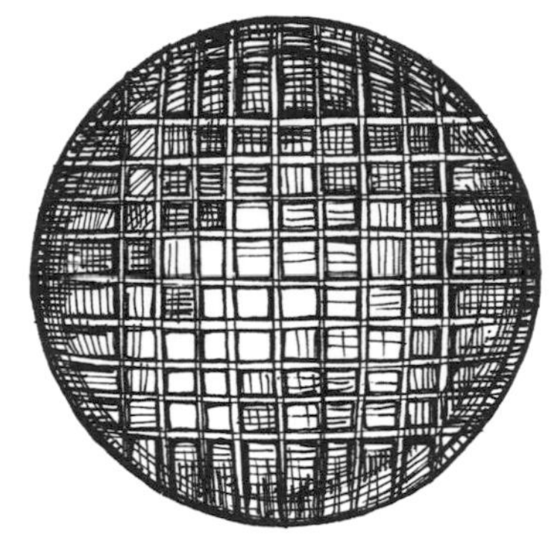

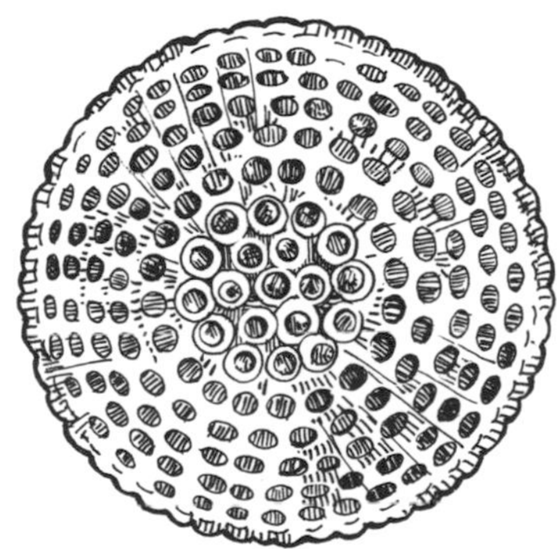

HASKELL 1898
The next innovation came from two Americans: an amateur duffer named Coburn Haskell and a B.F. Goodrich Company employee named Bertram Work. Their patented creation, referred to as the Haskell ball, consisted of a liquid or solid core wrapped in rubber thread and covered in hardened gutta-percha or balata sap. The result was extra yards off the tee.

DIMPLED HASKELL 1905
The modern golf ball was born with the twentieth century, when William Taylor decided to invert the bumps on balls, essentially turning pimples into dimples. Dimples, which maximize lift while reducing drag, remain the signature feature of golf balls today.

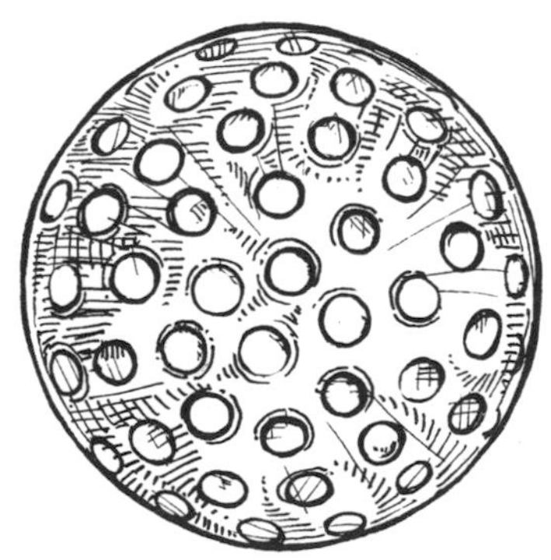

MESH 1930s
As golf's popularity exploded, so did the variety of balls. One of the more popular was the mesh pattern, named for its square dimples.

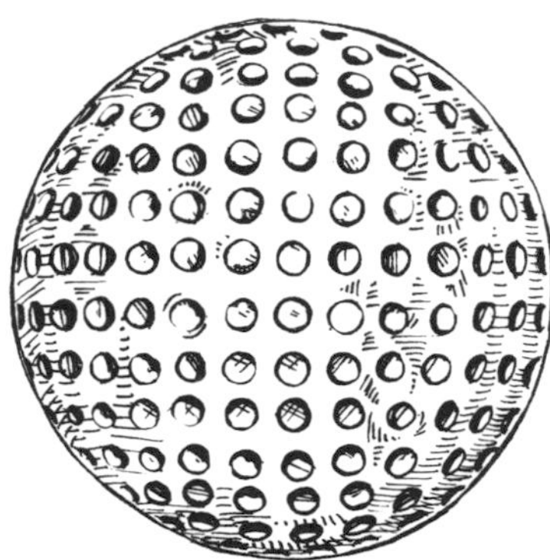

SURLYN 1960s
Variations of the Haskell ball were the standard until American chemical giant DuPont developed a new plastic trademarked as Surlyn. Highly durable, this polymer was quickly adopted by ball makers everywhere and continues to be used today.

Golf's two primary governing bodies, the United States Golf Association (USGA) and the Royal and Ancient Golf Club of St. Andrews (R&A), have exacting specifications for shape (balls must be symmetric), weight (capped at 1.620 ounces), diameter (not to exceed 1.680 inches), velocity, and distance capabilities (the latter two have changed over time), but there are myriad potential constructions in addition to the four most common types described at right. Today's golfers can choose from more than one thousand balls approved by the USGA and the R&A.

Modern Golf Ball Varieties

There are hundreds of ways to construct a modern golf ball.
Here are four of the most common.

---

① **TWO-PIECE** Large solid core/dimpled Surlyn or urethane cover.
② **THREE-PIECE** Large solid core/thin mantle/dimpled Surlyn or urethane cover.
③ **FOUR-PIECE** Large solid core/thin outer core/thin mantle/dimpled Surlyn or urethane cover.
④ **FIVE-PIECE** Gradual progression from soft core to dimpled Surlyn or urethane cover.

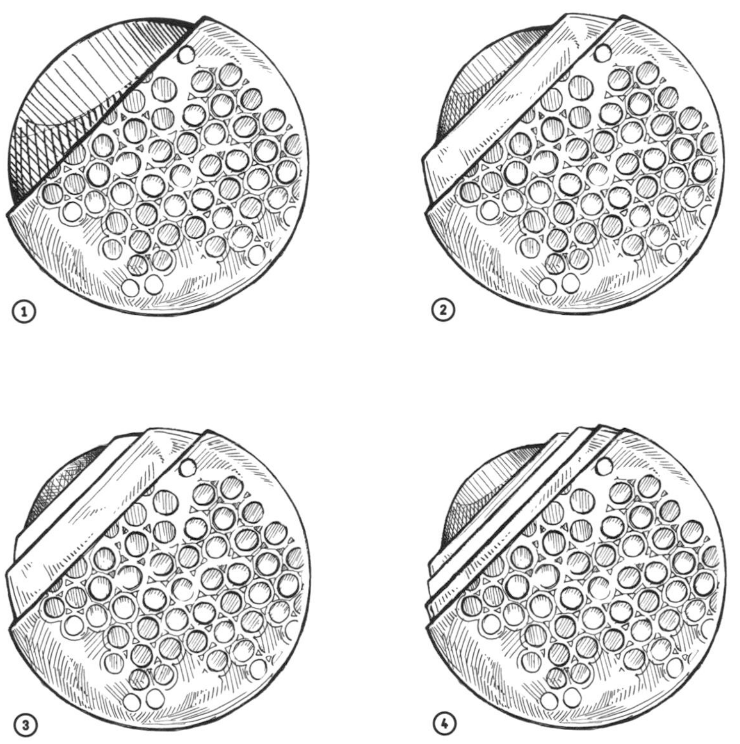

ICE HOCKEY

LIKE MANY OF THE SPORTS FEATURED IN THIS BOOK, ICE hockey was the brainchild of boredom. Concocted by British soldiers garrisoned in eastern Canada at the beginning of the nineteenth century, it shares colonial roots as well. And like two other empire first cousins, cricket and golf, it is one more variation on the stick-and-ball idea. There is a crucial difference, though: because nothing much remained unfrozen during those unyielding Canadian winters, hockey was developed to be played on ice.

Many of His Majesty's soldiers were Irish conscripts, so the early game was sometimes referred to as "hurling on ice," invoking a millennia-old Gaelic game that requires players to get a ball over a goal or between its posts using a stick. Surely, those weather-besting soldiers were also inspired by lacrosse and its antecedent, a local First Nations game called *tooadijik*. In fact, they may have used sticks fashioned by members of the Mi'Kmaq tribe.

Whatever its source, ice hockey was an unregimented pond game until the 1850s. For one thing, players used whatever they could muster—a ball, a boot heel, frozen dung—for a puck. (That word almost certainly derives from the Scottish Gaelic *puc,* which means to hit or strike. The name hockey may come from the French word for shepherd's crook, *hoquet,* or from a possibly apocryphal British officer, a certain Colonel Hockey, who used the game to keep his troops in shape.) In 1872 James Creighton, a young engineer and athlete from Nova Scotia, moved to Montreal, bringing word of the game, along with sticks and, most important, special skates—boots with rounded metal blades affixed with metal clamps—to play it. Within three years, Creighton was angling to stage this game at the Victoria Skating Rink, an indoor facility used mainly for figure skating competitions.

Trouble was, the trajectory of the hockey ball was hard to control, which was not an obstacle during an outdoor match but posed a potentially significant danger to spectators in an enclosed space. So Creighton crafted a substitute: a flat, circular piece of wood. The first indoor ice hockey game was played on March 3, 1875, and "aroused city-wide interest," according to one player. Many in the crowd were turned off by the violent antics, but others were quite amused, and the sport spread quickly. Two years later, a list of seven rules was printed in the *Montreal Gazette*—the oldest set in existence today. Soon hundreds of amateur clubs were facing off throughout the region, and by the early 1880s competitions were being held to crown a national champion.

One of the sport's earliest enthusiasts was also among its most influential. After watching several championship tournaments, Lord Stanley of Preston, the governor-general of Canada, purchased a silver bowl to reward the top team. In 1893 he presented his cup to the Montreal Amateur Athletic Association, who had "defeated all comers during the late season." On that day, Canada hailed its national pastime—and one of the sports world's most famous pieces of hardware, the Stanley Cup.

JAMES CREIGHTON'S RULES OF HOCKEY (1877)[1]

RULES	NOTES
1st **The game shall be commenced and renewed by a Bully[2] in the centre of the ground. Goals shall be changed after each game.[3]**	*1. These seven rules were derived from an earlier set of thirteen, known as the Halifax rules, which were never published.* *2. What we call a face-off. A referee placed the puck between two players' sticks, which often meant bruised hands if he didn't pick them up fast enough. Beginning in 1914, refs dropped the puck instead, sparing their appendages the mutilation.* *3. Teams still switch sides after each period (formerly known as games), although since 1910 there have been three rather than two. One reason for the change was to provide an extra opportunity to clean and resurface the ice.*
2nd **When a player hits the ball,[4] any one of the same side who at such moment of hitting is nearer to the opponents' goal line is out of play,[5] and may not touch the ball himself, or in any way whatever prevent any other player from doing so, until the ball has been played. A player must always be on his own side of the ball.**	*4. The ball was hockey's projectile of choice until the late 1800s, when Creighton's flattened wooden pucks were introduced. Rubberized versions debuted in the 1880s and are still used today.* *5. No forward passes were allowed. Rather, in a nod to rugby, players skated forward with the puck until impeded, at which point they passed backward to a teammate who would surge forward again. To increase pace and scoring, the National Hockey League, which was founded in 1917, instituted the forward pass in 1929.*

RULES	NOTES
3rd **The ball may be stopped, but not carried or knocked on by any part of the body. No player shall raise his stick above his shoulder. Charging from behind, tripping, collaring, kicking or shinning shall not be allowed.**[6]	*6. At the time, a penalized player wasn't removed from the ice until after a third infraction; instead, the "penalty" was to restart play with a bully. Sending a player off the ice for each infraction, for two-, three-, or five-minute terms, began in 1904, but his team could slot in another player until his return. Only with the birth of the NHL were penalized teams forced to play a man short. Fighting regulations weren't instituted until 1922, when, as now, the infraction earned a five-minute banishment.*
4th **When the ball is hit behind the goal line**[7] **by the attacking side, it shall be brought out straight 15 yards, and started again by a Bully; but, if hit behind by any one of the side whose goal line it is, a player of the opposite side shall hit it out from within one yard of the nearest corner, no player of the attacking side at that time shall be within 20 yards of the goal line, and the defenders, with the exception of the goal-keeper, must be behind their goal line.**	*7. This rule was altered once enclosed (indoor) rinks reconfigured the standard field of play. There were no longer out-of-bounds areas in any sense that rules needed to address.*
5th **When the ball goes off at the side, a player of the opposite side to that which hit it out shall roll it out from the point on the boundary line at which it went off at right angles with the boundary line,**[8] **and it shall not be in play until it has touched the**	*8. See note 7.*

RULES	NOTES
ice, and the player rolling it in shall not play it until it has been played by another player, every player being then behind the ball.	
6th **On the infringement of any of the above rules, the ball shall be brought back and a Bully shall take place.[9]**	*9. The punishment for breaking the rules was increased over time in response to growing public outcry over on-ice violence. After two players died from injuries sustained during games in 1905 and 1907, many people (including jurors) advocated for harsher penalties to force the game to be safer. The founders of the NHL built their new league around an emphasis on player safety.*
7th **All disputes shall be settled by the Umpires, or in the event of their disagreement, by the Referee.[10]**	*10. In 2000, the NHL began to employ two referees (to go along with the two linesmen) to keep an eye on things.*

PRIZEWORTHY

ICONIC SPORTS HARDWARE

Arguably the most recognizable championship trophy in the United States, the Stanley Cup is not the only one a self-respecting fan should know on sight.

①

②

① AMERICA'S CUP When the New York Yacht Club won the inaugural One Hundred Sovereign Cup in 1851—its schooner *America* defeated fifteen boats from the Royal Yacht Squadron in a race around the Isle of Wight—the group promptly changed the name of the prize to America's Cup. It took 132 years, when the cup was won by an Australian boat, for the Yanks to give it up.

② THE ASHES Australia beat England in an 1882 test match in London and a newspaper ran a snide obituary for English cricket, announcing that "its ashes" had been taken Down Under. Ivo Bligh, England's captain, vowed to bring those ashes back. And he did. Some ladies in Melbourne presented him with an urn said to be filled with the ashes of a cricket ball. The vessel now resides at the Marylebone Cricket Club, but the two countries still compete for a Waterford crystal replica.

③ **BORG-WARNER TROPHY** Although the Indianapolis 500 is run every May, the winner doesn't receive the Borg-Warner Trophy—a miniature replica, to be exact—until an awards dinner the following January. The actual prize, named in 1935 for the auto parts supplier, is always on display at the Indianapolis Motor Speedway and features a bas-relief sculpture of the face of every winner since 1911.

④ **CLARET JUG** After Young Tom Morris won his third (British) Open Championship in a row, the Challenge Belt awarded to the victor was retired. But when Morris won his fourth Championship, in 1872, the new prize, a claret jug, wasn't ready. He got a medal instead, which is why every winner since then has, too. The jug was ready in 1873. Every year it is quickly engraved on-site with the victor's name before the presentation.

⑤ **COMMISSIONER'S TROPHY** For most of baseball's long history, no official trophy was awarded to the World Series champion. Instead, a commemorative object, usually a ring, was given to players, coaches, and employees by the winning team. MLB finally got its act together in 1967 and started presenting its champs with the Commissioner's Trophy, which was redesigned by Tiffany in 1999.

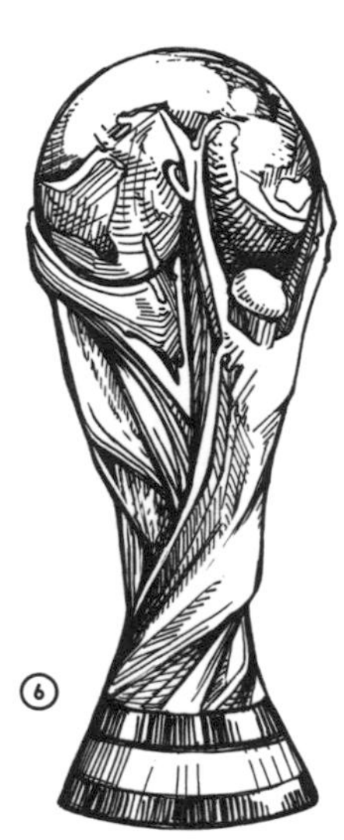

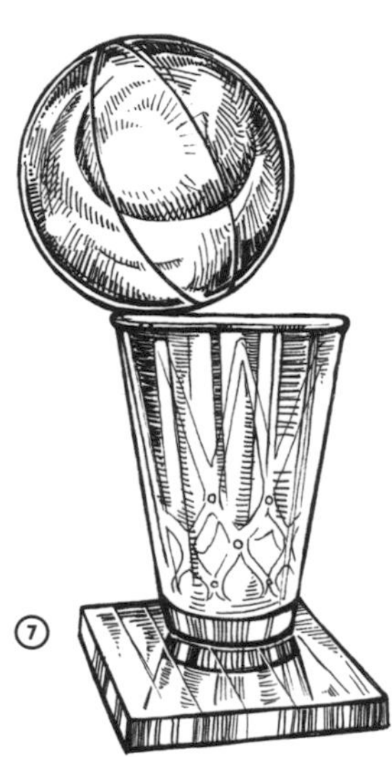

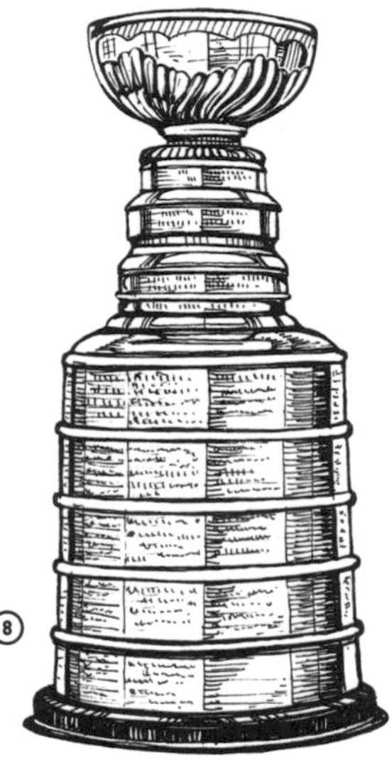

⑥ FIFA WORLD CUP TROPHY Incredibly, the original trophy given to the winning country in the world's most prestigious soccer tournament was stolen twice. Named for Jules Rimet, FIFA president when the tournament started in 1930, the trophy was snatched and recovered in 1966, then handed over permanently to Brazil after that country won it for the third time. (To replace it, the gold trophy awarded since 1974 was commissioned.) But in 1983, Rimet's prize was purloined from the Brazilian Football Confederation—and never found.

⑦ LARRY O'BRIEN NBA CHAMPIONSHIP TROPHY Lawrence O'Brien was President Lyndon Johnson's postmaster general before being named NBA commissioner. The league's top prize was named for him when he retired in 1984. Before that the trophy honored Walter Brown, original owner of the Boston Celtics, who was instrumental in the 1949 merger of leagues that created the NBA.

⑧ STANLEY CUP Each year every player on the NHL's reigning championship team gets to spend at least one day with the Stanley Cup during the off-season, to do as he pleases. (Sleeping with it and drinking from it are typical activities.) Etched with the names of each player on every title team, the Cup, first awarded in 1893, may be the most mistake-filled commemorative: for example, Hall of Fame goaltender Jacques Plante's names have been incorrectly rendered as "Jack," "Jocko," and "Plant."

⑨ VINCE LOMBARDI TROPHY Every year the Super Bowl winner receives a trophy to keep forever, and every year Tiffany makes a new one. So it has been since the first one was awarded, in 1967, to the Green Bay Packers, winner of the AFL-NFL World Championship Game. (The trophy was renamed in 1970 to honor the legendary—and recently deceased—former Green Bay head coach.) The one exception? After the Baltimore Colts, winner of Super Bowl V, skipped town for Indianapolis in 1984, Charm City won the right to keep the team's hardware.

⑩ WIMBLEDON TROPHIES When a gentleman wins the most prestigious Grand Slam tournament in tennis, he is presented with a silver chalice engraved "The All England Lawn Tennis Club Single Handed Championship of the World." The winner of the women's singles title hoists a platter called the Venus Rosewater Dish. But since 2007, all winners have received the same prize money.

KICKBALL

DODGEBALL. RED ROVER. NEWCOMB. KILL THE GUY WITH the Ball. Duck on a Rock. For most Americans, these games recall a specific stage of life and a particular part of the day—childhood and recess, respectively. School-yard games have been a staple of free time for kids since, well, the invention of school. Because most of these activities emerge from young imaginations ("Wouldn't it be fun if . . ."), their origins are often lost over the years. But we actually know the history of one of the most popular and enduring playground games of all.

Kickball is the brainchild of Nicholas C. Seuss (no relation to the "Dr." of children's books fame), who supervised Cincinnati's park playgrounds in the second decade of the twentieth century. Always on the hunt for organized ways to keep Queen City tykes from running wild, Seuss needed a game that didn't require exceptional skills (so kids of all ages could play) or special equipment (as there's nothing like a trip to the park for losing gloves, bats, and rackets). Seuss's solution was simple, fun, clever—and blatantly and unabashedly derivative. He called it "Kick Base Ball," sometimes spelled "Kick Baseball." The name was apt, because the rules for his sport borrowed liberally from America's burgeoning national game. A baseball being too difficult for a child—or anyone, really—to kick, a basketball of the era was used instead (or a volleyball for younger players). After kickball was included in *The Playground*, a monthly publication for recreational directors, in 1917, it quickly became a staple of elementary school gym classes, in part as a way to teach the rules of baseball.

A century later, kickball remains largely a kids' pursuit, but adults have a soft spot for it, too. Maybe it's the lure of the oversize red ball (developed in the 1950s, the recognizable orb has achieved iconic status) or the simplicity of the rules and ease of play. It could be that kickball is especially suited for grown-up socializing. (Relative to other sports, consuming large amounts of beer doesn't much diminish the necessary skills.) But it's just as likely the game's ability to bridge the gap between childhood and adulthood that explains its allure (that's Christopher Noxon's argument in *Rejuvenile: Kickball, Cartoons, Cupcakes, and the Reinvention of the American Grown-up*).

The first recorded adult kickball match took place in 1922 in Clinton County, New York, at a teacher conference. The educators were assigned numbers to create teams: odds on one side, called Yale; evens on the other, called Princeton. It was a hot day, so they played only three innings. Yale won, 3–2. And the little game that could was on its way to offering some big-boy and -girl fun.

CINCINNATI PLAYGROUNDS' RULES FOR "KICK BASE BALL" (1917)

RULE I. ARRANGEMENT OF GAME.

Any number of players may take part in this game. The players are divided into two teams, (a) the kickers and (b) the fielders.

RULE II. OBJECT OF THE GAME.

The object of the game is to kick the ball out into the field and reach one or more bases before the fielders get possession of the ball.

RULE III. THE DIAMOND.

The diamond is laid out with a 35-foot base line.[1] The bases are two feet square. A 10-foot serving line is marked in rear of home base.[2]

---

1. Kickball is typically played on a diamond of softball dimensions, with bases 60 feet apart.

2. The 10-foot serving line creates a box that resembles the batter's box in baseball.

RULE IV. THE BALL.

Regulation basket ball is used.[3] For smaller children use a volley ball.

---

3. The "basket ball" referenced here is not bouncy or orange—this was the early 1900s, remember. It resembled a soccer ball.

RULE V. THE LINE UP.

The kickers are lined up according to size in rear of serving line.[4] The fielders are arranged at irregular intervals within the diamond.[5]

---

4. The organizing principle of lining up by size has since given way to more strategic lineups.

5. Twelve players were scattered around the infield area, all inside the baselines. Today no more than eleven players take the field at a time, with a handful in the outfield.

RULE VI. THE FOUL LINE.

The foul line must be drawn from home plate to the outer edge of first and third base and to the boundary of the field. A foul line is also drawn ten feet in front of home base.

RULE VII. KICKING THE BALL.

The ball may be kicked (a) from the ground; (b) as a drop kick; (c) as a bounce kick.[6]

6. That's right, there was no pitcher. Pitchers were introduced in the 1920s, although for a while they were often members of the kicking team. Drop and bounce kicks were eliminated once pitchers became standard.

RULE VIII. THE SERVING LINE.

The ball must be kicked from the rear of the serving line; stepping on or over the line constitutes a foul.

RULE IX. CHOICE OF INNING.

The choice of inning shall be decided by flipping a coin.

RULE X. THE GAME.

Nine innings constitute the game. If the score be a tie at the end of the ninth inning, play shall continue until a decision is reached.[7]

7. According to the World Adult Kickball Association (WAKA), a regulation kickball game lasts five innings these days, and there are no extra innings. Formed in 1998 by a group of guys looking to meet new people, WAKA reigns over more than forty thousand players in leagues in thirty-five states. Each league is coed, current rules stating that teams must field a minimum of four men and four women.

RULE XI. SCORING OF RUNS.

One run shall be scored every time a base runner, after having legally touched the first, second and third base, shall touch the home base before three players are put out. The team scoring the greater number of runs wins the game.

RULE XII. BASE RUNNERS.

A kicker becomes a base runner instantly after he makes a fair kick. Any number of base runners may be at one base at the same time.[8]

THE BASE RUNNER IS OUT:

1. **If hit with the ball before reaching the first base.**
2. **If ball reaches home base before base runner reaches second, third, or home base.**
3. **If a fly ball is caught.**
4. **In kicking two fouls.[9]**
5. **Interfering or being hit with the ball while running from one base to another.[10]**
6. **In leaving bases before fly ball is caught.**
7. **In leaving the base while ball is out of play.**

---

8. No more bunches on bases. Players run the bases as they do in baseball.

9. Four fouls make an out now.

10. Alas, more civilized heads have prevailed. Throwing the ball at a runner is not allowed.

MULTIPLE CHOICE

ROCK-PAPER-SCISSORS VARIATIONS

Whatever the sport and wherever the playground, one team has to hit, bat, kick, or serve first. And one of the most common ways to decide such matters is a game most Westerners know as rock-paper-scissors (Roshambo, to some). But the origins of RPS are older than you think, and there are variations aplenty.

ROCK-PAPER-SCISSORS Rock-paper-scissors came to England and France in the late 1800s, as increased trade between Europe and Asia sparked a host of cultural exchanges. The game's origins date back at least to China's Han Dynasty, roughly 200 BC to AD 200. But though there were many different versions of this "zero-sum hand game"—in which A is beaten by B, B is defeated by C, and C is topped by A—the modern version Westerners know originated in Japan in the nineteenth century.

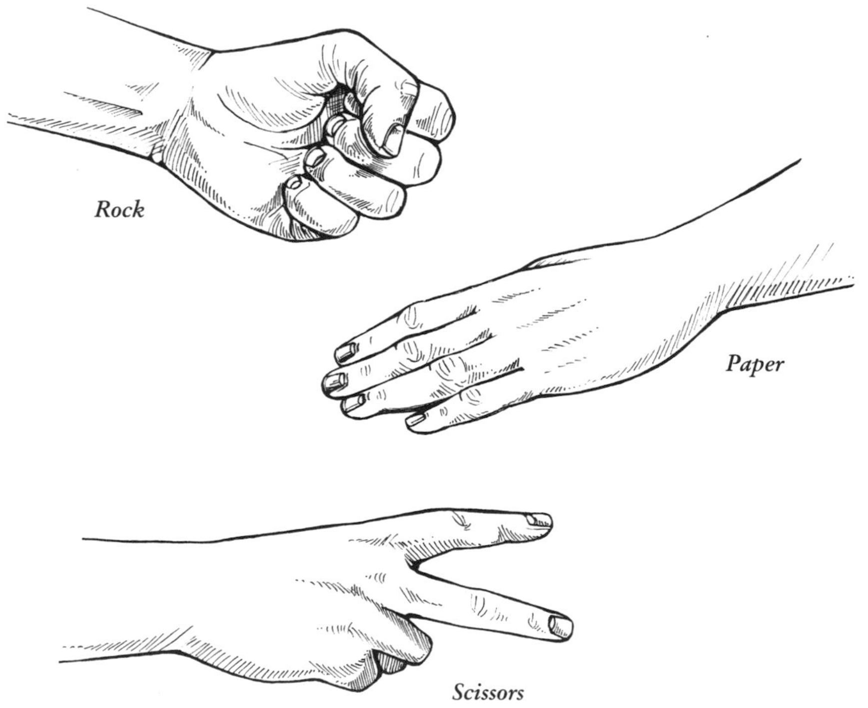

ROCK-PAPER-SCISSORS—SPOCK-LIZARD This twenty-first-century edition was invented by the blogger Sam Kass (with his friend Karen Bryla) to address the problem faced by players who had learned each other's throwing tendencies. Adding two more options, they theorized, would lessen the chance of ties. This five-way version received a major boost in popularity when it was referenced multiple times on *The Big Bang Theory*. (Characters on the sitcom are a bit obsessed with Star Trek's Lieutenant Commander Spock.) For the record: scissors cut paper, paper covers rock, rock crushes lizard, lizard poisons Spock, Spock smashes scissors, scissors decapitate lizard, lizard eats paper, paper disproves Spock, Spock vaporizes rock, and rock crushes scissors.

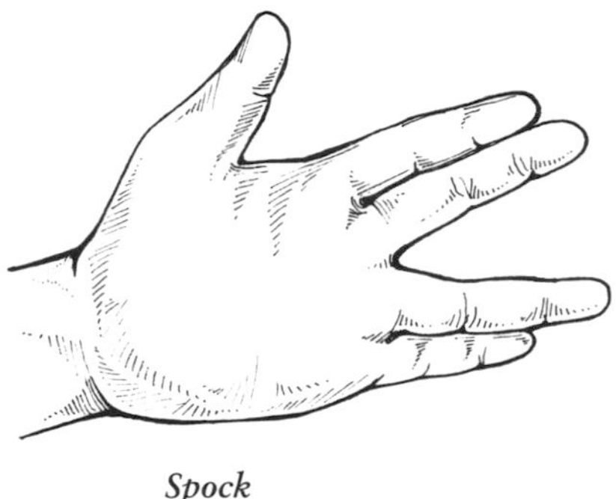

Spock

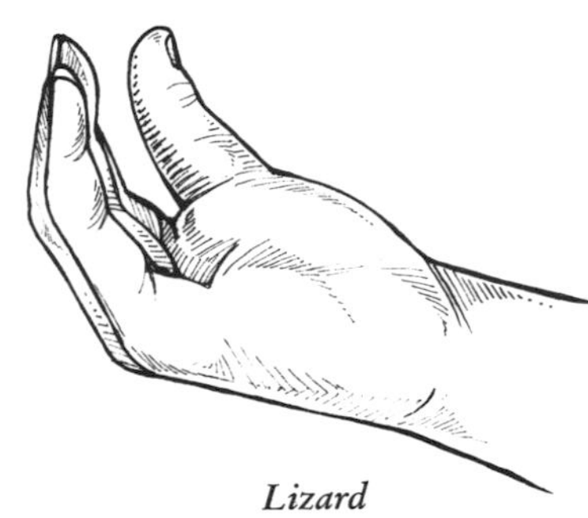

Lizard

FROG-SLUG-SNAKE In this nineteenth-century Japanese zero-sum hand game, frog is beaten by slug, slug is killed by snake, and snake is bested by frog. Confused naturalists will be comforted by the strong likelihood that in translating this game from an earlier Chinese version, Japanese players misinterpreted the Chinese characters representing a poisonous centipede for ones designating a less-menacing slug.

Frog

Slug

Snake

FOX–HUNTER–VILLAGE HEAD

Both hands are required for this nineteenth-century RPS ancestor, also from Asian cultures, in which a supernatural fox is killed by a skilled hunter, who is beaten by a wise village head, who falls prey to the fox.

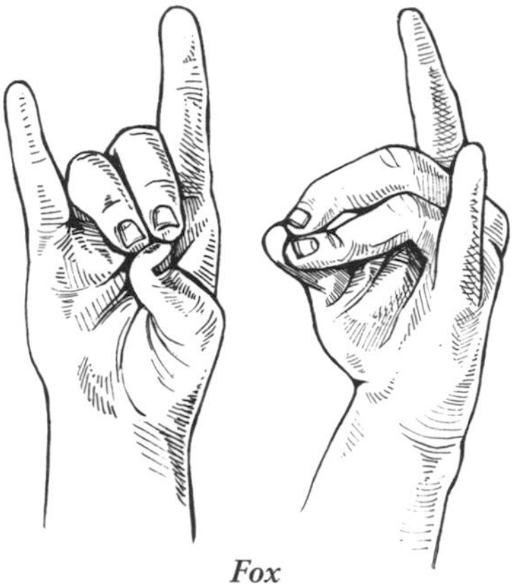

Fox

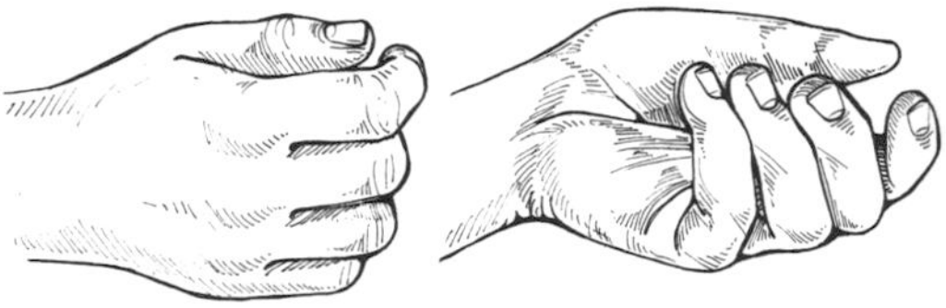

Hunter

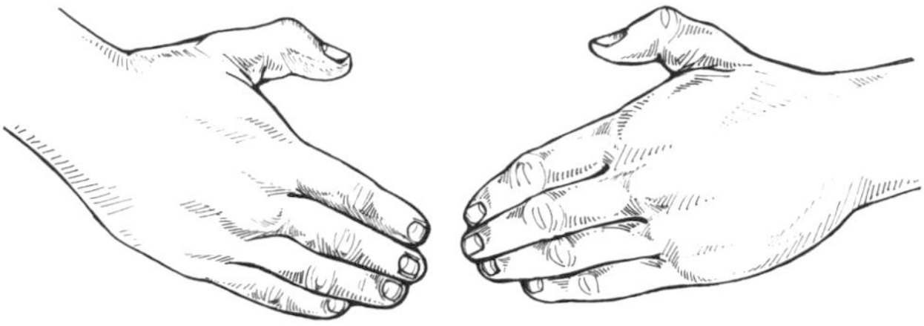

Village Head

Zero-sum hand games are a human invention, but they have origins—or at least analogues—in nature. Exhibit A: the common side-blotched lizard, indigenous to the Pacific Coast of North America. Female side-blotched lizards will choose an orange-sided male over one with blue markings, a blue-sided male over one with yellow markings, and a yellow-sided male over one with orange markings.

The World RPS Player's Responsibility Code

The World Rock Paper Scissors Society (WorldRPS.com) is an amusing organization founded in the first decade of the twenty-first century (no matter what the website waggishly claims) with the primary tongue-in-cheek goal of bringing order and rigor to RPS. That mission included the establishment of the player responsibility code reproduced here, the enforcement of which appears to be purely self-directed.

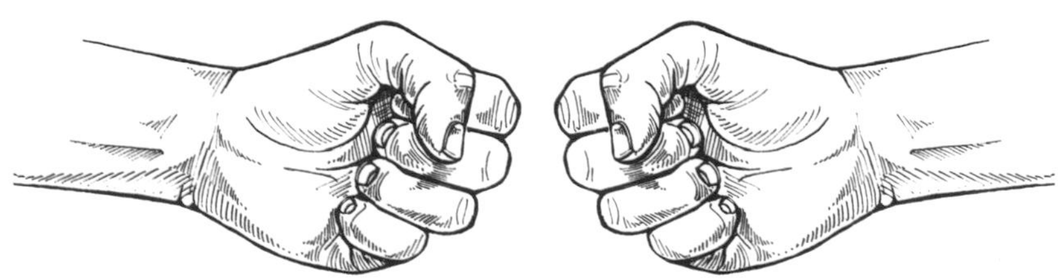

1. Safety First! Always ensure that all players have removed sharp jewellery and watches.

2. Ensure agreement, before the first round, on priming conventions (we recommend the standard 3 prime shoot).

3. Always establish what is to be decided or whether the match is to be played for honour.

4. Pre-determine the number of rounds required to win the match (remember odd numbers only).

5. Encourage novice development by explaining blunders in judgement with a mind towards being helpful. Don't berate.

6. Think twice before using RPS for life-threatening decisions.

7. Always respect foreign cultures. When abroad consider yourself an ambassador of the World RPS Society.

MIXED MARTIAL ARTS

THE URGE TOWARD VIOLENCE RUNS DEEP IN US. WE CAN ONLY speculate about what other than competition for mates and food motivated our ancestors to fight. But we know for certain that combat as sport is nearly as old as civilization itself. The ancient Greeks, who created democracy and produced seminal works of art and thought, still found time and reason to enjoy a good tussle, which at the time was almost exclusively hand-to-hand. As preparation for war, naked men competed in a sometimes deadly grappling and striking sport called pankration. By 648 BC it was an Olympic event.

These days, our fiercest brawls, outside of bars, take place in an octagonal cage, where male and female devotees of mixed martial arts (MMA) strive to force opponents to submit using a range of international combat styles. That defining feature—the mixed part—is a relatively new addition to the ageless stable of combat sports. It arose at the end of the nineteenth century, as a kind of grown-up iteration of a playground challenge: my fighting tradition can beat up your fighting tradition! In the ports of Japan, newly opened to the world, American sailors versed in wrestling and boxing challenged practitioners of the local martial arts, such as karate and *kenpo,* in bouts known as *merikan.* These fights, in which the reputation of a particular style hinged on its representative's dominating victory or bloody defeat, extended far beyond Japan's borders and to many other forms of fighting: muay Thai, jujitsu, Greco-Roman wrestling. As the twentieth century dawned, styles began to mix, and the matches focused as much on the fighters as the forms.

One hybrid was taking shape in South America: Brazilian jujitsu, aka BJJ, a combination of Japanese judo (itself a mix of medieval jujitsu techniques) and European "catch wrestling" (which emphasizes submission holds). To help disseminate the new discipline, its chief proselytizer, Carlos Gracie, issued the now-famous Gracie Challenge: a cash-prize, all-combat invitational in the carnival tradition of *vale tudo,* or "no-holds-barred" fighting. Carlos and his kin—the first generation of an MMA dynasty that continues today—took on all comers: wrestlers, boxers, even acrobatic capoeira fighters. After conquering Brazil, some of the Gracies moved to California, where new challenges were delivered, and new fans made.

In the early 1990s, the head of the family branch in the United States, Rorion Gracie, was in the market for an outlet to showcase BJJ. Teaming with a marketer and a filmmaker, he created another *vale tudo*/Gracie Challenge hybrid, this one a caged event, broadcast on pay-per-view TV. His Ultimate Fighting Championship (UFC) premiered on November 12, 1993, in Denver. Fighters of all weight classes converged, drawn from the worlds of BJJ, boxing, kickboxing, sumo, *savate* (French kickboxing), American *kenpo,* shootfighting (Japanese wrestling), and tae kwon do. The rules for UFC 1, drawn up before the event, were spare, designed to foster a not-quite-lawless brand of street fighting. By the time the BJJ fighter was crowned as victor, American fight fans had witnessed a new type of sports combat. And they liked it.

"RULES AND REGULATIONS FOR UFC 1" (1993)

RULES	NOTES
1st **5 five-minute rounds,[1] 1 minute rest in between.**	*1. All UFC title bouts remain five rounds each, with five minutes per round divided by one-minute rests. Actually, most governing bodies require similar specs, even when a title belt is not on the line.*
2nd **Fight to be held in a circular pit,[2] 20 feet in diameter (to be designed by John Milius).**	*2. The founders of MMA figured the sport's rough nature could lead to athletes tumbling out of more traditional rings. The pit was usurped by an octagonal cage—30 feet wide, with eight walls each 5½ feet tall—that may not have been designed by Hollywood screenwriter John Milius at all. The eight-sided ring made it hard for one fighter to trap another in corners and neutralized any advantage for wrestlers and boxers used to either round or square fighting areas.*
3rd **Fighters wear clothing according to their style (i.e., Karate/Judo gi, boxer trunks, etc.).[3]**	*3. In 2000 California and New Jersey passed what is now known as the Unified Rules of Mixed Martial Arts, which covered a wardrobe: trunks, cup and mouthguard, and gloves (4 to 6 ounces).*
4th **Fight can be stopped as follows: knockout (standard 10 count), submission, corner throw in a towel, choke-out, doctor's intervention.[4]**	*4. Sounds ominous, but the hype surrounding the event was worse, promising that bouts would be stopped only by knockout, submission, or death.*

RULES	NOTES
5th **Punches, kicks, elbow strikes, joint locks and/or chokes are permitted.[5]**	*5. But there were some limits. At the first rules meeting, Rorion Gracie reportedly proclaimed: "There is no biting. We are men not animals."*
6th **Target areas for all strikes include head and body with the exception of the eyes and groin.[6]**	*6. The groin was actually fair game in UFC 2, but it and a lot more was deemed off-limits when the sport was more officially and comprehensively codified in 2000. Here is the worst of today's banned mayhem.* • *Biting or spitting at an opponent* • *Fishhooking (inserting fingers into the mouth or nose and pulling)* • *Intentionally placing a finger in any orifice, or in any cut or laceration of an opponent* • *Small joint manipulation* • *Throat strikes of any kind, including, without limitation, grabbing the trachea* • *Kneeing or kicking the head of a grounded opponent*
7th **6 ounce boxing gloves or Kenpo gloves[7] are required if a fighter's art employs closed fist strikes to the face and head, otherwise bare-knuckles are permitted.**	*7.* Kenpo, *or* kempo, *gloves pad the knuckles but leave the fingers and palm free. But in the beginning, few fighters wore gloves, feeding the sport's nasty reputation.*

RULES	NOTES
∞ *8th* ∞ **No point system is in effect;[8] a fight shall continue into overtime rounds until one fighter scores a knock-out, submission hold, or a choke-out.**	*8. Like boxing, UFC bouts are now determined by three cage-side scorers, but UFC honcho Dana White awards postfight bonuses for submissions and knockouts that are often larger than the fight purse itself.*
∞ *9th* ∞ **Fight shall not be interrupted in the event of a clinch and/or fall to the ground.[9]**	*9. No longer an official rule, but don't tell that to fans, who routinely boo when fighters (usually wrestlers) employ what's derisively called "lay and pray"—taking the fight to the ground and keeping it there. These days, refs often step in during long lulls to stand the fighters up.*

SCALE MODELS
WEIGHT CLASSES OF FIGHTING SPORTS

What's a fight if it's not fair, and what's fairer than a fight pitting two athletes of a similar size against each other?

(Note: All weights, including those converted from kilograms, are rounded to the nearest pound.)

MEN'S BOXING (PROFESSIONAL)

Grose's Classical Dictionary of the Vulgar Tongue, an 1823 compendium of British slang, defined "light weights" as "a pugilistic expression for gentlemen under twelve stone," thus creating the first-ever boxing weight class: up to 12 stone, or 168 pounds. Other dictionaries asserted their own conceptions of "light weight," so the National Sporting Club of London resolved the squabbles in 1909, with a full list of weight-class specifications.

CLASS	WEIGHT IN POUNDS
Minimum Weight	<105
Junior Flyweight	108
Flyweight	112
Junior Bantamweight	115
Bantamweight	118
Junior Featherweight	122
Featherweight	126
Junior Lightweight	130
Lightweight	135
Junior Welterweight	140
Welterweight	147
Junior Middleweight	154
Middleweight	160
Super Middleweight	168
Light Heavyweight	175
Cruiserweight	200
Heavyweight	>200

WOMEN'S BOXING (PROFESSIONAL)

Women have been boxing, often illicitly, since the early 1700s. But it took a trail of legal battles for the women's amateur game to be recognized by USA Boxing in 1993, with the inclusion of weight classes. Fully sanctioned women's boxing in the United States began shortly thereafter.

CLASS	WEIGHT IN POUNDS
Pinweight	<101
Light Flyweight	106
Flyweight	110
Light Bantamweight	114
Bantamweight	119
Featherweight	125
Lightweight	132
Light Welterweight	138
Welterweight	145
Light Middleweight	154
Middleweight	165
Light Heavyweight	176
Heavyweight	>189

MEN'S JUDO (OLYMPIC)

Judo is built on the principle that softness controls hardness: a weak man can defeat a stronger opponent by avoiding his attack and throwing him off balance, thus diminishing his power. The idea seems counter to the institution of weight classes, but as judo gained popularity, the delineation became necessary for recognition as an official sport; the first weight distinctions were set in the sport's home country for the 1964 Tokyo Olympics.

CLASS	WEIGHT IN POUNDS
No official class name	<132
	146
	161
	179
	198
	220
	>220

WOMEN'S JUDO (OLYMPIC)

Women practiced a form of judo different from men's until the 1960s. British suffragettes used judo to fight policemen at the beginning of the twentieth century, and increasing numbers learned the art for self-defense. Before long, the sport was being associated with independence and freedom, and had become an unlikely tool of progress. The first sanctioned women's competitions were held in 1975, after weight classes were already used for men.

CLASS	WEIGHT IN POUNDS
No official class name	106
	115
	126
	139
	154
	172
	>172

MEN'S MIXED MARTIAL ARTS (UFC)

Like judo, mixed martial arts originated from a principle that would seem to resist weight classes: pitting any style of fighter against another. But MMA overseers realized that the "outlaw" sport needed to be seen as more regulated. In 2001 the New Jersey State Athletic Control Board issued a set of rules (including weight distinctions) that have since been adopted universally.

CLASS	WEIGHT IN POUNDS
Strawweight	115
Flyweight	125
Bantamweight	135
Featherweight	145
Lightweight	155
Welterweight	170
Middleweight	185
Light Heavyweight	205
Heavyweight	265
Super Heavyweight	No limit

WOMEN'S MIXED MARTIAL ARTS (UFC)

With a large number of organizations promoting women's MMA, rules and regulations vary from competition to competition. But the most-adopted regulations, which provide weight-class boundaries, are those published by the UFC.

CLASS	WEIGHT IN POUNDS
Strawweight	115
Bantamweight	135

MEN'S SUMO (USA SUMO)

Amateur sumo conforms to divisions in weight because it is working toward a spot in the Olympics; professional sumo wrestlers are divided into categories based on success. Though the weight classes have been in place since 1992, sumo has yet to be added to the Summer Games.

CLASS	WEIGHT IN POUNDS
Lightweight	187
Middleweight	253
Heavyweight	>253

WOMEN'S SUMO (USA SUMO)

In professional sumo, women are banned from even setting foot in the ring, but that hasn't stopped them from donning *mawashis* (sumo thongs) and competing anyway, often against male opponents. Supported by the International Sumo Federation (partly in response to the 1994 International Olympic Committee's declaration that the Games would not consider single-sex sports), the first all-women's tournament was held in Europe in 1996. The religious aspects of professional men's sumo were absent, but the same weight classes were represented.

CLASS	WEIGHT IN POUNDS
Lightweight	143
Middleweight	176
Heavyweight	>176
Open Weight	Unrestricted

MEN'S GRECO-ROMAN WRESTLING (OLYMPIC)

How does Greco-Roman wrestling differ from the freestyle version? (Both are men's Olympics events.) Holds below the waist are not permitted. Although Greco-Roman weight classes are typically a few pounds heavier than their freestyle analogues, the wrestlers themselves generally have leaner body masses.

CLASS	WEIGHT IN POUNDS
No official class name	130
	146
	165
	187
	216
	287

WOMEN'S FREESTYLE WRESTLING (OLYMPIC)

At every level of competition, including the Olympics since 2004, women's wrestling is of the freestyle variety. Its ranks are growing on high school and college campuses, in part because of what it could lead to—a gig in the increasingly popular world of women's mixed martial arts.

CLASS	WEIGHT IN POUNDS
No official class name	106
	117
	128
	139
	152
	165

POKER

THE DEBATE OVER WHETHER POKER IS A SPORT HAS RAGED forever—or at least since 2003, when ESPN, by then America's de facto decider of such things, expanded its coverage of the World Series of Poker, the game's marquee event. To be fair, sports fans love to argue, and disagreements like this one are nothing new; opinions about stock car racing and golf fly freely. Like stock car racing, which critics deride as nothing more than driving in circles, poker demands stamina and focus. Participants must concentrate for long periods while maintaining a keen awareness of competitors' behavior. Like golf, which haters dismiss as a long walk punctuated by minor demonstrations of hand-eye coordination, poker is a test of will and strategy, rewarding discipline over long stretches of monotonous play.

Such parsing would have amused card players of yesteryear, who were mostly just interested in gambling. Poker has its roots in a card game similar to dominoes played by a Chinese emperor in the tenth century. (The Chinese invented the playing card a while earlier.) There are also elements that connect poker to a sixteenth-century Persian game. But poker's closest cousin—and most likely the source of its name—is a game called *poque,* a seventeenth-century French game based on earlier Spanish and German games (*primero* and *Poch*, respectively). Rules varied from town to town, but the same combinations reigned everywhere: a pair, three of a kind, a "flux" (aka a flush, a hand of same-suited cards). More crucially, all the games thrived under the assumption that the winning hand didn't necessarily need to be the best hand, owing to the betting—and acting—skills of the players. In *Bohn's New Hand-Book of Games,* a book first published in 1850 that contains the earliest surviving rules of "modern" poker, the game is alternatively called "bluff."

Poque was brought to the New World by the French. The game took off, in part because of its popularity as a riverboat pastime, with the French-accented port of New Orleans as its hub. After the Louisiana Purchase in 1803, poker (its name now anglicized) began a slow transformation into the game we play today.

In his memoirs, the English actor Joseph Cowell reported playing "draw poker" in New Orleans in the 1820s, using a twenty-card deck. (Our fifty-two-card deck—thirteen cards each in suits of clubs, diamonds, spades, and hearts—is a "French deck," but it was one of many varieties that vied for broad adoption. The four suits in a forty-card "Italian deck," for example, were cups, coins, clubs, and swords.) In Cowell's account, five cards each were dealt to four players, who then bet on which player's hand formed the best combination. There was just one round of betting; the deal itself was the "draw" that gave the game its name, and no replacement cards were taken (or available, for that matter). Gradually, as poker became a favorite amusement of frontiersmen, professional gamblers, and other American risk lovers, the fifty-two-card deck became the standard: more cards meant more people could play, and more people meant more robust betting. Such progress was slow, because players needed time to adapt to changes in what were often very high-stakes affairs. In the 1856 edition of *Bohn's New Hand-Book,* for example, a run of five consecutive cards, aka a straight, wasn't listed among usable hands.

The no-draw poker that Bohn describes is very much the basis for all the variations that followed: five-card stud (four cards revealed and one card down, known only to the player to whom it is dealt), seven-card stud (three cards down and four revealed, from which the best five-card hand is made), and, of course, Texas Hold'em (two cards down to every player, with all players sharing five common cards revealed in the middle of the table). Arguably the most popular version of poker today, hold'em is the game featured in the World Series of Poker's main event, which draws thousands of players annually, each of whom antes $10,000 for the right to compete against professional sharps and amateur enthusiasts alike. And as golfers will argue, nothing yells sports more than a serious pro-am tournament.

BOHN'S RULES OF 52-CARD POKER (1856)

Depends more on hazard than another game played with cards, as it is not always the case that the best hand is the winning one; for if an adversary risks more money than you think your hand would justify you in doing, he wins, although he may have an inferior hand to yours in point of worth; whence the game is termed as above. It is played by a full pack of cards, and by any number of persons under ten.[1]

1. Ten could play with one fifty-two-card deck because no cards were discarded and redrawn as is the way today.

ON DEALING

In commencing the game, the cards are dealt one to each player, the lowest card designating the dealer. In case a tie occurs, it is decided by another deal; the ace being the lowest card, the deuce next, &c. The dealer commences on his left, and gives "one" at a time, until each player receives "five cards," being the number required. It is at the option of a player either to accept or reject a faced card; in case the latter, it is placed at the bottom of the pack, and the card following the one faced is given him. In case of a misdeal, the "pool" is doubled, each player putting up an additional stake, the deal going to the next one on the left.

ON BETTING

An equal stake is deposited in the "pool," which lies in the middle of the table, by each of the parties, who play on their own account. "Counters" or "chips"[2] are generally used, the valuation of which must be agreed upon on commencing; and should no limitation be restricted to in betting, he that puts the largest number of "chips" in the pool, or bets on his hand the highest, is entitled to all that is up, unless met by an adversary, in which case an equal amount must be put up, the better hand of course winning. Should one of the party over-reach the amount that is in possession of an adversary, a "*sight*"[3] may be demanded.

***Premiums*[4] are occasionally played, the amount decided upon at commencement of the game. A "flush"[5] being the lowest hand to which a holder is entitled, next a "full," all the fours beginning at "deuces," and ending with "four aces."**

2. Poker chips weren't standardized until the early 1900s, when casinos and other manufacturers started to produce the decorated clay versions in use today. Before that, gold nuggets, coins, or other small things of value acted as chips.

3. Poker players without the requisite cash today ask to "Go light"—in friendly games, anyway. Good luck making the request in a tournament.

4. A cash bonus for certain exceptional hands.

5. Flush, as in full—of one suit.

VALUE OF CARDS

***One Pair.*—Two cards of any colour being of equal value—thus, two deuces the lowest pair, two aces the highest single pair.**

***Two Pair* is the next in value to a single pair of aces, deuces and trays[6] being the lowest, kings and aces the highest two pair.**

***Three,* of equal value, rank next to the two highest pair. Three deuces beat aces and kings.**

A *Flush,* or "five cards" of the same suit, then follows, beating three aces. Should two "flushes" come together, it is decided by the one having the highest cards.

***Full Hand,*[7] consists of three of equal value, and one single pair—thus, three deuces and two trays beat a "flush."**

***Four* of equal value is the last combination. Deuces, four of which beat a "full," and rank next in value. The only two certain winning hands are four kings with an ace, and four aces;[8] the fortunate holder of either of these can rest easy in regard to a certainty of getting whatever amount he should stake, together with his adversary's.**

Should two or more hands come together of equal value in pairs, the better hand is decided by the highest side cards.

6. We spell it with an e*—treys—but either way it means threes.*

7. Or a full house, which is the more common term even if it makes less sense. And sometimes it's called a full boat. Why? As with many etymologies in this particular realm, it's because some guy once lost his (boat) to another guy holding just that hand.

8. The highest hand of all today is the royal flush, an ace-high straight flush. The odds of pulling one are 1 in 649,750, or 0.0000015 percent. A person is more than fifty times more likely to get struck by lightning in his or her lifetime.

Pass.—The person on the left of the dealer having the first privilege either to put a certain sum in the pool or pass his hand, and so on in rotation to the dealer; should all decline betting, the hands are thrown up, making a "*double head*," the one on the left taking the deal.

Call.—When an adversary wishes to meet the amount put in the pool by any one preceding him, this term is used.

Run Over.—Should you wish to bet more or "bluff" off your adversary.

Sight.—Not having funds enough to meet the stake put in the pool, entitles you to see an adversary's hand for such an amount as you have.

Double Head.—Should no one enter for the pool, the stakes are doubled, the deal passing to the left.

Treble Head.—When the cards have been twice dealt, and no bets for the pool, &c., the pool always belonging to the *board* until a bet is made.

Blind.[9]—The one left of the dealer has the privilege of putting up a limited number of "*chips*" before raising his hand, he passing. Should a party see fit to call the blind, must put twice the number in the pool, with the privilege of running over the blind; on coming around, the one who first entered either makes his blind good by putting up equally with the one who called, or passes his hand. Should no party see the blind, he is entitled to the pool.

---

9. "Blind" is used because the player makes the bet without seeing his cards. Its purpose is to build the pot a bit before the real action transpires, making it more enticing to play on.

HANDY GUIDE

TEXAS HOLD'EM HOLE CARD NICKNAMES

Poker players never met a slang phrase they didn't like, especially when describing the two cards dealt to begin a Texas Hold'em hand. There are dozens of such "hole card" handles, with the logic behind most being an obvious reference to the number or the shape of the letter on each card. Here are some of the more inventive.

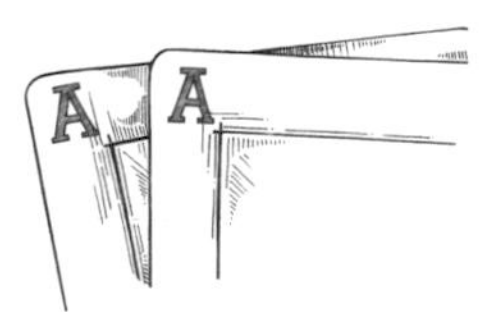

BULLETS; SHARP TOPS
Aces are killers, and *A*s are pointy.

COWBOYS; KING KONG
In other words, alpha males.

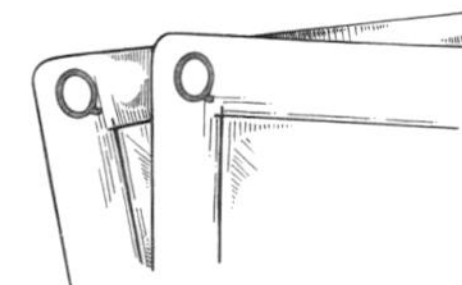

LADIES; SNOWSHOES
It is, after all, *Her* Highness; Q, if you squint, looks like a snowshoe.

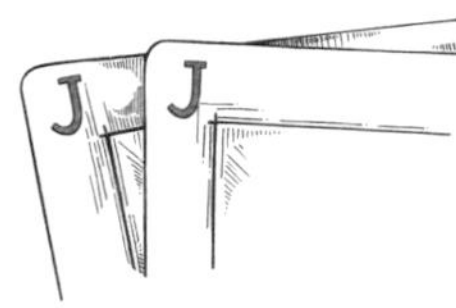

FISHHOOKS; JAYBIRDS
J, even if you *don't* squint, looks like a fishhook; a *J* (jay) by any other name is still a bird.

BARBARA FELDON; POTHOOKS
Barbara Feldon is the actress who played Agent 99 in *Get Smart*. We're not entirely sure what a pothook is, but we'd bet one looks like a 9.

SNOWMEN; PIANO KEYS
An 8, in any season, looks like two giant balls of snow stacked one on the other; a piano has 88 keys.

WALKING STICKS; HOCKEY STICKS
Depending on whether the view is right side up or upside down.

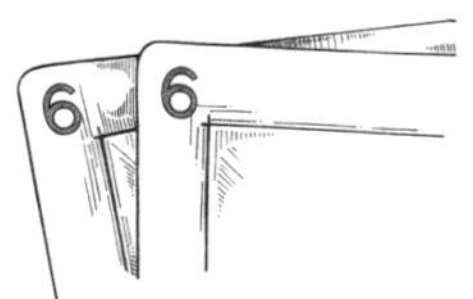

ROUTE 66; CHERRIES
A cultural reference to the famous U.S. highway of song and show; a 6 looks like a cherry with its stem.

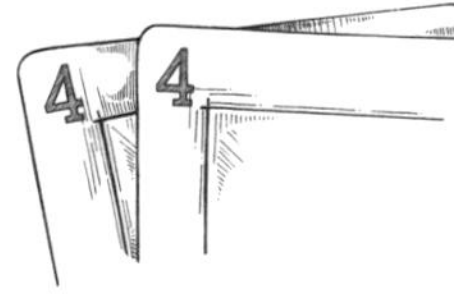

MAGNUM; SAILBOATS
As in the .44-caliber handgun; a 4 looks like a sail.

CRABS; TREYS
Tilt your head and a 3 looks like a certain crustacean; Old French for three.

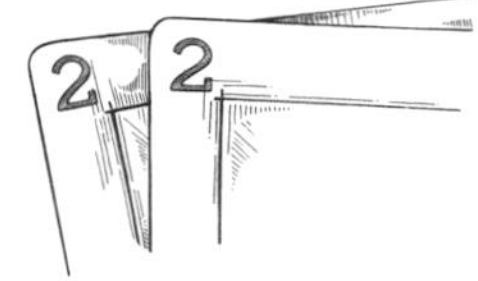

DUCKS; DEUCES
A 2 looks like a duck on a pond (yes, it looks more like a swan, but let's not quibble); Old French for two.

ASHTRAY; LUCKY 13
A pun, because "ash" begins with *A*, and "tray" (aka "trey"—see 3-3) means 3; 1 "pip" on an ace + 3 = 13.

CANINE; FIDO
Say it out loud—and the obvious extrapolation.

JACKSON FIVE; MOTOWN
Conjuring a famous pop family and its equally famous record label.

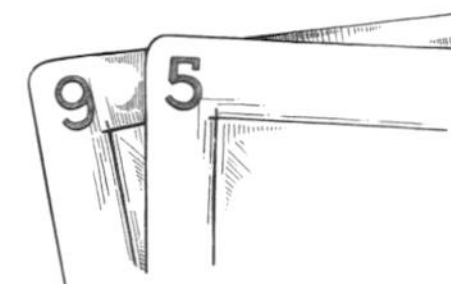

DOLLY PARTON; HARDWORKING MAN
A dated reference to a movie starring the country-singing icon; and a secondary reference to an honest day's labor.

ORWELL; BIG BROTHER
The rare literary reference (to the author of *1984*, if you missed that high school assignment); and the book's ubiquitous government overseer.

BOMBER; PICK UP
A military reference to the B-52 air force strategic bomber; a prank card game called 52-pickup.

AK-47; MACHINE GUN
Two references to the Russian assault weapon.

WALTZ; WALTER PAYTON
Time signature for most waltzes; the number worn by the Chicago Bears Hall of Fame running back.

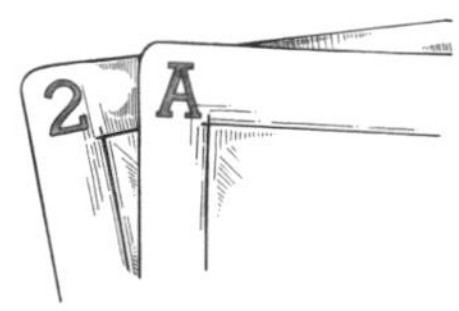

BLACKJACK; TWENTY-ONE
The former a card game in which the ideal hand total is the latter.

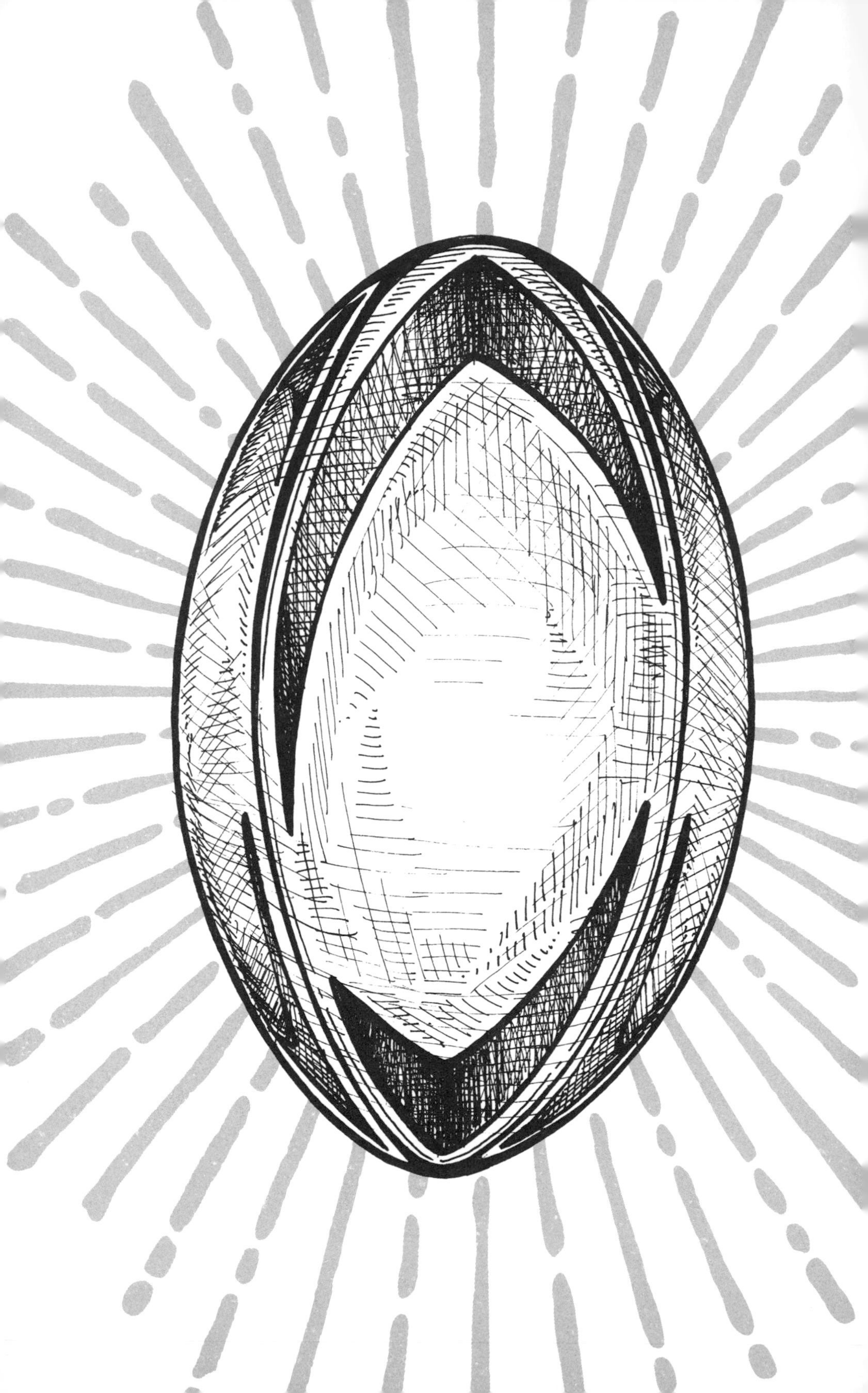

RUGBY

IF IT'S TRUE THAT ONE SHOULD NEVER LET FACTS GET IN THE way of a good story, then a British prep school boy named William Webb Ellis "invented" rugby in 1823 when he picked up the ball and ran with it in the middle of a soccer game. Young William's mythic act of rebellion at Rugby School sparked the first great schism in English sports, setting up a lasting rivalry between supporters of association football, aka soccer, said to be a gentleman's game played by rogues, and partisans of the more physical, tackling game known as union football, aka rugby, said to be a rogue's game played by gentlemen. His alleged deed also had consequences far beyond the United Kingdom. Popular throughout the British Empire, rugby also fathered American football, which, despite featuring more violence and stoppages in play, embraces the same premise: trying to advance a ball into an opponent's protected territory.

History, of course, is rarely so simple. Soccer—the kicking-only version of this branch of the sports family tree—is generally accepted as the one "true" football (except maybe in America). But games that sanctioned running with the ball probably came before those that prohibited it. In England, such games date back at least to the Middle Ages and likely originated with Celtic tribes that played "folk" or "mob" football. In these chaotic spectacles, teams made up of an unlimited number of players, typically hailing from neighboring areas, tried to carry an inflated animal bladder over a designated boundary, by any means necessary, on "fields" marked in pastures and city streets. The melees that inevitably resulted led to local authorities banning such games as early as the twelfth century—at least for regular folk. Among the few places where football remained acceptable were the campuses of England's elite public schools, namely the "Sacred Seven": Charterhouse, Eton, Harrow, Rugby, Shrewsbury, Westminster, and Winchester. Each school developed its own brand of the rowdy game, the rules of which were dictated in part by the quirks of the local playing areas: most of these schools were fashioned after monasteries, so their open spaces were generally paved with cobblestones. Because such a surface was not especially inviting to those in the mood for tackle football, it was inevitable that the students would favor sports that emphasized ball handling over the brute force of the ancient folk games.

At Rugby School, however, there was (and still is) a large grassy stretch on what's called "the Close," and it was on this field that Webb Ellis and his mates developed their kind of football. His spiritual descendants were so pleased with the parochial creation that in 1845 they did what no one had done before—they wrote down the rules to the game. The backlash was nearly twenty years in the making, but when students at Harrow, Charterhouse, and other schools formed the Football Association and compiled a rule book of their own for the kicking version of football they played, the result was seismic.

To be fair, though, the dominance of soccer in the early decades of both games, not to mention its continued supremacy, was at least in part rugby's own fault. In the late stages of the nineteenth century, internal politics in the sport forced a second rift, this one between two camps of ruggers: those convinced the game should remain an amateur diversion and those who thought players should be paid (at least when they missed work to compete). The two factions—rugby union and rugby league, respectively—at first played by the same rules, but eventually significant differences, from number of players per side to approach to possession and scoring, emerged.

Meanwhile, William Webb Ellis continues to be credited with inventing rugby—the sport's World Cup trophy bears his name—proving once and for all that a good story conquers all.

"THE LAWS OF FOOTBALL AS PLAYED AT RUGBY SCHOOL" (1845)

RESOLUTIONS

That only in cases of extreme emergency,[1] and only by the permission of the heads of the sides, shall anyone be permitted to leave the Close, after calling over, till the game be finished, and consequently, that all dressing take place before that time.

That the punishment for absenting oneself from a match without any real and well-grounded reason, be left to the discretion of any praeposter.[2] That whenever a match is going to be played, the school shall be informed of it by the Head of School in such a manner as he shall think fit, some time before dinner on the day in question.

That no unnecessary delay take place in the commencement of matches, but as soon as calling over be finished the game be commenced. That the old custom, that no more than two matches take place in the same week, be strictly adhered to, of which, one must always take place on Saturday, without some strong cause to the contrary.

That all fellows not following up be strictly prohibited from playing any game in goal, or otherwise conducting themselves in any way which shall be deemed prejudicial to the interests of their side.

That in consequence of the great abuse in the system of giving notes to excuse fagging,[3] etc., and otherwise exempt fellows from attendance at the matches, no notes shall be received which are not signed by one of the Medical officers of the school and countersigned by the Head of House or by a master when the case specified is not an illness.

---

1. *If at times these rules sound overwrought or overly specific (when to get dressed?), cheeky, or in other ways somewhat less than bureaucratic, it is because they were written by three high school kids. (A fourth was enlisted to illustrate.)*
2. *A resident adviser, specifically an upperclassman tasked with keeping an eye on the younger kids.*
3. *A chiefly British word for toil or drudgery. In English public schools, it was tradition for younger students to be put in service of upperclassmen. So who exactly was guilty of a "great abuse" in this case is an open question.*

That all fellows at Tutor during calling over, or otherwise absent, shall be obliged to attend as soon after as possible.

That the Head of School take care that these resolutions be generally known among the school, and as far as the case may be shall apply equally to the big sides.

That Old Rugbeians shall be allowed to play at matches of Football, not without consent, however, of the two heads of the sides.

RULES

i. FAIR CATCH is a catch direct from the foot.

ii. OFF SIDE. A player is *off his side* if the ball[4] has touched one of his own side behind him, until the other side touch it.[5]

iii. FIRST OF HIS SIDE is the player nearest the ball on his side.

iv. A KNOCK ON, as distinguished from a *throw on,* consists in striking the ball on with the arm or hand.

v. TRY AT GOAL.[6] A ball touched between the goalposts may be brought up to either of them, but not between. The ball when *punted* must be within, when caught without the line of goal: the ball must be place-kicked and not dropped,[7] even though it touch[ed] two hands, and it must go over the bar and between the posts without having touched the dress or person of any player. No goal may be kicked from touch.[8]

vi. KICK OFF FROM MIDDLE must be a place-kick.

---

4. *The first rugby balls were round, but through the years they became more ovoid in shape. At first they were not all equal in size, because each conformed to the particular animal bladder from which it was made.*

5. *This isn't the clearest way to describe what remains a core principle of all rugby versions (we've used union as our reference point throughout): the ball can only be passed backward, and is thus advanced mostly through runs. A teammate who finds himself in front of the ballcarrier—say, after passing it to him—can't receive the ball until his colleague moves ahead of him. Because he is off his side.*

6. *Now as then the point of the game was to make tries, or plays that resulted in a team advancing the ball across the line. At first, though, the try was not in itself a scoring play but merely offered teams a chance—a try—to kick the ball through or over the goalposts to score.*

7. *What is now known as the conversion can be either drop-kicked or placekicked.*

8. *Out of bounds.*

vii. KICK OUT must not be from more than ten yards out of goal if a place-kick, not more than twenty-five yards if a punt, drop, or knock on.
viii. RUNNING IN is allowed to any player on his side, provided he does not take the ball off the ground, or take it through touch.
ix. CHARGING is fair, in case of a place-kick, as soon as the ball has touched the ground;[9] in case of a kick from a catch, as soon as the player's foot has left the ground, and not before.
x. OFF SIDE. No player being off his side shall kick the ball in any case whatever.
xi. No player being off his side shall hack, charge, run in, touch the ball in goal, or interrupt a catch.
xii. A player when off his side having a fair catch is entitled to a fair *knock on,* and in no other case.
xiii. A player being off his side shall not touch the ball on the ground, except in touch.
xiv. A player being off his side cannot put *on his side* himself, or any other player, by knocking or throwing on the ball.
xv. TOUCH. A player may not in any case run with the ball in or through touch.
xvi. A player standing up to another may hold one arm only, but may hack him or knock the ball out of his hand if he attempts to kick it, or go beyond the line of touch.
xvii. No agreement between two players to send the ball *straight out* shall be allowed on big-side.[10]
xviii. A player having touched the ball straight for a tree,[11] and

---

9. Because allowing such encroachment made it virtually impossible to get off a kick, today the defense cannot move to block the ball until the kicker's leg begins to move forward.

10. Big-side refers to a team made up of the top players at the school—basically, the varsity. Apparently, in games of such import, players couldn't possibly be trusted with making decisions involving the run of play.

11. The pitch at Rugby School, though rare for its vastness, was not without its hazards. Trees—three elms, to be precise—dotted the field. The rules couldn't very well ignore them. In this particularly local instance, it seems the team in possession when the ball hit said tree got to retain possession, restarting the attack from anywhere near the tree, as their opponent yielded.

touched the tree with it, may drop from either side if he can, but the opposite side may oblige him to go to his own side of the tree.
xix. A player touching a ball off his side must *throw* it *straight out.*
xx. All matches are drawn after five days, but after three if no goal has been kicked.[12]
xxi. Two big-side balls must always be in the Close during a match or big-side.
xxii. The discretion of sending into goals rests with the heads of sides or houses.[13]
xxiii. No football shall be played between the goals till the Sixth match.[14]
xxiv. Heads of sides, or two deputies appointed by them, are the sole arbiters of all disputes.
xxv. No strangers, in any match, may have a place-kick at goal.[15]
xxvi. No hacking with the heel, or above the knee, is fair.
xxvii. No player but the first on his side, may be hacked, except in a *scrummage.*
xxviii. No player may wear projecting or iron plates on the heels or soles of his shoes or boots.
xxix. No player may take the ball out of the Close.
xxx. No player may stop the ball with anything but his own person.
xxxi. Nobody may wear cap or jersey without leave from the head of his house.
xxxii. At a big-side, the two players highest in the School shall toss up.

---

12. *Wow. Today eighty minutes, split into two forty-minute halves with a rest in between, is more than enough. But this rule alludes to a fundamental problem of the unsophisticated early game: it was very difficult to score.*
13. *In other words, the captain of the team decided who got to play.*
14. *The Sixth match was the one played by the sixth form, Britain's equivalent of American high school's juniors and seniors. Again, kids—sixth formers, to be exact—wrote these rules, so it's no surprise that they included this warning to any and all to stay off their field until their scheduled recreation or competition time.*
15. *This may well be the first written prohibition in sports against ringers. The rule makers knew enough about their constituency—other prep school kids—to know any of them might well recruit some non-student help if given the chance.*

xxxiii. The Island[16] is all in goal.
xxxiv. At little-sides[17] the goals shall be four paces wide, and in kicking a goal the ball must pass out of the reach of any player present.
xxxv. Three Praepostors constitute a big-side.
xxxvi. If a player takes a punt when he is not entitled to it, the opposite side may take a punt or drop, without running if the ball has not touched two hands.
xxxvii. No player may be held, unless he is himself holding the ball.
As these Rules have now become the Laws of the game, it is hoped that all who take an interest in Football will contribute all in their power to enforce their observance.[18]

---

16. Another geographic quirk of the Rugby School campus. And it was in play.

17. Little-sides, of course, are the younger kids, for whom the field was truncated and the rules governing kicked goals less stringent; the wee ones didn't have to worry about clearing goalposts, just the outstretched arms of their tallest peers.

18. In 1871, rugby's laws—the basis for both rugby union and rugby league—were standardized by the Rugby Football Union.

TAKING AIM
THE GOALS OF SPORTS

There are numerous ways to mark success on fields of play, among them the acquisition of territory and the surrender of opponents. One of the most common is the placement of a ball (or puck) in (or through) a defined target. Goals, nets, baskets . . . a rose, by any other name, still counts on the scoreboard.

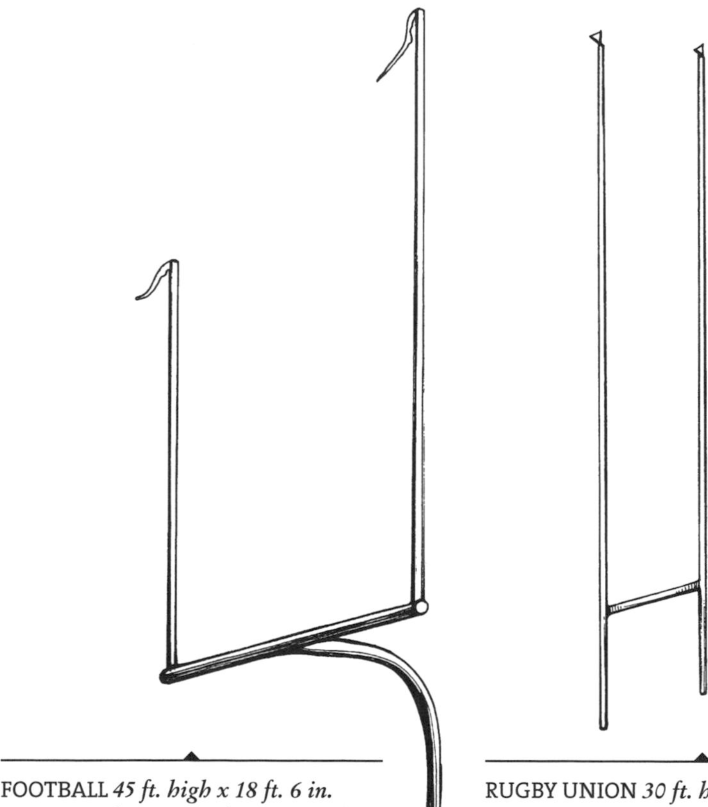

FOOTBALL *45 ft. high x 18 ft. 6 in. apart; crossbar: 10 ft. above ground*
Player safety was a factor when the NFL moved its posts from the goal line to the back of the end zone in 1974, but the main impetus was to encourage teams to continue drives instead of attempting long field goals.

RUGBY UNION *30 ft. high x 18 ft. 5 in. apart; crossbar: 9 ft. above ground*
Football once used H-shaped goalposts but switched to a Y-shaped design in 1967 to cut in half the possibility of players colliding with support posts. This is not as much of a concern in rugby, because players don't spend much time around the posts.

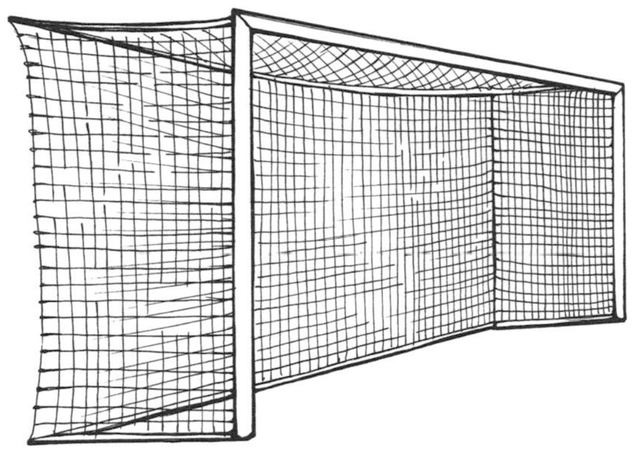

SOCCER *24 ft. x 8 ft.*
Use of the word "score" in sports is thought to derive from a long-ago practice in soccer, in which goals were recorded by notching—or scoring—wooden goalposts.

AUSTRALIAN RULES FOOTBALL *Goal (middle) posts: 20 ft. high, 21 ft. apart; behind (outside) posts: 10 ft. high, 21 ft. from goalposts*
Australian rules football uses four separate goalposts, set in a straight line. Kicking the rugby-style ball between the inner two results in six points, while kicking it between an inner and an outer post racks up one. Hitting any of the posts also nets a point.

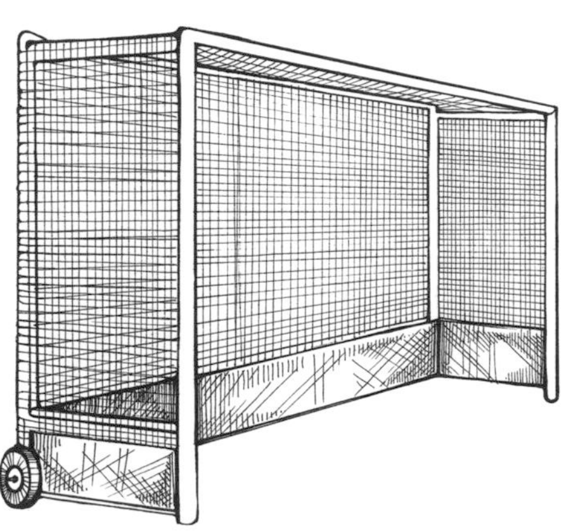

FIELD HOCKEY *12 ft. x 7 ft.*
Relative goal size and ball speed make field hockey goaltender one of the most challenging positions in all of sports.

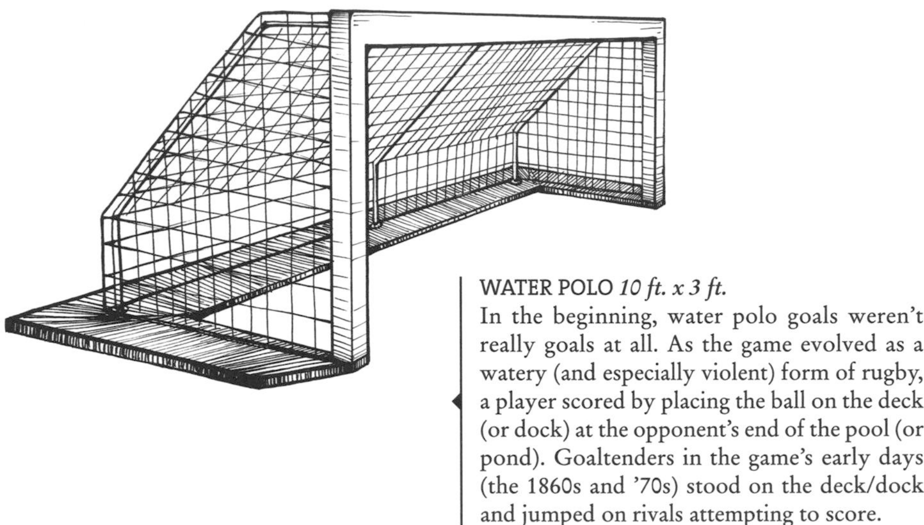

WATER POLO *10 ft. x 3 ft.*
In the beginning, water polo goals weren't really goals at all. As the game evolved as a watery (and especially violent) form of rugby, a player scored by placing the ball on the deck (or dock) at the opponent's end of the pool (or pond). Goaltenders in the game's early days (the 1860s and '70s) stood on the deck/dock and jumped on rivals attempting to score.

NETBALL *Basket ring: centered, 15 in. diameter, 6 in. from pole, 10 ft. above court*
Although the same height above the ground as a regulation basketball hoop, a netball goal has no backboard and a rim that is several inches smaller in diameter.

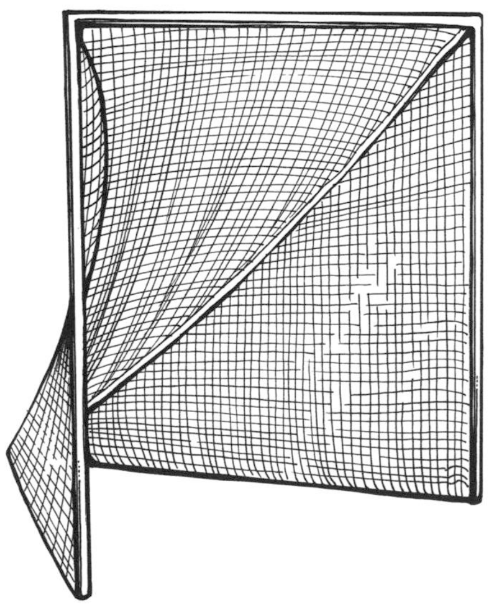

LACROSSE *6 ft. x 6 ft.*
The triangular base is intended to make it easier for players to circumnavigate the goal.

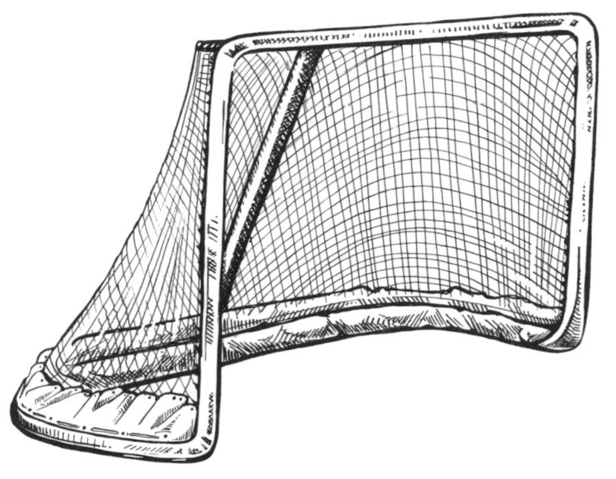

ICE HOCKEY *6 ft. x 4 ft.*
The National Hockey League once secured goal nets to metal poles embedded in, and protruding 8 inches above, the ice. (The poles slipped into sleeves in a goal's side posts.) The setup was a hazard to anyone who rammed into the net, so in 1984 the league switched to magnets that adhered to ¾-inch metal anchors in the ice. The pull is strong enough to steady the net in most situations while allowing it to pop free in hard collisions.

BASKETBALL ***Backboard: 6 ft. x 3.5 ft.; basket ring: centered, 18 in. diameter, 6 in. from backboard, 10 ft. above court***
Early basketball backboards were less about shooters and more about fans. The first, made of wood or chicken wire, were added in the mid-1890s to block those seated above the hoop from interfering with the ball.

SOCCER

THE EARLIEST REFERENCE TO KICKING BALLS FOR SPORT comes from a Chinese military manual dating from the third century BC, which describes an exercise wherein soldiers booted leather orbs into tiny nets stretched between bamboo poles. An alternative account that features victorious Anglo-Saxon barbarians and the head of a conquered Danish prince circa AD 500 might appeal more to the bloodthirsty among us. Something in the human condition makes kicking anything almost irresistible.

Happily, something in the animal condition makes this a desire easy to slake: bladders, specifically those of slaughtered livestock. According to the British author James Walvin, these organs were pretty much "unsuitable for most other purposes, but ideal to inflate and play with." (His is the most succinct explanation for why this book has multiple references to animal organs.)

Football, at its most basic, was ubiquitous in many cultures throughout the Middle Ages. But the game that has become the most played and watched in the world took shape among English public (that is, private) school boys in the early nineteenth century. Different schools played by different rules, and the prime point of disagreement centered on the legality of picking up the ball. Using one's hands is modern soccer's cardinal sin, but the practice was common in the game's formative years. In fact, playing the match in halves may have emerged as a compromise between rival football factions: carrying the ball was allowed in one half but prohibited in the other.

And that's how the game might have been played today if not for an 1863 meeting of prominent English football clubs—held at a London pub, appropriately—at which the negotiations mainly centered on the hot-button running-with-the-ball issue. The group called itself the Football Association, and after roughly half a dozen get-togethers, they agreed on a list of thirteen rules, three of which specifically dealt with a prohibition against carrying the ball. Participants who had insisted that it was an essential part of the game walked out in protest. The great divide between soccer and rugby (named after Rugby School, where it was honed) has persisted ever since.

Those pub confabs were also inadvertently responsible for the nomenclatural differences between what the sport was called in America (soccer) and how pretty much the rest of the world referred to it (football). The British, especially the upper crust, have always liked to shorten names, a clubby affectation meant to imply familiarity or fondness. So a rugby football player was known in some circles as a "rugger," while an association football player was known as a "soccer" ("assocer" didn't trip off the tongue quite so well). Although the second nickname never caught on in Britain, it did here for a perfectly good reason: Americans were already falling for a game they called football, so another term was needed for the British import. That's why this chapter, written by Americans for a primarily American audience, is about soccer—though, of course, it's really about football.

THE FOOTBALL ASSOCIATION'S RULES OF SOCCER (1863)

RULES	NOTES
∞ *1st* ∞ **The maximum length of the ground shall be 200 yards,[1] the maximum breadth shall be 100 yards, the length and breadth shall be marked off with flags; and the goals shall be defined by two upright posts, 8 yards apart, without any tape or bar across them.**	*1. Two hundred yards is one long run. Today's internationally sanctioned matches are played on fields that are between 110 and 120 yards long (and 70 to 80 yards wide). The span of the goal remains the same.*
∞ *2nd* ∞ **The winner of the toss shall have the choice of goals. The game shall be commenced by a place kick from the centre of the ground by the side losing the toss; the other side shall not approach within 10 yards of the ball until it is kicked off.**	
∞ *3rd* ∞ **After a goal is won, the losing side shall kick off and goals shall be changed.[2]**	*2. One goal change, at halftime, suffices now.*
∞ *4th* ∞ **A goal shall be won when the ball passes between the goal posts or over the space between the goal posts (at whatever height),[3] not being thrown, knocked on, or carried.**	*3. Goals don't reach to the heavens anymore. Since 1875 a crossbar has topped off the target at a height of 8 feet.*
∞ *5th* ∞ **When the ball is in touch,[4] the first player who touches it shall throw it from the point on the boundary**	*4. Out of bounds.*

RULES	NOTES
line where it left the ground, in a direction at right angles with the boundary line.[5]	*5. The throw-in no longer has to be perpendicular to the touchline; it can go forward or backward from the point of the throw at any angle. Nor is it made by the first player who reaches it; rather the team that did not kick it out gains possession, and any member can throw in.*
∞ 6th ∞ **When a player has kicked the ball any one of the same side who is nearer to the opponent's goal line is out of play and may not touch the ball himself[6] nor in any way whatever prevent any other player from doing so until the ball has been played; but no player is out of play when the ball is kicked from behind the goal line.**	*6. This is an early version of offside, and it has since been tweaked. Players on the side with possession can position themselves in front of the ball as long as there is an opposing player—besides the goalkeeper—between him and the opposing goal. The implementation of this rule caused the most interclub friction in the early attempts to codify the game; some clubs didn't even recognize offside as an infraction, while others called for three opponents between the player in question and the goal.*
∞ 7th ∞ **In case the ball goes behind the goal line, if a player on the side to whom the goal belongs first touches the ball, one of his side shall be entitled to a free kick from the goal line at the point opposite the place where the ball shall be touched. If a player of the opposite side first touches the ball, one of his side shall be entitled to a free kick (but at the goal only) from a point 15 yards from the goal line opposite the place where the ball is touched. The opposing side shall stand behind their goal line until he has had his kick.[7]**	*7. This kick is now taken from the corner, and has been since 1872; the attacking team is awarded it and the defense does not need to stand idly by.*

RULES	NOTES
8th **If a player makes a fair catch[8] he shall be entitled to a free kick, provided he claims it by making a mark with his heel at once; and in order to take such kick he may go as far back as he pleases, and no player on the opposite side shall advance beyond his mark until he has kicked.**	*8. Wait—players could use their hands? As rules 9, 11, and 12 make perfectly clear, that's not allowed (excepting the goalkeeper, of course). This rule is the last vestige of the more rugby-like versions of football. It didn't last beyond the 1870s, and players could only catch the ball, not advance it.*
9th **No player shall carry the ball.**	
10th **Neither tripping nor hacking shall be allowed[9] and no player shall use his hands to hold or push his adversary.**	*9. There are no rules, however, governing diving—that is, embellishing a fall after a trip. Today's fans see this as a major oversight.*
11th **A player shall not throw the ball or pass it to another.**	
12th **No player shall take the ball from the ground with his hands while it is in play under any pretence whatever.**	
13th **No player shall wear projecting nails, iron plates, or gutta percha on the soles or heels of his boots.**	

SPHERES OF INFLUENCE

THE BALLS OF SPORTS

Soccer is the world's most popular ball sport, but it's hardly the only one.

(Note: Balls are measured by inches in circumference.)

---

1. SQUASH BALL *5 in.*
2. TABLE TENNIS BALL *5 in.*
3. GOLF BALL *5.3 in.*
4. TEAM HANDBALL *5.9 in.*
5. PELOTA (JAI ALAI) *6.75 in.*
6. SNOOKER BALL *6.9 in.*
7. RACQUETBALL (ALSO PADDLEBALL) *7 in.*
8. POOL BALL *7.2 in.*
9. ROUNDERS BALL *7.5 in.*
10. BANDY BALL *7.7 in.*
11. LACROSSE BALL *8 in.*
12. TENNIS BALL *8.2 in.*
13. SLIOTAR (HURLING) *8.7 in.*
14. BASEBALL *9 in.*
15. CRICKET BALL *9 in.*
16. FIELD HOCKEY BALL *9 in.*
17. WIFFLE BALL *9 in.*
18. PICKLE-BALL *9.25 in.*
19. POLO BALL *10.25 in.*
20. CROQUET BALL *11.4 in.*
21. SOFTBALL *12 in.*
22. BOCCE BALL *13.3 in.*
23. TAKRAW (SEPAK TAKRAW) *17 in.*
24. BROOMBALL *18.9 in.*
25. KORFBALL *25.6 in.*
26. RUGBY BALL *26 in.* *(12 in. long)*
27. VOLLEYBALL *26 in.*
28. BEACH VOLLEYBALL *26.5 in.*
29. BOWLING BALL *27 in.*
30. WATER POLO BALL *27 in.*
31. SOCCER BALL *27.2 in.*
32. FOOTBALL *28 in.* *(12 in. long)*
33. NETBALL *28 in.*
34. BASKETBALL *30.7 in.*
35. KICKBALL *31.46 in.*

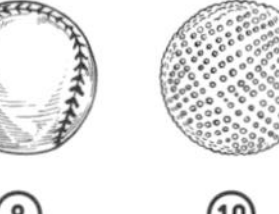

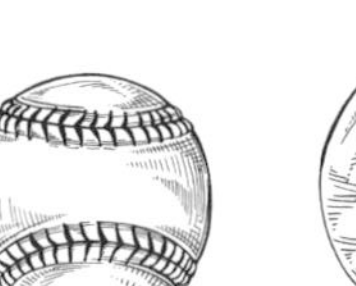

23
24
25
26
27
28
29
30
31
32
33
34
35

STOCK CAR RACING

THE STORY GOES THAT THE FIRST AUTOMOBILE RACE TOOK place on the day they built the second car. And while that's impossible to prove, it does align nicely with our understanding of human nature. Most of us are captivated by things that go fast, whatever the means of transport: feet, horses, cars, boats, planes. The German inventor Karl Benz is credited with unveiling the first motorized auto in 1886, and slightly more than a year later a French newspaper publisher sponsored the first known race. The 1.2-mile sprint between two Parisian landmarks was won by Georges Bouton—who was the clear favorite, if for no other reason than he was the only competitor to show up.

Stateside, the first auto race occurred on November 28, 1895, on a 70-mile stretch between Chicago and Evanston, Illinois. The victor was Frank Duryea, who with his brother Charles had recently developed America's first gasoline-powered car. Like many early automakers, the Duryeas were bicycle builders until, with petroleum looming as the world's primary fuel source, they turned their attention to horseless carriages. Racing was the ideal showcase for the newfangled motorized vehicles, and as a new century dawned carmakers and mechanics gathered in large numbers at such events to display their creations.

By today's standards, these early competitions were somewhat less than thrilling, with top speeds falling short of 10 mph. Fortunately, car manufacturing moved more quickly: by the mid-1930s, 300 mph seemed within reach, at least for vehicles specifically designed to achieve high speeds. Of course, those cars demanded particular kinds of open roads upon which to go from zero to whatever in safety. With its wide expanse of hard-packed sand, Daytona Beach, Florida, was already America's unofficial racing mecca, drawing drivers and spectators since Ransom E. Olds (as in Oldsmobile, maker of the REO Speed Wagon) and Alexander Winton raced each other there in 1903. It was in Daytona that the British racing enthusiast Malcolm Campbell flashed along the beach at 276 mph in 1935. But, soon after, the harder-packed salt flats of Utah beckoned serious speed chasers, leaving the city fathers of Daytona Beach searching for a way to regain the nation's attention (and tourism dollars).

Their solution was a race between ordinary factory-built cars, and in 1936 Milt Marion and his Ford V8 won the first stock car race, on Daytona's closed beach-and-road course. The focus on stock cars would prove doubly beneficial. First, it emphasized American know-how in an endeavor that had been dominated by European makes. Second, stock cars provided a relatable spectator experience: fans could easily imagine themselves behind the wheels of those familiar sedans. But that payoff would take time. The 1936 race was a financial failure, and Daytona's days as a hotbed of racing appeared at an end.

A combination of commerce and criminality saved the day. For many early racers, driving fast wasn't merely a sporting pursuit; it was a way to stay out of jail. Throughout Prohibition, makers of moonshine needed to transport their product from mountain stills to thirsty towns throughout the Deep South. As cars went faster and became easier to come by, distillers began to hire drivers who enjoyed the challenge that outrunning the law presented. These bootleggers, who often became local legends, regularly met up at county fairs for races that burnished reputations and paid a little extra cash—on the rare occasion that an unscrupulous promoter didn't "lose" the gate receipts instead.

Bill France Sr., a little-known mechanic who finished fifth to Marion in that money-losing Daytona race, saw a business opportunity in bringing order to these seat-of-the-pants competitions. In January 1947 France founded the National Championship Stock Car Circuit, a yearlong tour of forty races that featured an ongoing points system and the promise of $1,000 to the series winner. That December, France made good on that promise, handing Truman "Fonty" Flock the champion's check. Shortly after, he convened a meeting of prominent drivers, mechanics, and promoters at Daytona's Streamline Hotel, to guarantee his circuit would have lasting direction. When the group emerged after four days of confabbing, the National Association for Stock Car Auto Racing was ready to roll. The rules for NASCAR's inaugural season were in place in time for the first race the following February—in Daytona.

THE NATIONAL ASSOCIATION FOR STOCK CAR AUTO RACING'S "1948 RULES AND SPECIFICATIONS"

Rule 1. Cars eligible—1937 models and up[1] through 1948. '37 and '38 models must have four-wheel hydraulic brakes.

Rule 2. Later models must be run in the same model chassis.

Rule 3. Foreign[2] manufactured cars will not be permitted.

Rule 4. If a car is a convertible[3] type, it must be run with top up and in proper place and must be equipped with safety hoops mounted to frame.

Rule 5. All cars must have full stock fenders, running boards, and body if so equipped when new, and not abbreviated in any way other than reinforcement.

---

1. *Decade-old car models remained eligible because most racers were soldiers in World War II, and when they returned home, they went back to racing (and running moonshine) in the same cars they'd left behind. It also took time for Detroit assembly lines to be refitted for nonmilitary use. The next season, NASCAR ran its first "Strictly Stock" or "New Car" race, which was open to cars no older than three years.*
2. *NASCAR founder Bill France Sr. staunchly believed in giving the American people what they'd never seen before—race cars that looked like what they drove. That meant sticking to domestic nameplates. Until Toyota entered NASCAR full-time in 2004, the only foreign car to win a Grand National race was Al Keller's Jaguar, in a makeshift road race on the tarmac of the Linden, New Jersey, airport on June 13, 1954.*
3. *NASCAR ran a separate Convertible Division between 1956 and 1959, but many races mixed roofed and open-air rides, including the inaugural running in 1959 of what has become the sport's signature event, the season-opening Daytona 500. Race legend Richard Petty's first career win came in a Convertibles competition at the Columbia Speedway in South Carolina in 1959. Luckily, given the dangers, a lack of Detroit factory support shuttered the series soon after.*

Rule 6. Stock bumpers and mufflers must be removed.[4]

Rule 7. Crash bars may be used no wider than frame, protruding no farther than 12 inches from body.

Rule 8. All doors must be welded, bolted, or strapped shut.[5] **Doors blocked will not be permitted.**

Rule 9. Fuel and oil capacities may be increased in any safe manner. Any extra or bigger tanks must be concealed inside car or under hood.[6]

Rule 10. Wheelbase, length, and width must be stock.

Rule 11. All cars must have safety glass. All headlight and taillight glass must be removed.

Rule 12. All cars must have full windshield in place and used as windshield.[7] **No glass or material other than safety glass may be used.**

Rule 13. Cars must be equipped with rear view mirror.

Rule 14. All cars must be subject to safety inspection by Technical Committee at any time.

Rule 15. All cars must have four-wheel hydraulic brakes or any brake manufactured after 1947.

---

4. *Why no stock bumpers? Because the protruding chrome ornaments of the day broke off too easily—becoming dangerous projectiles—or hooked themselves into other cars on contact. Why no stock mufflers? Because the louder the race car, the more awesome the race car!*
5. *The most common way to keep doors closed was to tie a leather strap to the door and its frame. (More often than not, the belt was yanked right from a driver's pants.) By 1967 mandatory unibody construction had done away with doors altogether.*
6. *Call it the most misguided rule of the bunch. Looking to keep their cars on the track while rivals pitted, mechanics flooded cars with fuel—including inside the doors, frame, and roll bars. That meant crashes inevitably led to massive flash fires. Glenn Roberts—he of the unintentionally prescient nickname Fireball—died in a terrible conflagration at the Charlotte Motor Speedway in 1964. Afterward, NASCAR mandated strict fuel cell regulations, including a rubber aircraft membrane to prevent crash-caused gashes to the tank.*

Rule 16. Piston displacement in any car is limited to 300 cu. in., except where motor is used in same body and chassis it was designed and catalogued for. Under 300 cu. in. motors may be interchanged in same manufacturer's line.

Rule 17. Any block can be oversize. The only truck blocks permitted to be used in any Stock Car will be 100 H. P. Ford[8] Blocks, which are fundamentally same as passenger car. These may only be used in models up to 1947 Fords. (Stock interchangeable passenger car blocks must be used in all cars through 1947.)

Rule 18. Cars may be run with or without fan or generator.

Rule 19. Any flywheel may be used.

Rule 20. Any part may be reinforced.

Rule 21. Any interchangeable wheel or tire size[9] may be used.

Rule 22. Any rear end arrangement may be used.

Rule 23. Any radiator may be used, providing stock hood will close and latch properly. Hoods must have safety straps. All cars must have hoods on and must be stock hood for same model car.

Rule 24. Any type battery ignition may be used, excluding magnetos.

Rule 25. Any type of manufactured spark plug may be used.

---

7. *Racers had to be forced to use windshields, especially on dirt, because the glass—and thus their view—ended up caked in mud. Modern stock cars coat windshields with a stack of plastic tear-offs, which are yanked away one by one during pit stops to maintain unsullied sight lines.*

8. *Any leeway given to teams running Fords was no accident. The legendary Ford Flathead engine was the weapon of choice for bootleggers, so anything bearing Henry's signature was their preferred racing machine, too. There were fifty-two races in NASCAR's original 1948 Modified Division championship schedule: all were won by a Ford.*

9. *As stock cars became more restrictedly uniform in the 1970s, so did tires. Before then, showing up with the best trick tire, no matter how goofy, could be the winning edge. Johnny "Mad Man" Mantz won NASCAR's first asphalt speedway race, the 1950 Southern 500 at Darlington, by bolting on bulky truck tires and cruising along on the apron while the other seventy-four cars popped rubber like birthday balloons on the high-banked turns.*

Rule 26. Any model manufactured flat type cylinder heads may be used. Cylinder heads may be machined to increase compression.

Rule 27. Heads allowed with overhead valves only when coming as standard or optional equipment from factory.

Rule 28. Any valve springs may be used.

Rule 29. Multiple carburetion[10] will be permitted. Any type carburetion may be used.

Rule 30. Superchargers allowed only when optional on stock equipment by manufacturer.

Rule 31. Water pump impellers may be cut down.

Rule 32. Altered camshafts will be permitted.

Rule 33. Altered crankshafts may be used.

Rule 34. All drivers must be strapped in and must wear safety helmets.[11] Belt must be bolted to frame at two points and must be aviation latch type quick-release belt.

Rule 35. Regulation crash helmets must be used.

---

10. *Carburetion remained the NASCAR norm until long after its use in streetcars became obsolete. Teams started to rely on old-school, four-barrel carburetors during the JFK administration and held on until 2012. That's when they finally switched to fuel injectors, used in every new American passenger car since 1990.*

11. *This rule and the one that follows it were revolutionary for their time, representing the first real effort to force roughneck racers to protect those necks. These safety requirements changed slowly over the decades, until they were pushed into overdrive by Dale Earnhardt's death in the 2001 Daytona 500. Six-point harnesses and custom-fit seats quickly became the norm; NASCAR mandated head and neck restraints and conducts detailed inspections to guarantee those seats and belts are mounted properly.*

START YOUR ENGINES
MOTORSPORT VEHICLES

NASCAR is far from the world's only (or biggest) high-revving competition. If a vehicle has an engine, someone somewhere is redlining it.

DRAG BOAT
The fastest drag boat is the hydroplane. It's designed to trap air underneath the hull, so it essentially rides atop a cushion of air with only a few inches of boat touching water. Hydroplanes can reach 260 mph.

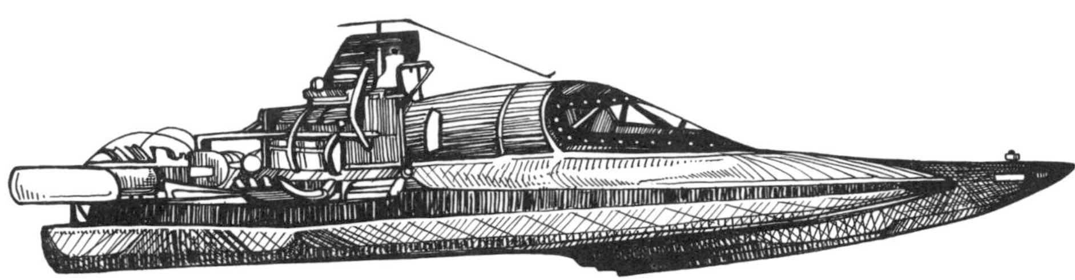

POWERBOAT (F_1H_2O)
A tunnel-hull design offers F1 powerboats increased maneuverability and an acceleration of zero to sixty in fewer than two seconds. Races aren't the straight shots of drag boat contests; drivers experience 4.5 g's of force as they whip around sharp bends. Despite that, cockpits remained open until the 1990s, when an enclosure was mandated to protect drivers in the event of a crash.

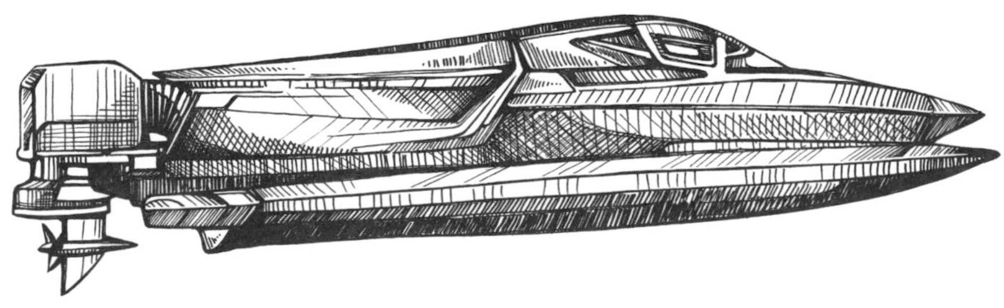

SNOWMOBILE (SNOCROSS)

The first snowmobile was invented in Canada in 1937, but Snocross, a racing competition derived from motocross, wasn't added to the Winter X Games until 1998. Snocross racers fly more than 100 feet in a single jump and take straightaways at speeds of up to 60 mph when they are not navigating a course of many obstacles.

MOTORCYCLE (MOTOGP)

The first season of MotoGP was in 1949, which makes it the oldest motorsport world championship circuit. Today its races span the globe: fourteen countries on four continents.

MIDGET CAR

These compacts have a high power-to-weight ratio. Instituted in the 1930s, midget racing has long served as a minor league to NASCAR, including for some of its biggest names, such as Jeff Gordon and Tony Stewart.

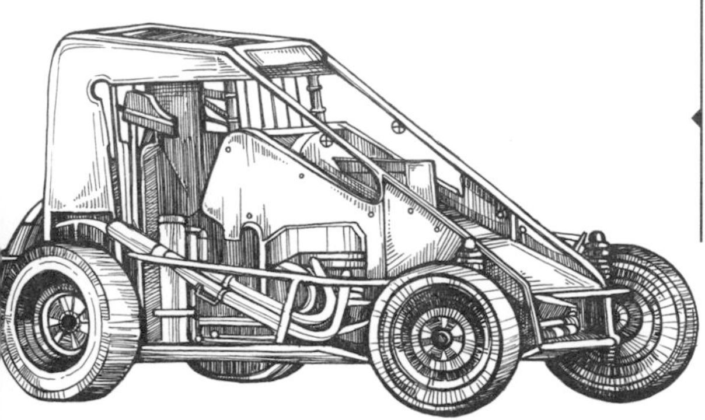

OPEN WHEEL (INDYCAR)
IndyCar is America's most popular form of open-wheel racing and therefore synonymous with the sport as a whole. It is the country's fastest form of auto racing, with cars topping out at around 230 mph on oval racetracks like the world-famous Indianapolis Motor Speedway—home of the equally famous 500 that gave the sport its name.

OPEN WHEEL (FORMULA 1)
Similar in size and speed capability to IndyCars, F1 race cars run much slower because they compete on twisty road courses. People seem to think it's worth it, though, as it is the most expensive motorsport in the world, with team budgets in the hundreds of millions of dollars.

TRUCK (NASCAR TRUCK SERIES)
The NASCAR version of truck racing takes place almost exclusively in the United States, featuring pickups that more closely resemble race cars than worksite vehicles. The Camping World Truck Series is another one of those minor-league stops on the way to the big leagues. Sprint Cup stars Kyle Busch, Kevin Harvick, and Carl Edwards all started their careers in trucks.

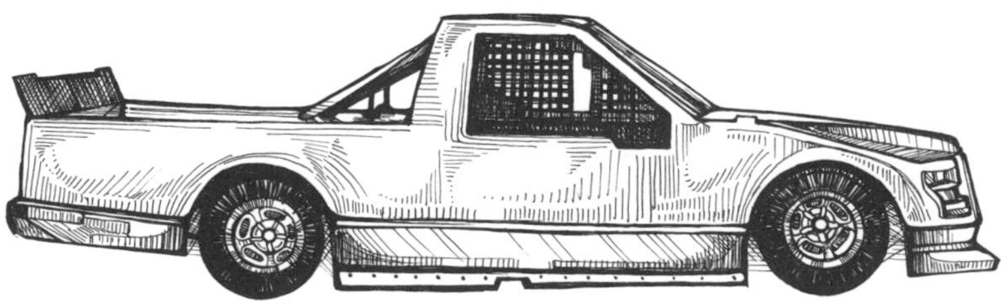

TRUCK (INTERNATIONAL AUTOMOBILE FEDERATION)
Another European-centric circuit, this one run by the IAF (often called the FIA to give the French name, Fédération Internationale de l'Automobile, its due). Unlike many other forms of motor racing that feature purebred vehicles, FIA trucks look a lot like regular semitrailer trucks. With many components similar to those of stock semis, vehicles reach a maximum speed of 100 mph.

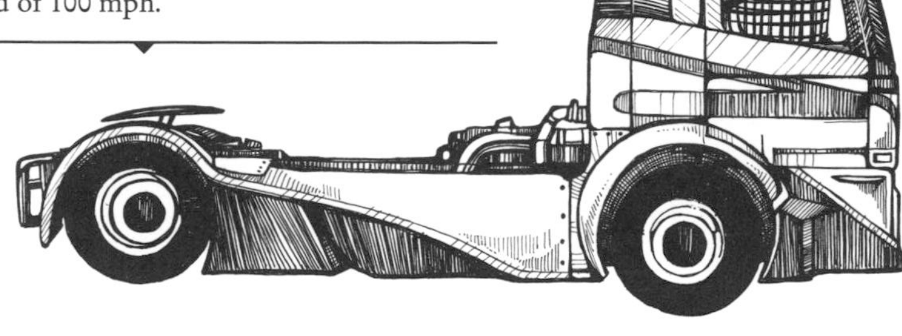

STOCK CAR (NASCAR)
Although meant to evoke cars fans might buy at local dealerships, NASCAR's rides are anything but. Vehicles in the dominant Sprint Cup Series are high-tech, custom-crafted versions of their showroom counterparts, and race winners are as much a reflection of team engineering skill as driver talent. That said, the current "Gen 6" of the circuit's highly regulated design iterations are meant to return the sport to its roots, with tougher-to-handle cars emphasizing driver prowess and styles crafted to more closely resemble showroom models.

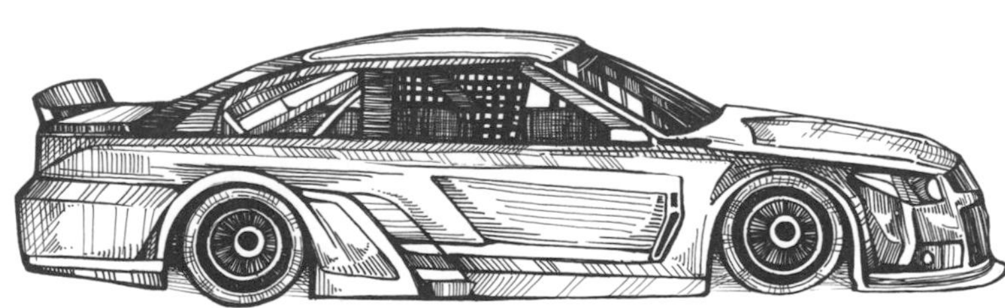

TENNIS

"STICK AND BALL" BEGAT "RACKET AND BALL." FIRST, THOUGH, the sport we know as tennis had to wend its way through "hand and ball." Hints of a game in which the palm was used as the means of knocking a projectile back and forth date to the second century BC. More specific evidence suggests a germ of tennis emerged around the year AD 1000. European monks played a courtyard game called *jeu de paume* (game of the hand) behind the walls of their medieval monasteries. It is thought that the good brothers were apt to warn opponents of an imminent serve by yelling, "*Tenez,*" which means "to take"—as in, "Are you ready to take my serve?" The name "tennis" likely springs from these etymological roots.

Over the next centuries, the game evolved—for example, gloves were donned to protect the hands—and was adopted by the nobility. Elaborate indoor courts were soon being built in manor houses and palaces across Europe. The most familiar features of tennis (court, net, that weird scoring system, and—because a blue blood's palm is at least as delicate as a monk's—the tennis racket) can be traced to the indoor game that bloomed on the Continent around the middle of the fourteenth century.

Played exclusively indoors—often in palaces, no less—tennis was mostly a rich man's game. (The homes of regular folks just didn't have that kind of space.) And it might very well have stayed that way if not for the ingenuity of two Englishmen. On August 31, 1830, Edwin Beard Budding of Stroud, in

Gloucestershire, received a patent for the first lawn mower, an invention that meant grass could be cut shorter and more uniformly than had previously been possible with sickle and scythe. Suddenly, the back gardens of England's emerging middle class were ideal locales for a spate of new sports such as lawn bowls and croquet. Around the 1860s, croquet—with its restrictive rules and slow pace—began to lose its new-toy luster, particularly among members of the younger generation who were looking for something more athletic and challenging.

Walter Clopton Wingfield sensed an opportunity. The retired and well-connected army captain filled the need in 1873 by marketing to the world a product called Sphairistike—Greek for "skill with the ball." (Others in England at the time were reacquainting themselves with the ancient game, but it was Wingfield who rushed the net.) His portable kit featured a net, rackets adapted from the indoor version, an india rubber ball, and instructions for laying out an hourglass-shaped playing area replete with baselines and service boxes that could accommodate two to four participants at a time. The new game was an instant hit, although the name proved a harder sell. Within a year, Wingfield's friend Arthur Balfour, the future British prime minister, convinced him to reclaim its original one. (The court shape wouldn't last, either.) Thus was lawn tennis born, and with it one of the game's three primary court surfaces. Today one of the sport's four Grand Slam events is played on grass at Wimbledon, aka the All England Lawn Tennis & Croquet Club (the sports were reversed in the name back then)—where the first tournament was played in 1877. The rules of the game were standardized a year later.

Wingfield, to his credit, made no claim to having "invented" a new game. His patent application specifically stated he was merely trying to simplify "the ancient game of tennis" so it could be played in the "open air." Unfortunately, despite his efforts to remake the scoring system to one based on 15 "aces," or points, that 15, 30, 40 weirdness survives.

THE ALL ENGLAND CROQUET AND LAWN TENNIS CLUB'S "RULES OF LAWN-TENNIS" (1878)

The Court is 27 feet in width, and 78 feet in length. It is divided across the middle by a net, the ends of which are attached to the tops of two posts, A and A,[1] which stand 3 feet outside the Court on each side. The height of the net is 4¾ feet at the posts, and 3 feet at the centre. At each end of the Court, parallel with the net, and at a distance of 39 feet from it, are drawn the *Base-lines,* C D and E F, the extremities of which are connected by the *Side-Lines,* C E and D F. Half-way between the Side-Lines, and parallel with them, is drawn the *Half-Court-line,* G H, dividing the space on each side of the net into two equal parts, called the *Right* and *Left-Courts.* On each side of the net, at a distance of 22 feet from it, and parallel with it, are drawn the *Service-lines,* X X and Y Y.

In the three-handed and four-handed games,[2] the Court is 36 feet in width, and the height of the net at the posts, 4 feet. Otherwise, the Court is as above.

The balls[3] shall not be less than 2½ inches, nor more than 2⅝ inches in diameter; and not less than 1¾ oz., nor more than 2 oz. in weight.

Rule 1. The choice of sides and the right of serving during the first game shall be decided by toss: provided that, if the winner of the toss

---

1. *A diagram of a regulation court was included with these rules. We have not reproduced the layout here, because the dimensions of a modern tennis court are the same.*
2. *Four hands means four tennis players: doubles. The three-handed game—two against one—is these days called Canadian doubles, Australian doubles, or cutthroat depending on where it is played. (It is not an officially sanctioned game.) In both cases, they are no longer played on different-size courts.*
3. *Ball size hasn't changed, but the color has. Since 1972 all tennis balls used in sanctioned events are fluorescent yellow, which makes them easier to see for players and spectators alike. And why is a tennis ball fuzzy? To lessen the bounce and slow it down. Some of the first balls were covered in animal fur or even human hair for that purpose.*

choose the right to serve, the other player shall have the choice of sides, and *vice versa*. The players shall stand on opposite sides of the net; the player who first delivers the ball shall be called the *Server*, the other the *Striker-out*.[4] At the end of the first game, the Striker-out shall become Server, and the Server shall become Striker-out; and so on alternately in the subsequent games of the set.

Rule 2. The Server shall stand with one foot[5] outside the Base-Line, and shall deliver the service from the Right and Left Courts alternately, beginning from the Right. The ball served must drop within the Service-Line, Half-Court-Line, and Side-Line of the Court which is diagonally opposite to that from which it was served, or upon any such line.

Rule 3. It is a *fault* if the ball served drop in the net, or beyond the Service-Line, or if it drop out of Court, or in the wrong Court. A fault may not be taken. After a fault, the Server shall serve again from the same Court from which he served that fault.

Rule 4. The service may not be *volleyed*, i.e., taken before it touches the ground.

Rule 5. The Server shall not serve until the Striker-out is ready. If the latter attempt to return the service, he shall be deemed to be ready. A good service delivered when the Striker-out is not ready annuls a previous fault.[6]

---

4. This awkward term is no longer in use; to date, though, a better substitute has not surfaced.

5. Hmmm, that sounds like a foot fault. If both feet do not remain outside the baseline until the ball is struck on a serve, a point is now awarded to the receiver.

6. Not today it doesn't. But the point is replayed.

Rule 6. A ball is *returned,* or *in-play,* when it is played back, over the net, before it has touched the ground a second time.

Rule 7. It is a good service or return, although the ball touch the net.

Rule 8. The Server wins a stroke, if the Striker-out volley the service; or if he fail to return the service or the ball in-play; or if he return the service or ball in-play so that it drop outside any of the lines which bound his opponent's Court; or if he otherwise lose a stroke, as provided by Law 10.

Rule 9. The Striker-out wins a stroke, if the Server serve two consecutive faults; or if he fail to return the ball in-play; or if he return the ball in-play so that it drop outside any of the lines which bound his opponent's Court; or if he otherwise lose a stroke, as provided by Law 10.

Rule 10. Either player loses a stroke, if the ball in-play touch him or anything that he wears or carries, except his racket in the act of striking; or if he touch or strike the ball in-play with his racket more than once.

Rule 11. On either player winning his first stroke, the score is called 15 for that player; on either player winning his second stroke, the score is called 30 for that player; on either player winning his third stroke, the score is called 40[7] for that player; and the fourth stroke, won by either player is scored game for that player; except as below:—

If both players have won three strokes, the score is called deuce;[8] and the next stroke won by either player is scored advantage for that player. If the same player win the next stroke, he wins the game; if he lose the next stroke, the score is again called deuce; and so on until either player win the two strokes immediately following the score of deuce, when the game is scored for that player.

---

7. *The odd scoring system has been attributed to the quadrants of a clock face, with each point getting a player one quarter of the way to whole. What should be 45 is instead 40 because he or she has to win by two and the distance between 45 and 60 isn't easy to visualize as divisible by that number. "Love," tennis's term for zero, is from* l'œuf*—French for egg—because to early players that's what a zero looked like. (The French don't use "love," by the way. They just say zero.)*

8. *From* deux, *French for "two," because that's how many points a player needs to win by.*

Rule 12. The player who first wins six games wins a set; except as follows:—

If both players win five games, the score is called games-all;[9] and the next game won by either player is scored advantage-game for that player. If the same player win the next game, he wins the set; if he lose the next game, the score is again called games-all; and so on until either player win the two games immediately following the score of games-all, when he wins the set.

NOTE.—Players may agree not to play advantage-sets, but to decide the set by one game after arriving at the score of games-all.

Rule 13. The players shall change sides at the end of every set.[10] When a series of sets is played, the player who was Server in the last game of one set shall be Striker-out in the first game of the next.

---

9. *This phraseology has not stood the test of time, and, more important, neither has the scoring. Since the 1970s, except in certain tournaments that still require the final set to be won by two games (majors like the Australian and French Opens and Wimbledon and other prestigious events like the Olympics and the Davis Cup), tie breaks are played at 6–6: one game, first person to seven wins—although he or she has to win by two, of course.*

10. *Today in most tournaments players also change after the first, third, and subsequent odd games of each set, and after every six points in tie-break games.*

NOISEMAKERS
THE RACKETS OF SPORT

It may have taken a couple of centuries for the racket to catch on in tennis, but since then this particular swatter has gained many cousins among net and wall sports.

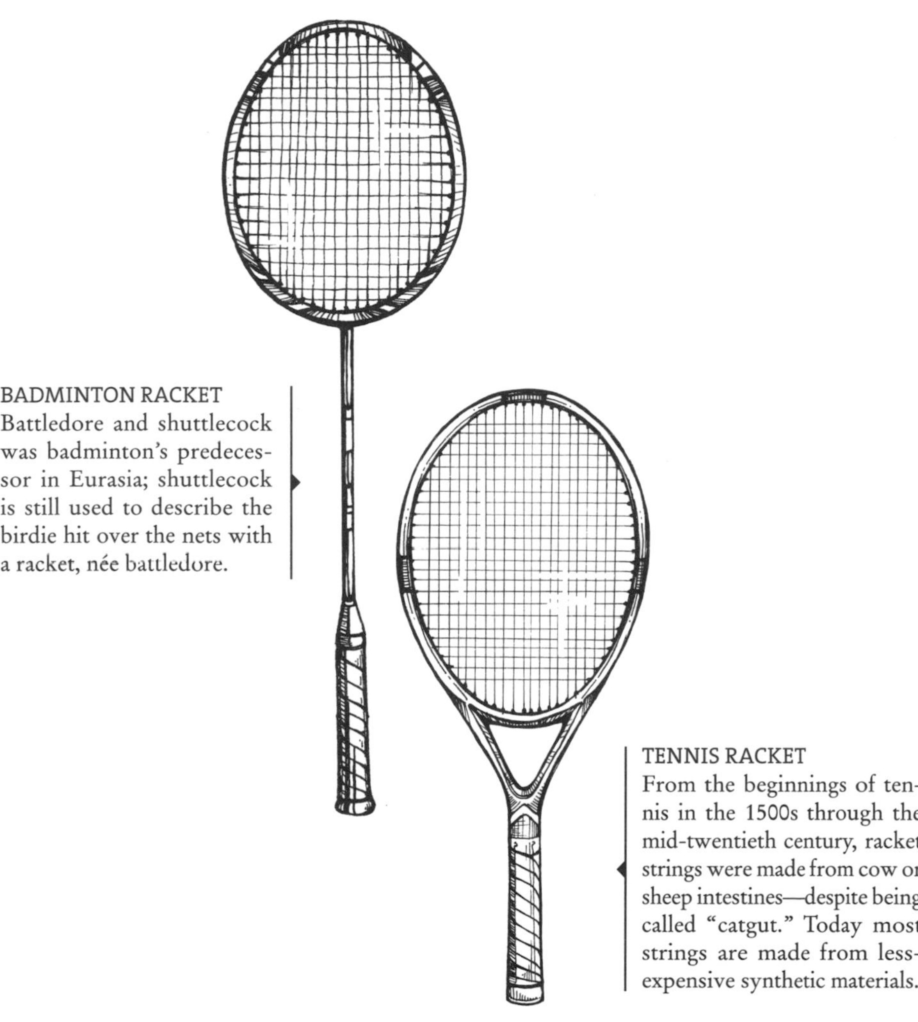

BADMINTON RACKET
Battledore and shuttlecock was badminton's predecessor in Eurasia; shuttlecock is still used to describe the birdie hit over the nets with a racket, née battledore.

TENNIS RACKET
From the beginnings of tennis in the 1500s through the mid-twentieth century, racket strings were made from cow or sheep intestines—despite being called "catgut." Today most strings are made from less-expensive synthetic materials.

QIANBALL RACKET

Qianball is a Chinese hybrid of squash and tennis, except both players are on the same side of the net and the ball is on a tether. (Watch on YouTube—it's cool.)

RACQUETBALL RACKET

Another sport invented in a YMCA, racquetball was the brainchild of Joe Sobek, a professional tennis and handball player who in 1950 devised a faster, indoor version of the two.

SQUASH RACKET

Squash was invented at Harrow, one of England's storied public schools. The name was a reference to its squashable ball, which was softer than the one used in a related, also British, game called racquets.

MATKOT RACKET
Popular in Israel and other seaside cultures, *matkot* (Hebrew for "rackets") is a cousin to beach tennis and was for many years also known as *kadima* (Hebrew for "forward").

PADDLE TENNIS PADDLE
Looking to keep neighborhood kids busy, an Episcopal minister in Manhattan invented the contained game of paddle tennis early in the twentieth century. (Manhattan then had few open fields but many roofs. So, like now.)

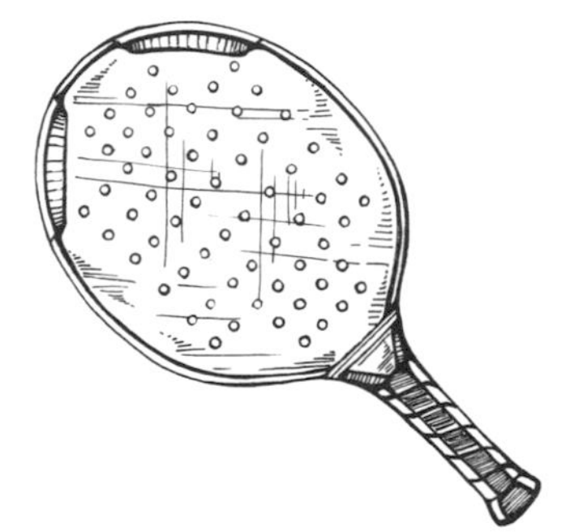

PICKLE-BALL PADDLE
Invented in the 1960s by three Seattle-area dads whose kids were bored, pickle ball can be best described as table tennis with a Wiffle ball played on a badminton court.

TABLE TENNIS PADDLE
Invented in England in the nineteenth century as a safe postdinner activity for the moneyed class, table tennis had many names, including whiff-waff and ping-pong, which most likely stemmed from the sounds of the game. In the early days of the twentieth century, a British company trademarked "Ping-Pong" and subsequently sold the U.S. rights to Parker Brothers—which is why the sport's professional associations refer to the game as table tennis.

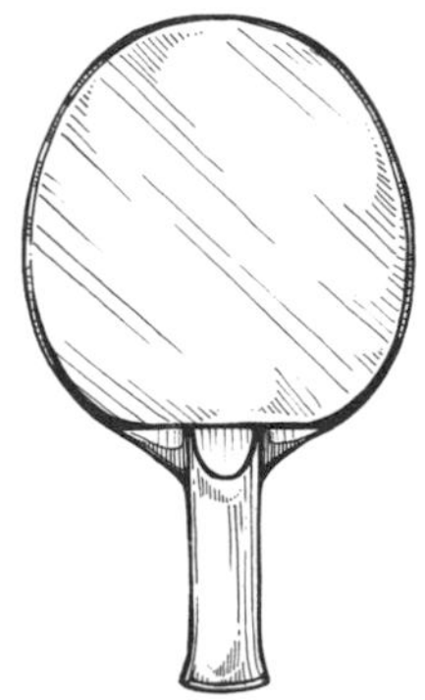

TENPIN BOWLING

IF SIR FLINDERS PETRIE IS RIGHT, BOWLING MAY BE THE world's oldest surviving noncontact sport. Some eighty years ago, the British archaeologist unearthed an Egyptian tomb from roughly 3200 BC that contained, along with a boy's mummified remains, what Petrie believed to be a ball and some rudimentary pins. And while the game's popularity has surely waxed and waned over the ensuing millennia, it should be no surprise that it has endured. Bowling is very much the people's sport. Top amateurs play the same game on more or less the same lanes as the pros, and are free to imagine that they can compete at a level few other recreational athletes can hope to achieve.

But no matter what was found in that young Egyptian's tomb, the skills needed for bowling—specifically the ability to throw or roll things as close as possible to other things—were prized in many cultures. In the first century AD, tossing stones close to other stones was the goal of a game played by Roman legionnaires. Germanic tribes—among the Romans' many conquests—were keen on throwing clubs called *Kegel* at a group of smaller sticks. A couple of centuries later, the man who would become Saint Boniface recognized the ubiquitous game as a means of furthering his own less-secular objective: converting those misguided German hordes to Christianity. Cleverly casting the sticks as *Heiden* (demons), he imbued the pastime with impressive if dubious moral significance: knocking down the small sticks demonstrated one's purity of spirit.

A similar game, absent the religious overtones, caught the fancy of British aristocrats in the Middle Ages. Theirs called for knocking down a set of pins by throwing or "bowling" a ball, which they did with gusto until 1366, when King Edward III had no choice but to outlaw the game to keep his soldiers focused on their duties. It would not be the last time bowling landed on the wrong side of the law.

European settlers, including all those German "keglers," brought their leisure activity with them when they colonized the New World, and by the end of the Colonial period, one version in particular—"ninepins"—was well ensconced. Soon after, the first known reference to the sport of bowling in American literature appeared: Washington Irving roused his famed snoozer Rip Van Winkle with a crash of ninepins.

Ninepins was typically played outside bars and taverns—"bowling alley" and "gutter ball" are terms that developed organically—and as a result the otherwise innocent game was closely associated with a pair of disreputable pursuits: drinking and gambling. That association soon caused many localities to once again declare the game illegal. Shockingly, this did not stop the American people from either drinking or gambling, and they soon arrived at an ingeniously simple way to skirt the law against the game: adding a tenth pin! (They also changed the name accordingly; once spelled "ten pin," it is now "tenpin.") By the end of the nineteenth century, more than two hundred tenpin alleys were open for business in New York City alone.

In an attempt to normalize the rules of play for all—drinkers, gamblers, and everyone else who enjoyed a few good rolls—a local restaurateur named Joe Thum brought together representatives of various New York bowling clubs. The American Bowling Congress (ABC) was established on September 9, 1895, and what the members agreed upon that day became the law of the lane.

THE AMERICAN BOWLING CONGRESS'S "RULES AND REGULATIONS GOVERNING THE GAME OF AMERICAN TEN PINS" (1901)[1]

All games of American Ten Pins, to be considered official, must be played and conducted in strict compliance with the following Rules and Regulations:

Rule 1. The alleys[2] upon which the game shall be played shall be not less than 41 nor more than 42 inches in width. The length from the center of No. 1 pin spot to the foul line shall be 60 feet. Back of the foul line there shall be a clear run of not less than 15 feet. The pin spots shall be clearly and distinctly described on or imbedded in the alleys,[3] and shall be so placed 12 inches apart from center to center. They shall be 2¼ inches in diameter. The pin spots numbered 7, 8, 9 and 10 shall be placed three inches from the pit edge of the alleys, measuring from the edge to the centers of such pin spots.

Rule 2. The pins shall be spotted on the pin spots placed upon the alleys according to the following diagram,[4] and the pins and spots shall be known by the numbers as follows.

Rule 3. Gutters shall be placed on each side of the alley, and shall begin at the foul line and extended parallel to the alleys to the pit.

---

1. *The United States Bowling Congress, formed in 2005 after a merger of the American Bowling Congress and the Women's International Bowling Congress, has rules dating back only to 1901. The game, however, changed little in the six years after the ABC was founded in 1895.*
2. *The first indoor bowling alleys were built in New York in 1840.*
3. *Lanes are commonly made of wood planks, thirty-nine of them to be exact, often of a hardwood like maple at the beginning and end of the lane, and a softer wood—or a synthetic—in the middle.*
4. *The diagram referenced describes the triangular setup common to the game today. While we're on the subject, the first automatic pinspotter debuted in 1946, designed by sporting goods manufacturer AMF. Before that, pins were set by hand and balls returned to bowlers by pinboys after each roll.*

From a point opposite No. 1 pin, they shall decline so that where the gutter enters the pit it shall be 3½ inches below the alley surface.

Rule 4. The gutters shall be from 8¾ to 9 inches in width, and in all cases shall be of such width that the surface or the side cushions or partitions shall be 12 inches from the center of the 7 or 10 pin spot respectively.

Rule 5. The pit shall be not less than 10 inches in depth, measuring from the top of the pit mat, or cushion, to the alley surface, and shall be not less than 2½ feet in width from the alley edge to the surface of the rear swinging cushion.

Rule 6. The side and center partitions shall be two feet in height above the alley surface, and shall extend from a point opposite No. 1 pin spot to the rear cushion wall: Such partitions may be covered with one layer of leather of not to exceed one-half inch in thickness, no other covering shall be permissible. The side partitions shall be so placed that the surface thereof facing the alleys shall be 12 inches from the center of the corner pin spot.

Rule 7. The rear swinging cushion shall in all cases have for a covering material of a dark color, and shall be so constructed as to prevent the pins from rebounding onto the alleys.

Rule 8. The foul line shall be clearly and distinctly marked upon or imbedded in the alleys, in dark-colored paint, or inlaid with dark-colored wood or other material, and shall be not more than one inch in width; the center point of the foul line shall be 60 feet from the center of the No. 1 pin spot. The foul line, wherever possible, shall be extended from the alley surface to and upon the walls of the alleys.

Rule 9. The pins shall be of the following design and measurements: Fifteen inches in height, 2½ inches in diameter at the base, 15 inches in circumference at a point 4½ inches from their base, 11⅝ inches in circumference at a point 7¼ inches from their base, 5¼ inches in circumference at the neck, a point 10 inches from the base; 8 inches in circumference at the head, a point 13½ inches from the base. The taper from point to point shall be gradual, so that all lines shall have a graceful curve.

Rule 10. Sets of pins shall be of clear hard maple,[5] and of uniform weight, as near as possible. The pins shall be marked A. B. C. Regulation Pin, and there may be marked thereon the imprint of the manufacturer thereof.

Rule 11. The balls[6] shall not in any case exceed 27 inches in circumference. Any sized ball of less circumference than 27 inches may be used in the game.

---

5. Indigenous to North America, maple (especially sugar maple) is an especially hard and durable wood.

6. There is a maximum weight allowance for balls—16 pounds—but no minimum. Modern bowling balls, introduced in the 1980s, are made of polyurethane, but hardwood was the standard until the 1900s, followed by rubber (into the 1970s) and later plastic.

THE PLAY

Rule 12. In all team games there shall be an equal number of players on each team, and the full team membership shall appear for play at least fifteen minutes before play is called. Before the game is begun the Captains shall enter in the score book the names of the players on the teams. After play is begun no change shall be made in the rotation of the team as so entered. The team Captain may, at any time after play is begun, and before his team begins to play in the ninth frame, replace any of his players on the team by a substitute player, provided the player so removed has not made a strike or spare in the frame last rolled by him. A player once removed from a game can not be again played in the game from which he was removed.

Rule 13. Two alleys immediately adjoining each other shall be used in all games. The contesting teams shall successively and in regular order roll one frame on one alley, and for the next frame alternate and use the other alley, so alternating each frame until the game is completed.

Rule 14. In delivering the ball the player must not permit any part of his foot,[7] while any portion thereof is in contact with the alleys, to rest or extend on, over or beyond the foul line, nor shall any part

of his person be permitted to come in contact with any part of the alleys beyond the foul line, at any time before the delivered ball shall have reached the pins. A ball delivered contrary to the provisions of this rule shall be a foul ball, and shall be so declared by the umpire immediately such ball so becomes foul.

---

7. On that foot is, of course, a bowling shoe. Why? Indoor-only shoes mean no one is tracking outdoor muck onto the lanes. And smooth lanes and slippery soles encourage gliding approaches. Bowling shoes were created sometime after indoor alleys were introduced, probably around the 1880s.

Rule 15. No count shall be made on a foul ball, and any pins which are knocked down or displaced thereby shall be at once respotted. A foul ball shall count as a ball rolled against the player.

Rule 16. Pins which are knocked down or displaced by a ball which leaves the alley before reaching the pins, or from a ball rebounding from the rear cushions, do not count, and they shall be immediately respotted.

Rule 17. Every ball delivered, unless it be declared a dead ball by the umpire, shall be counted against the player.

Rule 18. Pins which are knocked down or displaced from any cause, except by a fairly delivered ball, shall in all cases be respotted.

Rule 19. Pins which are knocked down by another pin rebounding in the play from the side partition or rear cushion, are counted as pins down.

Rule 20. Should a player by mistake roll on the wrong alley, or out of his turn, or be interfered with in his play by another bowler or spectator, or should any of the pins at which he is playing be displaced or knocked down in any manner before his delivered ball reaches the pins, or should his ball come in contact with any foreign obstacle on the alleys, then the ball so delivered by him shall be immediately declared a dead ball by the umpire, and such ball shall not count, and shall be immediately rerolled by the player after the cause for declaring the ball dead has been removed.

Rule 21. Pins which are knocked down by a fair ball, and which remain lying on the alley or in the gutters are termed dead wood, and shall be removed before the next ball is rolled.

Rule 22. Should a standing pin fall by removing dead wood, such pin or pins shall be at once respotted.

Rule 23. Should a pin be broken or otherwise badly damaged during the game, it shall be at once replaced by another as nearly uniform with the set in use as possible. The umpire shall in all such cases be the sole judge in the matter of replacing such pin or pins.

Rule 24. Bowling balls used in the game and marked by their owners are considered private, and the other participants in the game are prohibited from using the same, unless the owner consents to such use.

Rule 25. Each player shall roll two balls in each frame, except when he shall make a strike, or when a second strike or spare is made in the tenth frame, when the player shall complete that frame by rolling a third ball. In such cases the frame shall be completed on the alley on which the first strike or spare is made.

Rule 26. A strike is made when the player bowls down the ten pins with his first ball delivered in any frame,[8] and is credited and designated in the score by an X in the upper right hand corner of the frame, and the count in such frame is left open until the player shall have rolled his next two balls, when all pins made, counting ten for a strike, shall be credited therein.[9]

Rule 27. A spare is made when the player bowls down all the pins with his second ball in any frame, and is credited and designated

---

8. *A particular rolling speed has been scientifically proven to maximize the chances of a strike: 17 mph at impact.*

9. *Imagine a bowler throws a strike on the initial roll of his first frame, then follows that by knocking down 5 pins in the first roll and 2 more in the second roll of frame No. 2. His total score for those first two frames is 24: 17 for frame No. 1 (10 for the strike and 7 for the total of the two rolls in frame No. 2) plus 7 (the total of the two rolls in frame No. 2).*

with a \ in the upper right hand corner of the frame in which it is made. The count in such frame is left open until such player shall roll his next ball in the succeeding frame, when the number of pins bowled down thereby shall be added to the ten represented by his spare, and the total shall be credited therein.[10]

Rule 28. A break[11] is made in all cases where the player does not secure either a strike or a spare in a frame, and in such cases only the number of pins knocked down are credited in the frame where the break is made.

---

10. Same theory as with a strike, but with half the benefit from the next frame. So: Imagine a bowler notches a spare on the second roll of her first frame, then follows that by knocking down four pins in the first roll and four more in the second roll of frame No. 2. Her total score for those first two frames is 22: fourteen for frame No. 1 (10 for the strike and 4 for the first roll in frame No. 2) plus 8 (the total of the two rolls in frame No. 2).

11. Today it's known as an "open frame."

Rule 29. If at the end of the tenth frame the team scores shall be a tie, another frame shall be immediately bowled, and play is so continued until at the close of even frames one of the teams shall have a greater number of pins than their opponents, which shall conclude the game.

Rule 30. In all contested games the Captains of the opposing teams shall select an umpire, whose duty it shall be to enforce all the rules and regulations of the game. He shall be the sole judge and decide all the plays, and immediately make his decision on all questions or points in the play. He shall immediately declare foul all balls delivered contrary to the rules in that respect, and in rendering his decisions he shall do so in a clear tone of voice. At the close of each game he shall declare the winner and sign the official score of the game.

Rule 31. After the umpire is selected he shall not be changed during the game, except on account of illness, or by the mutual consent of both Captains.

Rule 32. The umpire shall allow no unreasonable delay in the progress of the game, and should any member or team participating in the game refuse to proceed with the game for a space of five minutes after directed to do so by the umpire, he shall declare the game forfeited to the other team.

Rule 33. No appeal shall be allowed from the decision of the umpire, except for a clear misinterpretation of the rules or regulations.

Rule 34. The Captains of the opposing teams shall each select a scorer, who shall keep a correct score of the game, and after the completion of the game they shall sign the official scores. The scores shall be official when so signed by the scorers and umpire. No change shall be made in the scorers during the progress of the game, unless by incompetence, illness, or by the mutual consent of both Captains.

Rule 35. The umpire and scorers in a game shall be disinterested, and are not permitted to be interested, directly or indirectly, in any bet or wager on the game, and if either of the said officials shall at any time during the game be found to be so interested, he shall be immediately removed.[12] Should such removed official refuse to retire from the game on demand of either Captain, it shall be sufficient ground for sustaining a protest of the game in which such disqualified official served.

Rule 36. A member of a team club or association whose team, club or association is engaged in playing a contested game, who shall either directly or indirectly tamper with the alleys, pins, balls or in any manner whatsoever seek by unfair means to secure any advantage over his opponent, shall, upon proof thereof, be forever disqualified from participating in any match or tournament game, and the game in which such unfair advantage was so secured or attempted to be secured shall be declared forfeited by the umpire to the opposing team.

---

12. *It's worth noting that bowling was one of the earliest sports to address the possibility of officials compromised by gambling interests. This is doubtless a reflection of bowling's earlier, less savory history.*

Rule 37. A team failing to meet its schedule[d] engagements, unless such failure shall be occasioned by some unavoidable cause or by previous postponement had as provided by the rules governing such cases and in force in such tournaments, shall forfeit such scheduled games, and upon investigation of the case by the managing committee of such league, association or tournament, unless satisfactory reasons can be assigned for such default, the team or such of its members who cause such default, or the entire club, shall be expelled from membership in such league, association or tournament, as the case may be.

Rule 38. When a club, team or league is expelled, all games played by it in such tournament shall be null and void, and shall not be counted as games played.

Rule 39. When a game or games shall be forfeited under the rules, the team not at fault shall play its regular schedule[d] games the same as though they were actually contested, and the scores and averages so made shall be credited and recorded.

Rule 40. When a bowler is suspended or expelled from his club for non-payment of dues, or for conduct derogatory to the best interests of the game, he shall be prohibited and disqualified from thereafter playing in any club, team, league or tournament, and any such organization which shall knowingly play such disqualified player, after receiving written notice of his disqualification, shall forfeit all games in which such disqualified player has taken part, and such organization may be suspended from membership upon vote of the managing committee of such organization holding the tournament.

Rule 41. The manner and method of computing the scores and averages of the retired and substituted players under the provision of Rule 12 shall be fixed and determined by the rules of the organization in which such players are participating.

MEMORY LANE
NOTABLE PIN TYPES

Because bowling is a global sport but also hyperlocal, there's a wide variety of targets out there just waiting to be knocked down.

---

① **DUCKPIN** Some East Coast bowlers would have the world believe duckpin is "real" bowling—that is, more challenging than "regular" bowling. The cause for their pride: a softball-size ball (with no finger holes) and pins smaller, lighter, and wider at the base than traditional tenpins. Duckpin is a tenpin spin-off conceived in the early twentieth century by Baltimoreans seeking pins to match the small ball they practiced with. Their alley's managers, Wilbert Robinson and John McGraw (both fabled baseball figures), were avid duck hunters. When they saw the tiny pins (9.4 inches; 3 pounds, 12 ounces) toppled, one of them noted that the scene resembled a "flock of flying ducks"—and the name stuck.

② **CANDLEPIN** Developed before the standardization of tenpin, candlepin is also thought to be a more challenging version. Since the game's inception in the 1880s, no one has bowled a perfect score. (The highest-ever score, 245 out of a possible 300, has been achieved just twice.) The pin is one culprit: the cylinder (15.75 inches; 2 pounds, 8 ounces) tapers at both sides, making it hard to hit. The ball, which lacks finger holes, is another: with a weight equivalent to that of one of the pins, it is the smallest in any North American version of bowling (candlepin is most popular in eastern Canada and New England). Then again, the game offers extra chances: each turn consists of three rolls.

③ **FIVE-PIN** As Wiffle ball is to baseball, five-pin, played in Canada, is to tenpin (which still doesn't explain the hyphen). With a small, light rubber ball and pins 75 percent the size of regulation tenpins, the game persists as a less "strenuous" rendition. But what five-pin players may lack in physical strength they make up for in the mental acuity necessary for analyzing scoring strategies. Five-pin has a complex points system: the pins are arranged in a V, and each has a different value based on its position.

④ **NINEPIN** Although banned in the United States as a moral corruptor in the 1800s, the game doesn't seem especially evil. The rules, though, are quite involved. Bowlers take aim at a diamond of eight smallish pins (16 inches; 3.9 to 4.1 pounds)—sometimes connected by wire to a rack above—and hope against hope to leave a ninth (red) one in the middle upright.

⑤ **SKITTLE PINS** The roots of skittles, the great-granddaddy of most bowling variants, reach back to ancient Egypt and, in its modern iteration, to European lawn bowling in the Middle Ages. The rules of the game differ across Europe, but most pins are around 10 inches high, with the same body shape as tenpins. Though it has mostly disappeared in the United States, it remains a widely played recreational game.

⑥ **TENPIN** There are roughly four thousand bowling alleys in the United States, and all but a hundred or so offer tenpin (the rest feature candlepin, duckpin, or both). The standard regulation pin (15 inches tall; 3 pounds, 6 ounces, to 3 pounds, 10 ounces) is made of wood or plastic. Its mass is informed by the rules of physics, which deem that a pin should weigh 24 percent as much as the ball, the better to be knocked down—but not too easily so.

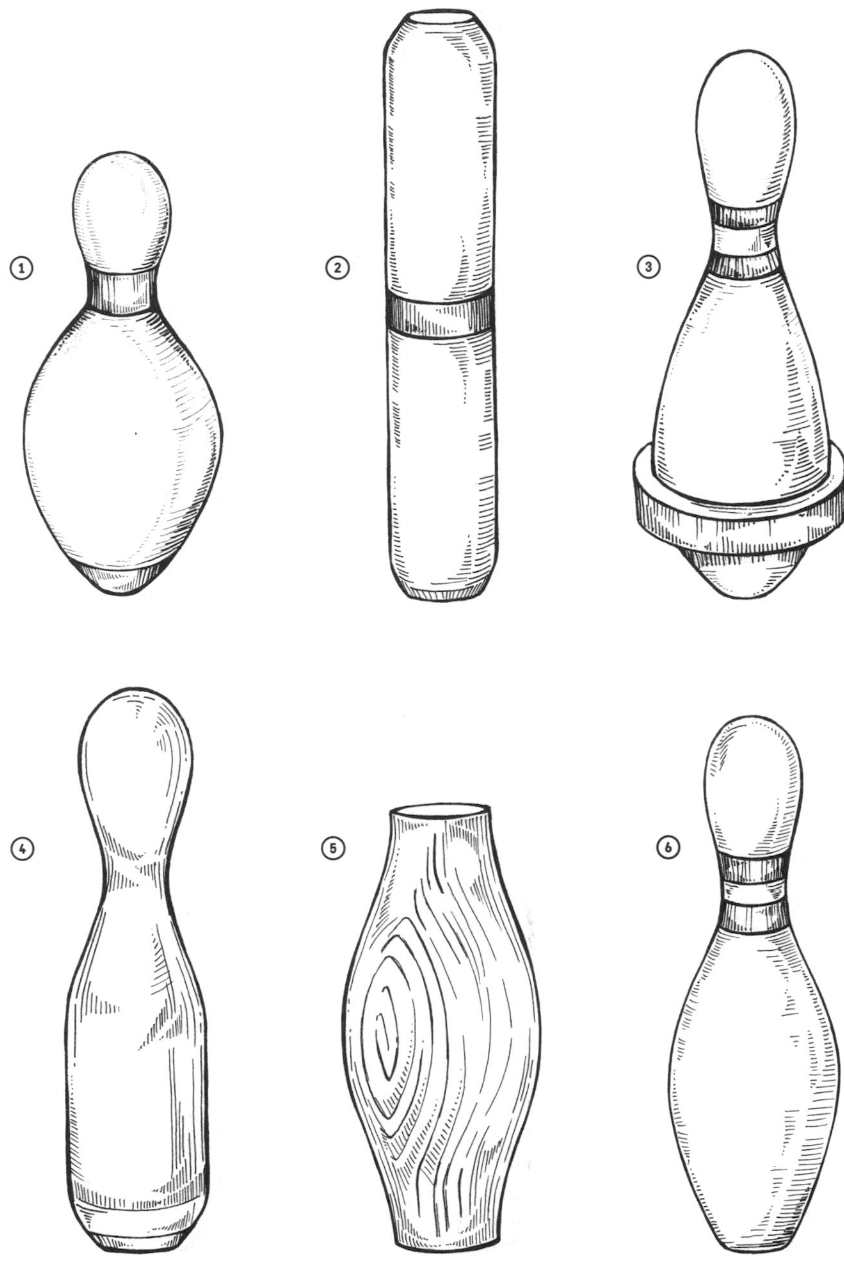

Tenpin Bowling

ULTIMATE

FOR MANY EVERYDAY OBJECTS, THE TRANSFORMATION TO an implement, projectile, or goal used in sports happened in a flash: one day a shepherd's crook, the next a golf club; yesterday's spear, today's javelin; Friday's fence gate, Saturday's cricket wicket. But at least one *objet de sport* mutated more slowly, with a quarter-century sojourn between ordinary utensil and bona fide sporting good. And like many great transformations, this one started with dessert.

One fine day in 1937, a seventeen-year-old named Walter Frederick "Fred" Morrison was tossing a pie pan back and forth with his girlfriend, Lucile Nay, on a Los Angeles beach. The five-cent pan sailed more smoothly than the popcorn-can lid the couple had been using, and before long a fellow sunbather approached them, offering to buy the upcycled toy for a quarter. Though only a lad, Morrison was savvy enough to recognize a 400 percent markup. A few twists, turns, and global military conflicts later, the commercial flying disc was born.

Morrison, a natural entrepreneur and inventor, continued to tinker with the design and construction of his flying pan. Capitalizing on America's obsession with UFOs in the late 1940s, he marketed a plastic disc as the Flyin-Saucer and, later, the Pluto Platter. It was a decidedly recreational product, a cute toy for young lovers and other idlers. Fred and Lucile, now married, traveled the fair circuit on weekends, demonstrating and selling. But in 1957, after twenty years of struggling to make the Pluto Platter soar, they sold their invention to Wham-O Manufacturing Company, a Southern California toy maker. Within a few months, execs at Wham-O had renamed the product Frisbee, likely a nod to the Frisbie Pie Company of Bridgeport, Connecticut, whose own pie tins were so often tossed by East Coast college students that "Frisbie-ing" had entered their vernacular. More crucially, Wham-O further refined the disc's shape—making it easier to throw accurately—and started to market it as a tool for a new sport in the early 1960s. That rebranding, which included the introduction of "professional" models, helped to turbocharge sales. And if none of the early iterations of Frisbee sports took off, one did lead directly to the sport played most seriously today, the one that boasts international participation and a decent shot at inclusion in the Olympic Games in the future. How *that* happened is a second tale.

At some point during the 1967–'68 school year at Columbia High School in Maplewood, New Jersey, a student named Joel Silver introduced "Frisbee Football," a game he had learned at camp the previous summer, to his friends. Silver, who went on to a career as a successful Hollywood producer (*Lethal Weapon, The Matrix,* and so on), was even then a man of action. He convinced the school's student council to form a team and set up a game against the student newspaper. (The paper won.) The first rules, written by Silver's friend Buzzy Hellring, were based on football: downs, lines of scrimmage, and running with the disc were all included. Dozens of players participated on each side as the high school crew continued to refine the homegrown game. But in 1970, Hellring, Silver, and their friend Jonny Hines "published" a revised set of rules, most notably by paring down the number of players, forbidding running with the disc, and generally bringing the sport more closely in line with hockey or soccer. By that time, Columbia High had begun to compete against other schools in the sport they had taken to calling Ultimate Frisbee. Within a year, a group of Garden State high schools had formed an Ultimate conference, and within five years—after devotees took their game to college—Yale hosted the first collegiate tournament, drawing eight teams.

It didn't take long for Ultimate to spread, nationally and internationally. Today, according to USA Ultimate, the governing body in America, an estimated 7 million people participate in the sport around the world. All thanks to a pair of high school boys separated by three decades and a whole continent but united by a mutual love for the ultimate flying saucer experience.

COLUMBIA HIGH SCHOOL'S "ULTIMATE FRISBEE OFFICIAL RULES" (1970)

Ultimate Frisbee[1] is a fast-moving, competitive game of Frisbee played by two equal-sized teams of about 5 to 10 players each.[2]

1. *Although "Frisbee" is a universally understood term for all manner of plastic flying discs, it's actually a trademark of Wham-O Inc., which means that only Wham-O's product can carry the name. Similarly, the game is called simply Ultimate by those who play it.*
2. *Regulation games are most commonly seven-person affairs these days.*

EQUIPMENT

The only equipment needed is one Frisbee of any size, although the Wham-O Master Tournament Model is recommended. Individual players may wear almost any aids they wish, including hats, helmets, or gloves as long as they do not endanger the safety of any other player. For example shoes with cleats are permissible but ones with sharp spikes are not. No player may carry any sort of stick, bat or racket.

PLAYING FIELD

The playing field may have any surface whatsoever, including grass, asphalt, sand, snow or the wood of a gymnasium floor. The two goal lines must be parallel and should be somewhere between 40 and 60 yards apart,[3] depending upon the number of players. The Ultimate Frisbee field has no lateral boundaries;[4] however, it is best to choose a field with natural boundaries created by a hill, a river or a wall.

3. *Regulation fields space the goal lines 70 yards apart. End zones add another 20 to 25 yards on either end.*
4. *You had to know the infinite sideline was too anarchic to last. Current field width is 40 yards.*

OFFICIALS

A referee or referees may officiate, and if so their decision must be final. If no referee is available the two teams play on an honor system, settling disputes by flipping a coin or by some other such method.

OBJECT

The object of the game is to gain points by scoring goals. The team with the most points at the end of the game, which may last for any time period agreed upon by the two teams—60 minutes is standard—is declared the winner.[5] If the score is even at the end of the specified playing time the contest is a draw, unless both teams agree to extend the playing time.[6] An alternate method is to play until one team reaches a specified score.[7] The game also ends when one team concedes defeat to the other.

A goal is scored when a player on the field successfully passes the Frisbee to another player on the same team standing on the opposite side of the goal line which that team is currently attacking.

5. *Games are more often played to a point total, usually fifteen or seventeen, than to a specific time limit.*
6. *This is a little too laid-back for today's results-oriented culture.*
7. *Ah, better. As suggested here, play usually goes on until there's a winner.*

THROW-OFF

Play begins with the Throw-off. The captains of the two teams determine, by the flip of a coin which team will elect to throw or receive;[8] the other team chooses which goal they will defend at the start. All players must stand on their own goal line until the Frisbee is released. One player, designated by the captain of the team which is throwing off, throws the Frisbee toward the opposite end of the field. As soon as he releases the Frisbee all players may leave their positions on the goal lines. No player on the team throwing may handle the Frisbee until it has been touched by a member of the receiving team. That latter team now may do one of two things with the Frisbee which is flying toward them: a) catch it, or b) allow it to fall to the ground without touching it. If a member of the receiving team successfully catches the Frisbee thrown, that player has possession of the Frisbee where it is caught, and if it is allowed to fall untouched to the ground the receiving team has possession where it lands and stops. If any member of the receiving team unsuccessfully attempts to catch the Frisbee thrown off and drops the Frisbee, or if the Frisbee comes in contact with any part of the body or clothing of any player on the receiving team and then

falls to the ground, the team having thrown gains possession of the Frisbee where it lands and stops.* Play continues immediately upon either team establishing possession of the Frisbee after the Throw-off.

* If the Frisbee which falls to the possession of the throwing team as specified in the last case above comes to rest in the end zone, the throwing team must bring it into play at the goal line.

---

8. The throw-off is now called a pull, and which team controls it is not always settled by a coin flip. In fact, USA Ultimate's official rules don't explicitly state how it is to be decided.

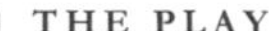

THE PLAY

The team which has possession of the Frisbee must attempt to move the Frisbee downfield into position so that they may score a goal by passing the Frisbee over the goal line. The Frisbee may be moved in only one way: it must be thrown. *No player may walk, run or take any steps while in possession of the Frisbee during playing time* or he shall immediately lose possession of the Frisbee to the opposite team. A player may propel the Frisbee in any way he wishes, using one or both hands. If the Frisbee touches the ground, a tree, a wall or any object other than the body or clothing of a player, the Frisbee falls to the possession of that team which did not last have possession. If the Frisbee touches the body or clothing of the referee he may decide which team has possession. Any time the Frisbee falls to the general possession of one of the two teams and is not under the control of any particular player, the captain of the team possessing the Frisbee may designate any member of his team, including himself, to take possession. *The Frisbee may never be handed from player to player.* In order for the Frisbee to go from the possession of one player to that of another the Frisbee must be at some time free in the air and touching no solid object. Likewise, the Frisbee may not be wrenched from the grasp of an opposing player, or knocked from his hand.

Members of the team which is not in possession of the Frisbee may gain possession in any of three ways: a) a player may catch

the Frisbee thrown by a member of the opposite team and gain possession immediately where he catches it; b) a player may strike the Frisbee while in flight with his hand or any part of his body causing it to fall to the ground, gaining possession where the Frisbee falls and stops; or c) a team gains possession of the Frisbee where it falls and stops whenever a member of the opposing team throws the Frisbee and it is not successfully caught by another member of the throwing team, unless a player on the team not in possession unsuccessfully attempts to catch the Frisbee. If a member of the team not in possession attempts to catch the Frisbee in flight and, in failing, touches the Frisbee with any part of his body or clothing, the Frisbee continues in the possession of the team which threw the Frisbee where it falls and stops. Cases where there is a dispute as to whether a player tried to catch the Frisbee and missed or merely blocked a shot, never intending to catch, must be decided by the referee or in the absence of a referee on the honor system.

While no player may run with the Frisbee, the player in possession may pivot on either foot, as in basketball. Also as in basketball,[9] any single player on the opposing team may "guard" a player in possession of the Frisbee and attempt to block his throw (although he may not knock the Frisbee out of the opponent's hand). The guarding player may not touch the body or clothing of the player whom he is guarding, nor may he grasp the Frisbee until it has left the hand of the man attempting to throw, but if he does do so the player throwing may take his throw again from the same spot.

---

9. Ultimate follows basketball and football in many ways. But here's one way it surpasses both: more flying discs are sold each year than basketballs, footballs, and baseballs put together.

END ZONES

Any time possession of the Frisbee changes from one team to the other and in the course of doing so crosses either goal line, the team gaining possession may choose to begin play at the goal line and may carry the Frisbee up to the playing field proper.

SCORING

Play continues until a goal is scored. As soon as a goal is scored the team having scored the goal throws off to the other team on the signal of the referee or the captain of the receiving team. Each time a goal is scored the teams switch the direction of their attack and defend the goal which they have just finished attacking. A team is awarded one point for each goal legally scored, and there is no other way to gain points.

FOULS

No player may strike the body of any other player in an attempt to gain possession or block a shot or a catch. Players must expect a certain amount of body contact when two or more jump up for a high throw. Any time a player commits a foul by striking the body of another player with any part of his body the team of the player who is fouled has the option of stopping play and taking possession of the Frisbee where it was at the moment when the foul occurred. Fouls are judged by the referee[10] or on the honor system.

Aside from fouls, play may only be stopped by the referee or by agreement of the captains of the two teams.

---

10. Though they are cited throughout, referees are not even mentioned in today's rules. Ultimate is one of the last remaining "gentlemen's sports," and it is assumed that no one competing at it would intentionally exploit its rules. Players are expected to call their own fouls.

GROUND RULES

Before the opening Throw-off the captains of the two teams may agree on any additional ground rules[11] necessary to adapt these rules of Ultimate Frisbee to the physical conditions of their playing field.

---

11. For friendly games, it is true that almost anything can be changed as long as the captains are on the same page. Since 2001 the most prestigious Ultimate tournament takes place every four years at the World Games.

A NOTE ON TEAM SIZE

While the CHS Varsity Frisbee squad, developers of Ultimate Frisbee, recommend 7 players as the optimum number for each team, this sport can be played with as many as 20 or 30 for each team, if a large enough field is available. Naturally, the skills needed in the game will diminish as the group gets too large.

ONE-HAND ULTIMATE

As proficiency with Ultimate Frisbee increases, a "one hand only" form of the game can be tried. In this variation the Frisbee may be caught cleanly in one hand only.[12] If two hands are used or if the player's body is employed to "trap" the Frisbee in any way, possession of the Frisbee is forfeit to the opposing team. The restriction applies to both teams, but a defending player may still use both hands or any part of his body to knock down the Frisbee in flight.

12. One-hand Ultimate never really caught on, but other variations have fared somewhat better. Indeed, Wham-O, in its efforts to market the Frisbee, invented or promoted "sports" like Guts, Double Disc Court, and Freestyle. Today some people play a half-court Ultimate game called Hot Box, and Frisbee Football is essentially Ultimate that allows for running with the disc.

MOVING PARTS
PROPELLED OBJECTS OF SPORTS THAT AREN'T BALLS

Most everything thrown, swatted, kicked, or caught is a sphere of some kind. Most, but not all.

ARROW

As any *Jeopardy!* champ knows, the English term for an arrow maker is "fletcher." That's because the toughest part of arrow making is the alignment of the feathers at the back of the shaft, to allow for stable flight. With the invention of fletching, arrows progressed from unreliable weapons of war and hunting to highly effective killing machines. It was much later that archery evolved beyond military training exercises to a full-fledged sport.

BADMINTON SHUTTLECOCK

High-quality shuttlecocks are composed of a rounded cork base encircled by a skirt of duck or goose feathers. (The more familiar "shuttles" have skirts of nylon or plastic.) A resemblance to the plumage of cockerels explains the latter half of the projectile's name; the former is thought to be a reference to the to-and-fro of play—shuttling. As a rule, it takes sixteen feathers to make each "birdie."

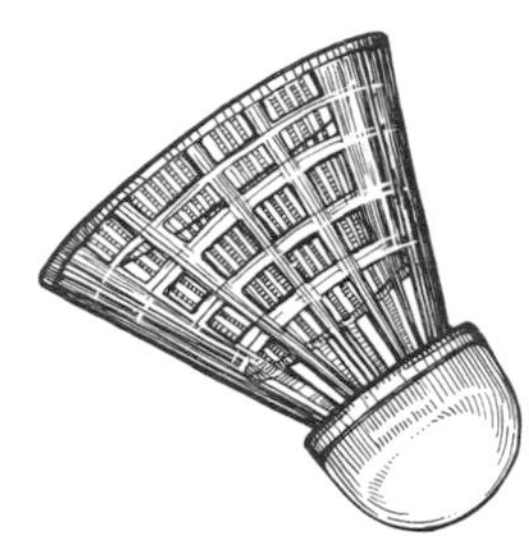

CABER TOSS

A staple of the Scottish Highland Games for centuries, the caber toss is a feat of strength and accuracy thought to have evolved from a real-world need to throw logs across rivers. Competitors stand as if in the center of a clock face holding the narrow end of a tapered log, then hurl it end over end toward twelve o'clock: the more accurate the toss, the higher the score. A typical caber, made from larch wood, is just under 20 feet long and weighs roughly 175 pounds.

CURLING STONE

Curling stones are made from granite, which exists pretty much everywhere on the planet. And yet nearly all curling stones are made from granite mined on a tiny island off the western coast of Scotland: Ailsa Craig. What makes that volcanic spew so special? The black-dotted mix of "Common Green" and "Blue Hone" granites is revered by serious curlers because it is durable and easily molded.

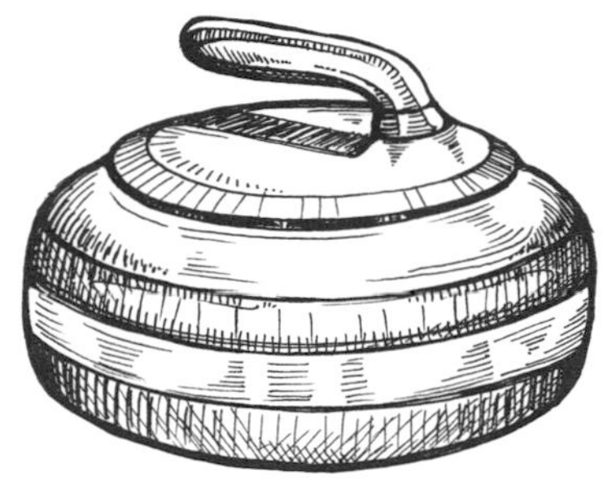

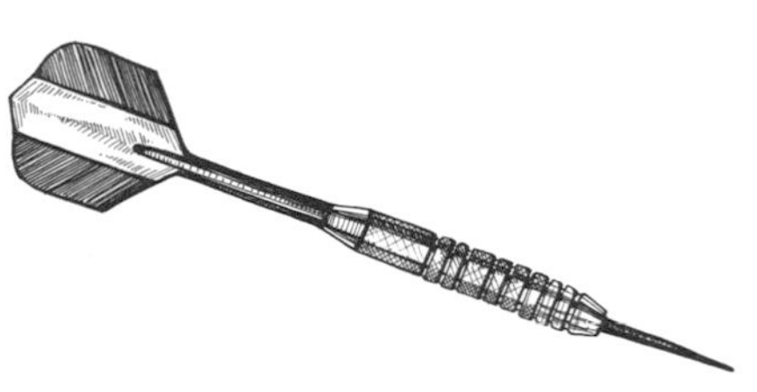

DART

Early dartboards were made from cross sections of trees, while early darts were sawed-off arrows. Darts were used in many cultures during close combat when there wasn't space or time for loading bows with arrows. Idle soldiers practiced their dart throwing, and from such beginnings a pub (and professional) sport was born.

DISCUS

As early as the eighth century BC, Greek athletes engaged in discus-throwing competitions, which are thought to have originated in prehistoric stone-throwing contests. (The flatter the stone, the more aerodynamic it is, by the way.)

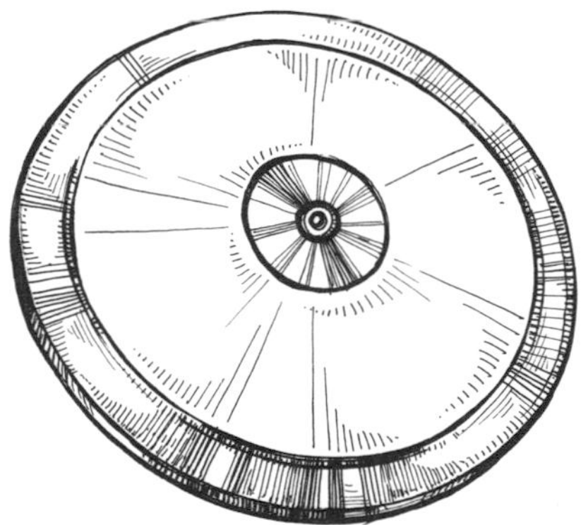

Ultimate

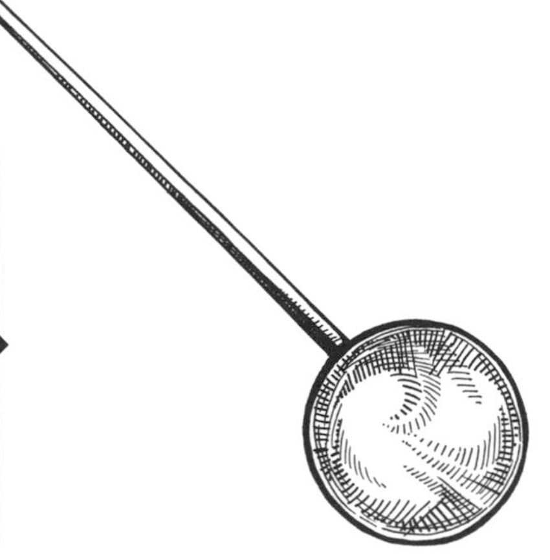

HAMMER

Why is a metal ball connected to a wire called a hammer? Most likely because in the early days of the sport—variations of which have thrived in Ireland, Scotland, and England for more than a millennium—the hammer in question was a wooden stick secured to a large rock. Indeed, at various Highland Games held regularly throughout Scotland, that's exactly the kind of hammer competitors continue to throw today.

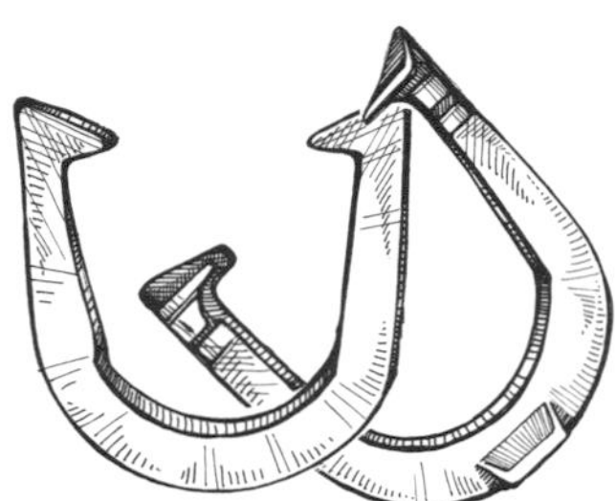

HORSESHOE

Which came first: the game of horseshoes or the ancient ring toss game called quoits? Either way, as far back as the Roman Empire soldiers competed to see who could toss discarded horseshoes closest to a stake in the ground, and that remains the essence of the game today (minus the world domination).

ICE HOCKEY PUCK

Modern hockey pucks are made from vulcanized rubber—and chilled before they are used in the pro game—but in the early days frozen cow dung was the puck of choice. When the fun moved indoors in the latter part of the nineteenth century, rubber pucks came into vogue; the earliest ones were made by sawing lacrosse balls in thirds and using the middle section.

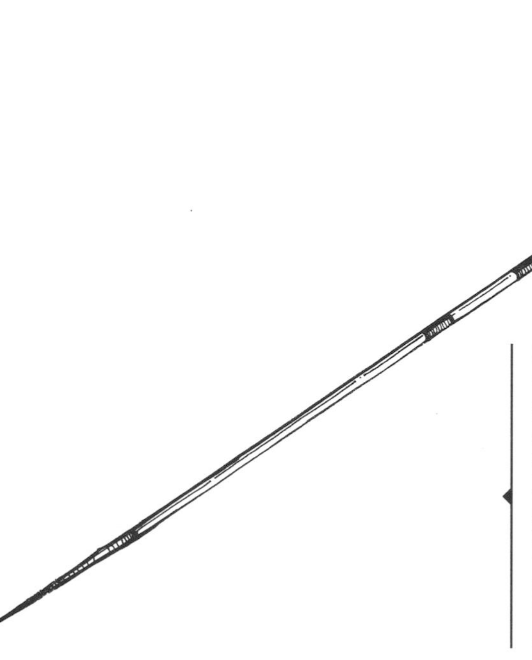

JAVELIN
Originally a weapon of war and hunting, the javelin is used almost exclusively in track-and-field events today, most notably in the Olympics. So good has the throwing technique of modern athletes become that in 1986 the sport's international governing body introduced design modifications—moving the spear's center of gravity forward, for starters—to reduce flight distances by about 10 percent.

SHUFFLEBOARD DISC
Shuffleboard's origins are shrouded in uncertainty, although it is known that the game was played in England in the sixteenth century; Henry VIII's ledgers record him paying a debt to a nobleman for losses at "shovillaborde." The modern discs, which are sometimes called weights, pucks, or biscuits, are made from plastic and metal (often chrome or aluminum).

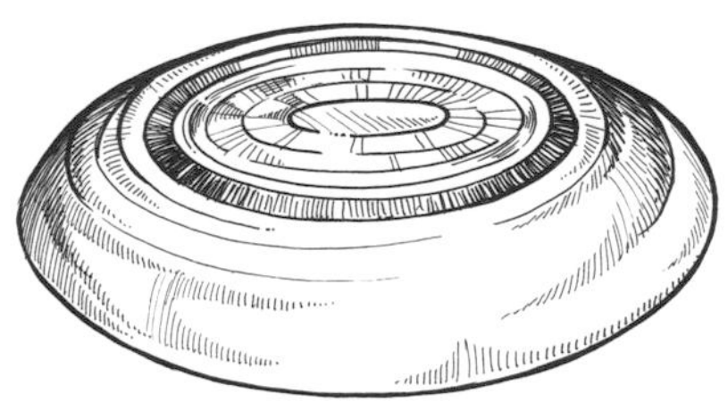

ULTIMATE DISC
Frisbee is an example of a "genericized trademark" (or "proprietary eponym"). That is, like Kleenex, Band-Aid, Jacuzzi, and many others, its trademarked name has come to represent its product category.

VOLLEYBALL

QUICK: WHICH IS THE MORE POPULAR SPORT IN THE UNITED States, basketball or volleyball? Most people would think basketball. And if revenue and media coverage are the gauge, it's clearly the correct answer. But in terms of number of participants, it's flat-out wrong. Volleyball is way more popular than basketball. *Way*. Today more than 46 million Americans play volleyball regularly. That's 20 million more than shoot hoops.

The comparison, we should explain, is not random. The two hard-court games have similar roots. Volleyball, like basketball, is a little more than a century old. Both originated within a five-year period in 1890s YMCAs, 8 miles apart in western Massachusetts. And each is the product of one man's imagination. William G. Morgan and James Naismith, the father of basketball, met in 1892 at the YMCA International Training School in Springfield. (Today it is Springfield College.) After graduation, Morgan became director of physical education at the Holyoke YMCA. There, needing a game for businessmen that called for even less physical contact than Naismith's newborn game, Morgan combined elements of handball, tennis, badminton, and, yes, basketball. He hung a tennis net 6½ feet above the floor, dividing a 25-foot-by-50-foot gymnasium court. The rules, his rules, came pretty easily. All that was left for Morgan to do was to come up with a name for his hybrid. Thus: Mintonette!

Wait—Mintonette? The name hinted at one of its precursors, badminton, but it didn't sound any more right back then than it does today. During an early demonstration of the game, one of Morgan's YMCA colleagues observed that the players seemed to be "volleying" the ball back and forth, and suggested respectfully that volleyball might be a better label. The freshly tagged game debuted in Springfield on July 7, 1896, and it was a big hit from the first serve. The YMCA network spread volleyball across New England, then to the rest of urban America and on to Canada, the Southern Hemisphere, and the Far East. In 1916 players in the Philippines developed the "set and spike" attack—passing the ball in a high trajectory so it could be driven over the net by a second player—calling that second hit the *bomba,* or kill, and it soon became the signature bit of volleyball action.

Toward the end of the First World War, thousands of volleyballs were provided to U.S. soldiers and their allies in military camps throughout Europe, as part of an official training regimen. Most were left behind when the troops returned home, to be picked up and played with by the locals. Today more than 800 million people across the world play volleyball at least once a week. Take that, basketball.

WILLIAM MORGAN'S RULES OF "VOLLEY BALL" (1896)

RULES	NOTES
∞ *1st* ∞ **Game. The game consists of nine innings.[1]**	*1. William Morgan cribbed aspects of many sports to invent his new one, and from baseball he took its duration. It was a short-lived imitation. In 1900 innings gave way to "first to twenty-one points." That win total has jumped around in the years since; currently, it's at twenty-five—by a margin of two.*
∞ *2nd* ∞ **Innings. An inning consists of: when one person is playing on each side, one service on each side; when two are playing on each side, two services on each side; when three or more are playing on each side, three services on each side.[2] The man serving continues to do so until out by failure of his side to return the ball. Each man shall serve in turn.**	*2. Now, of course, it's one server per possession. And for good reason: if everyone got a chance to serve during each possession, games would take hours.*
∞ *3rd* ∞ **Court. The court or floor space shall be 25 feet wide and 50 feet long, to be divided into two square courts, 25 x 25 feet, by the net. Four feet from the net on either side and parallel with it shall be a line across the court, the Dribbling Line. The boundary lines must be plainly marked so as to be visible from all parts of the courts. Note—The exact size of the court may be changed to suit the convenience of the place.[3]**	*3. Official court size was changed—not for convenience but for standardization—to 35 feet by 60 feet in 1912. And rule tweaks have long since rendered "the Dribbling Line"—a boundary up to which players could air-dribble (that is, pass the ball to themselves)—irrelevant. Under no circumstances can a player pass the ball to herself.*

RULES	NOTES
4th **Net. The net shall be at least 2 feet wide and 27 feet long, and shall be suspended from uprights placed at least one foot outside the side lines. The top line of the net must be 6 feet 6 inches from the floor.[4]**	*4. It didn't take long for the keepers of the game to realize that the original height wasn't high enough. The net has been raised over time, to its present 8 feet (7 feet 4 inches in the women's game). And not just any net will do: regulations include width (3 feet), material (4-inch square mesh of number 30 brown thread), and trim (¼-inch cable at the top and ¼-inch rope at the bottom).*
5th **Ball. The ball shall be a rubber bladder[5] covered with leather or canvas. It shall measure not less than 25 inches nor more than 27 inches in circumference, and shall weigh not less than 9 ounces nor more than 12 ounces.**	*5. Morgan's first volleyball was the bladder from inside a basketball. A year later, A.G. Spalding & Bros., which developed and manufactured the first official basketball, unveiled its volleyball.*
6th **Server and Service. The server shall stand with one foot on the back line. The ball must be batted with the hand. Two services or trials are allowed[6] him to place the ball in the opponents' court (as in tennis). The server may serve into the opponents' court at any place. In a service the ball must be batted at least ten feet, no dribbling allowed. A service which would strike the net, but is struck by another of the same side before striking the net, if it goes over into the opponents' court, is good, but if it should go outside, the server has no second trial.**	*6. Sorry, no more second chances: if the ball hits the net and doesn't go over or sails out of bounds, the server loses possession. (If a serve hits the net and goes over, it's in play.) No longer can a teammate give a serve a helpful push, either.*

RULES	NOTES
7th **Scoring. Each good service unreturned or ball in play unreturned by the side receiving, counts 1 score for the side serving. A side only scores when serving, as a failure to return the ball on their part results in the server being put out.[7]**	*7. Side-out scoring as described here—whereby only the serving team could score when it won a rally, while the receiving team simply earned the right to serve—lasted until 1999. Since then, teams score by winning a rally, whether they've served or not. The change was instituted to make the game faster and more appealing to fans.*
8th **Net Ball. A play which hits the net aside from the first service is called a net ball and is equivalent to a failure to return, counting for the opposite side. The ball hitting the net on first service shall be called dead and counts as a trial.[8]**	*8. Again, no second chances.*
9th **Line Ball. It is a ball striking the boundary line; it is equivalent to one out of court and counts as such.[9]**	*9. Today a line ball is rewarded with a point for pinpoint accuracy: if any part of the ball strikes the line it is in bounds.*
10th **Play and Players. Any number may play[10] that is convenient to the place. A player should be able to cover about 10 x 10 feet. Should any player during play touch the net, it puts the ball out of play and counts against his side. Should any player catch or hold for an instant the ball, it is out of play and counts for the opposite side. Should the ball strike any object other than the floor and bound back into the court, it is still in play.[11] To dribble the ball is to carry it all the time keeping**	*10. There is no team-size wiggle room today, not in sanctioned games, anyway: it's six to a side. (How much space they cover is for each player and the coach to decide.)* *11. Not so. If a ball hits a wall or a spectator or anything else that is out of bounds, the point is over.*

RULES

it bouncing. When dribbling the ball no player shall cross the Dribbling Line,[12] this putting the ball out of play and counting against him. Any player, except the captain, addressing the umpire or casting any slurring remarks at him or any of the players on the opposite side, may be disqualified and his side be compelled to play the game without him or a substitute or forfeit the same.

NOTES

12. As mentioned in Rule 3, "the Dribbling Line" became unnecessary once a 1916 rule prohibited any player from touching a ball twice unless another touched it in between. Four years later, the three-hits-and-over limit was instituted.

SIZING IT UP

DIMENSIONS OF TEAM-SPORT PLAYING AREAS

The volleyball court is one of the smallest fields of play; as many as forty-nine would fit inside a rugby union pitch, one of the largest. Here's a relative look at the standard sizes.

(Note: Some dimensions are rounded up to the nearest foot; others represent the minimum or maximum feet allowed when there is variability in field size.)

RUGBY UNION (PITCH) 472 ft. x 230 ft.

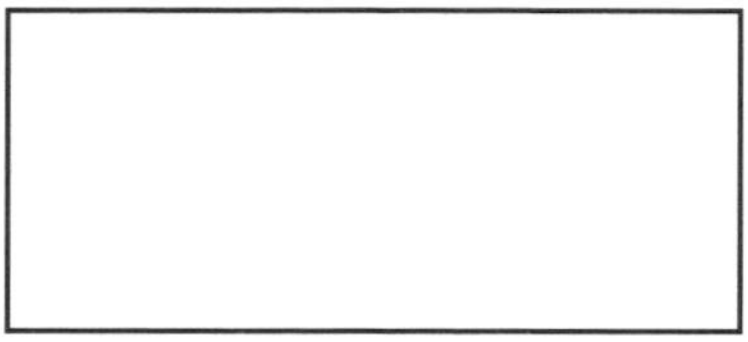

CANADIAN FOOTBALL LEAGUE (FIELD) 450 ft. x 194 ft.

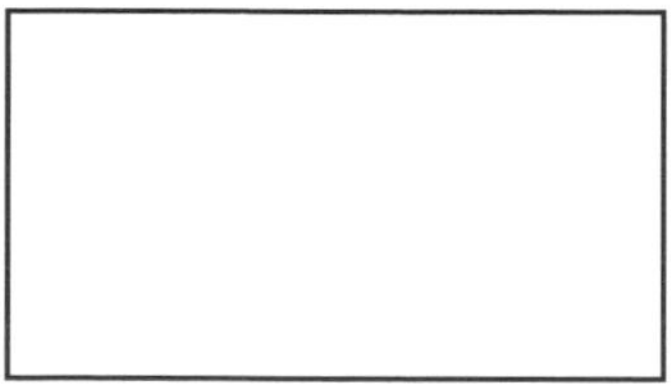

RUGBY LEAGUE (PITCH) 400 ft. x 224 ft.

ULTIMATE (FIELD) 361 ft. x 121 ft.

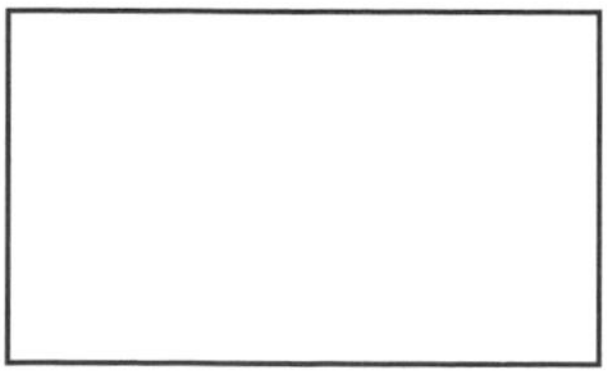

BANDY (RINK) 360 ft. x 213 ft.

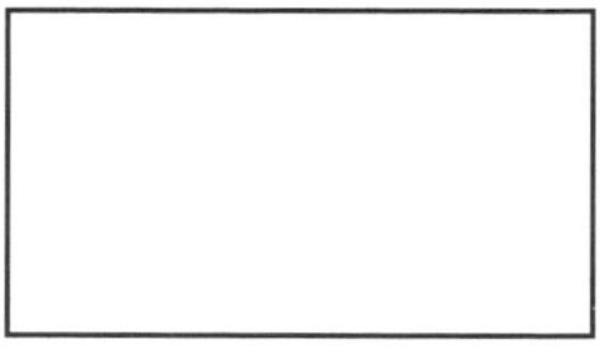

LACROSSE (FIELD) 360 ft. x 197 ft.

NATIONAL FOOTBALL LEAGUE (FIELD) 360 ft. x 160 ft.

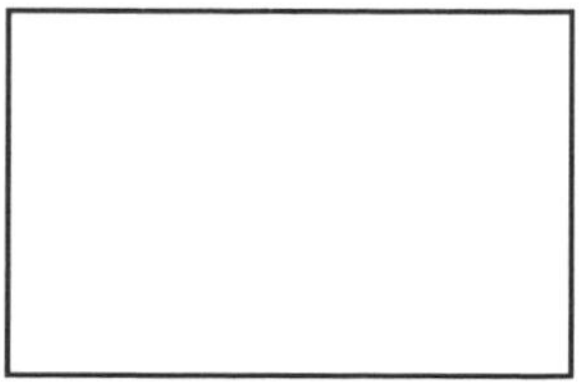

SOCCER (PITCH) 345 ft. x 223 ft.

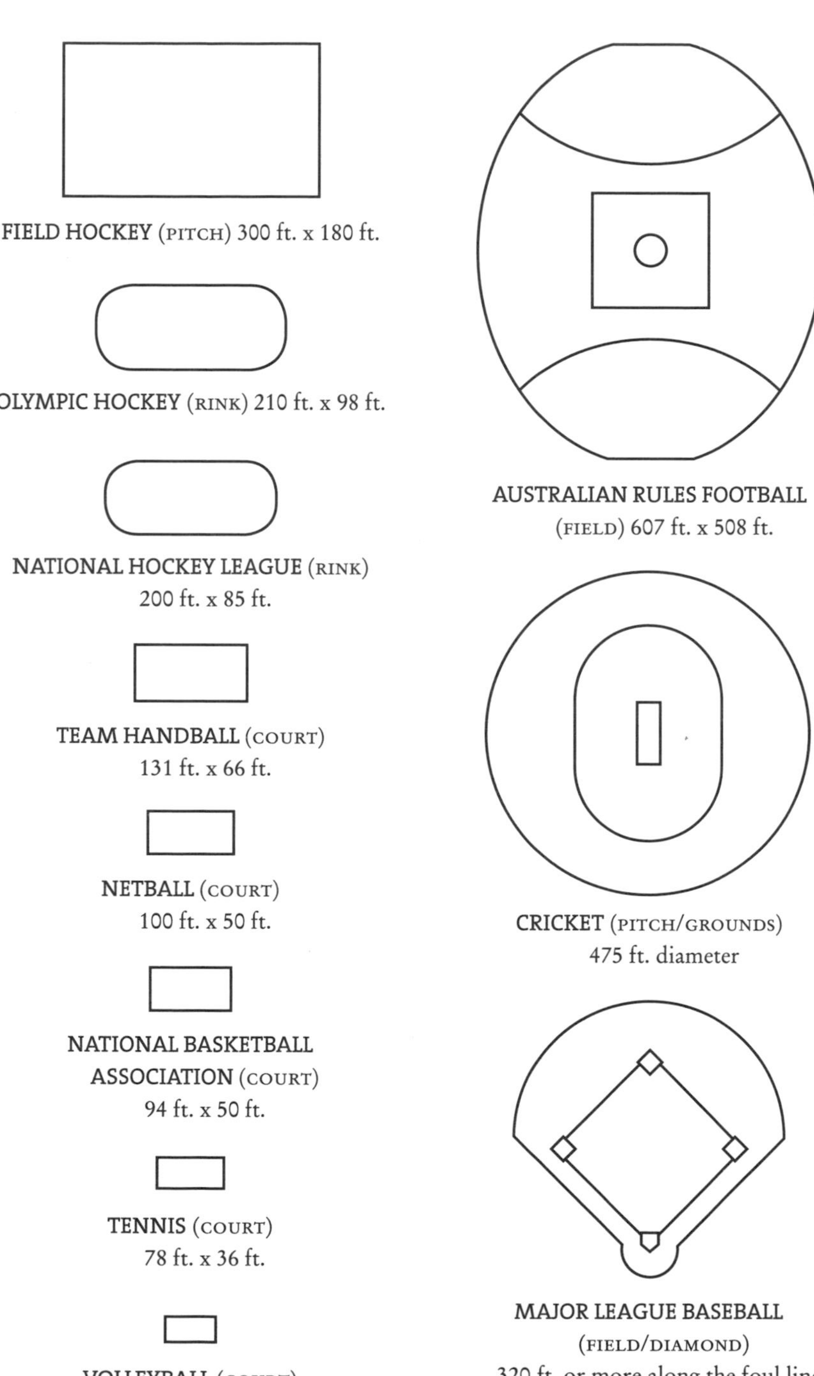
FIELD HOCKEY (PITCH) 300 ft. x 180 ft.
OLYMPIC HOCKEY (RINK) 210 ft. x 98 ft.
NATIONAL HOCKEY LEAGUE (RINK)
200 ft. x 85 ft.
TEAM HANDBALL (COURT)
131 ft. x 66 ft.
NETBALL (COURT)
100 ft. x 50 ft.
NATIONAL BASKETBALL
ASSOCIATION (COURT)
94 ft. x 50 ft.
TENNIS (COURT)
78 ft. x 36 ft.
VOLLEYBALL (COURT)
59 ft. x 30 ft.
AUSTRALIAN RULES FOOTBALL
(FIELD) 607 ft. x 508 ft.
CRICKET (PITCH/GROUNDS)
475 ft. diameter
MAJOR LEAGUE BASEBALL
(FIELD/DIAMOND)
320 ft. or more along the foul lines
and at least 400 ft. to center field

Play on Words

The terminology of various sporting locales explained.

COURT (VARIOUS BALL GAMES): From the Latin *cohort* and *cohors* ("yard" and "retinue," respectively), by definition a sporting court must be a quadrangle.

DIAMOND (BASEBALL): The infield as viewed from home plate to second base resembles the diamond suit in a deck of traditional (French) playing cards. Complications arise when trying to explain why "diamond" was ever used to describe the suit, which the French call *carreaux*, or "tiles." Something about the shape of French "tiles"—maybe the points—suggested diamonds to English-speaking card players in the fifteenth and sixteenth centuries.

FIELD (VARIOUS BALL GAMES): The original sites of most stick-and-ball games were meadows, pastures, and leas.

GRIDIRON (FOOTBALL): From Middle English for "griddle," devices for cooking meat that were made up of two sets of parallel bars intersecting at right angles. The boundaries and yardage markers of a football field mimicked the look.

GROUNDS (CRICKET): Early cricket games were often played on public commons dedicated to specific uses, which were more generally called "grounds."

PITCH (CRICKET, RUGBY, SOCCER): "Pitching the stumps" was an eighteenth-century term that referred to the primary act required to set up a cricket field: hammering in the wickets.

RING (VARIOUS FIGHTING SPORTS): During the early days of boxing in England, the spectators often encircled fighters (sometimes even holding a rope).

RINK (HOCKEY, CURLING): Scots back in the day (c. 1100 to 1500) used an Old French word (*renc*) for "rank" to describe jousting grounds, likely because competitors were military officers.

TRACK (VARIOUS RACING EVENTS): From a fifteenth-century French word for trail marks, reflecting the fact that most races, by whatever means, are held on a prepared course.

WIFFLE BALL

IT SEEMS QUAINT THAT WE EVEN CONTINUE TO USE THE word "play" when discussing what transpires in our various competitions. From multimillion-dollar contracts and minutely calibrated training regimens to international rivalries and global marketing initiatives, most of the sports in this book long ago became very serious business, not just for the athletes but for the leagues in which they toil and the fans who watch them go at it. But Wiffle ball—give or take a fiercely fought adult league—has remained true to its humble beginnings.

The game may be the only one in this collection whose guiding principle upends the trajectory of modern sports. Specifically, it can be seen as a sort of dialing back of baseball, a way to steal the game from the stadiums and return it to the backyards.

On a summer evening in 1953, twelve-year-old David Mullany was messing around with friends outside his Fairfield, Connecticut, home, hitting a thrown plastic golf ball with a broomstick. It wasn't exactly Ruthian-level stuff, but it did keep the neighbor's windows intact. Mullany's father, also named David, a former semipro pitcher and out-of-work car-polish entrepreneur, watched intently as his son tried over and over to put a little curve on the ball, eventually straining his young shoulder in the process. In an attempt to keep the boy from blowing out his arm before he reached puberty, Mullany Sr. began to investigate other materials that could be fashioned into a lightweight ball that might be more amenable to curving. His son and wife helped test his various prototypes, many of which he carved with a blade. (The former pitcher understood the use of imperfections and imbalance to manipulate a ball's flight.) None moved quite the right way.

Then, in one of those eureka moments that change the course of history, Mullany happened upon the spherical plastic packaging for Coty perfume. He cut eight perforations into one side, and his pitches began to break precipitously. Quick physics lesson: When the surface area of one side of a sphere is larger than the other, that side is subject to higher atmospheric pressure when in flight. The practical effect on the sphere is that it is "pushed" in the other direction. In the case of Mullany's ball, that would be toward the direction of the holes. If Mullany didn't know the exact science behind the action, he did know he had found what he was looking for: the Wiffle ball, its name derived from baseball's slang for striking out—whiffing. The missing *h* is a bit of a mystery but may well be simply a case of bad spelling. (Mullany family lore says it was to save money on any sign they might one day have to commission.)

The Mullanys peddled their balls from the trunk of the family car and at a neighborhood diner, for 49 cents each. After establishing themselves as a corporation, they soon closed a deal to sell at Woolworth's, with packaging that included Mullany's rules on how to play his game. And today, while baseball mints its billions, Wiffle balls are still made in the Mullanys' tiny fifteen-person factory in Shelton, Connecticut.

DAVID MULLANY'S RULES OF WIFFLE BALL (1954)

THE BALL

The Wiffle Ball was designed to take the place of baseball, stick ball and soft ball for boys and girls in back yards and city streets. It is made of a tough rubbery plastic—is light in weight and cannot be thrown or hit any great distance. The Wiffle Ball is also an excellent indoor ball.

THE CURVE

The Wiffle Ball is thrown like a baseball and will curve very easily.[1] The drawings below show how the ball should be held for curving and controlling the ball.[2]

1. *Yes, but only when they're new. Older, roughed-up balls display different aerodynamics. In fact, scuff the ball in just the right place and it will actually curve in the opposite direction. And that's just what pitchers in competitive leagues try to do, as there are no rules against doctoring the ball.*
2. *We did not reproduce the diagrams here because the grips are all wrong. The graphic artist didn't account for the fact that his model, David Mullany Sr., was a lefty when he drew his illustrations of right hands for the box.*

THE GAME

As stated above Wiffle Ball was designed for use in congested areas. Because the ball will not travel far when solidly hit, ball chasing and base running have been eliminated. An ordinary broom handle can be used as a bat if a Wiffle Bat is not available.[3] The size of the playing field is optional, but we recommend a minimum dimension 20 feet (8 paces) by approximately 60 feet long (23 paces). The field is laid out with foul lines and markers for single, double, triple and home run areas.

The minimum number of players required to play Wiffle Ball are two—the pitcher and batter—one player to a side. The maximum number of players that can compete are ten—five players to a side. If a full team is playing, each side will consist of catcher, pitcher, double area fielder, and home run area fielders. Fielders cannot move from one area to another when a full team is playing. However, any number of players up to ten can play Wiffle Ball. When more than

two players are playing, captains for each side are picked and they choose their respective teams alternately. As in baseball the game is played with one team at bat and one team in the field. The batting order of the team at bat shall be Pitcher 1st, then following the Catcher, Double area player, and home run area player.[4] The rules of play are similar to baseball. Three outs to an inning retire a side, nine innings to a game. In case of tie, additional innings are played. For a complete inning both sides must bat. An out for the batter can be made in three ways:

1. The batter can strike out only if he swings at a pitched ball and does not foul tip the third strike. Foul tips count as a strike for the first two strikes. A foul tip caught in back of the batter's box does not count as an out.

2. Fly balls caught in fair or foul territory.

3. Ground balls caught while ball is in motion in fair territory. Bunting is not allowed. The batter cannot obtain a base on balls.

---

3. The original Wiffle bat was made of wood. Today it is made of yellow plastic.

4. This is another one of those randomly quirky rules that never seem to stand the test of time. Teams can use their own discretion to choose their lineups.

SCORING

Single markers are placed approximately 24 feet from home plate[5] on foul line. Ball hit in single area (i.e. area between batter's box and single markers) and not caught, constitutes a single. Double markers are placed approximately 20 feet in back of single markers on foul line. Ball hit in double area (area between single marker and double marker) and not caught, constitutes a double. Triple markers are placed on foul lines 20 feet back of double markers. Ball hit in triple area (area between double markers and triple markers) and not caught, constitutes a triple. Ball hit beyond the triple markers and not caught, constitutes a home run.[6] The baseball rules of scoring runs apply. A player hits a single—his team has a man on first base (imaginary). The next player hits a single—his team now has an imaginary player on 1st base and 2nd base. The next player hits a home run—three runs score. The imaginary player on 1st and 2nd. And the home run. A player advances one imaginary base on a single, 2 bases on a double and three imaginary bases on a triple. A player

on 2nd base scores on a single, double or triple. A player on 3rd base scores on any hit.

---

5. *The modern layout for tournament fields makes hitting a single more of a challenge, putting the marker at 42 feet; the doubles marker is at 65 feet, and the triples marker can be as far away as 95 feet. But any ball (fair or foul) that is dropped, no matter where, is a single. And in any case, there is no base running.*
6. *Tournament rules do allow for a wall, between 4 feet and 16 feet high and no more than 125 feet to center field.*

HIT LIST

THE IMPLEMENTS OF SPORTS

Even ignoring rackets and paddles—see "Noisemakers," page 183—our games contain a cornucopia of sticks, bats, clubs, and other instruments used to hit, throw, shoot, hurl, knock, or whip projectiles.

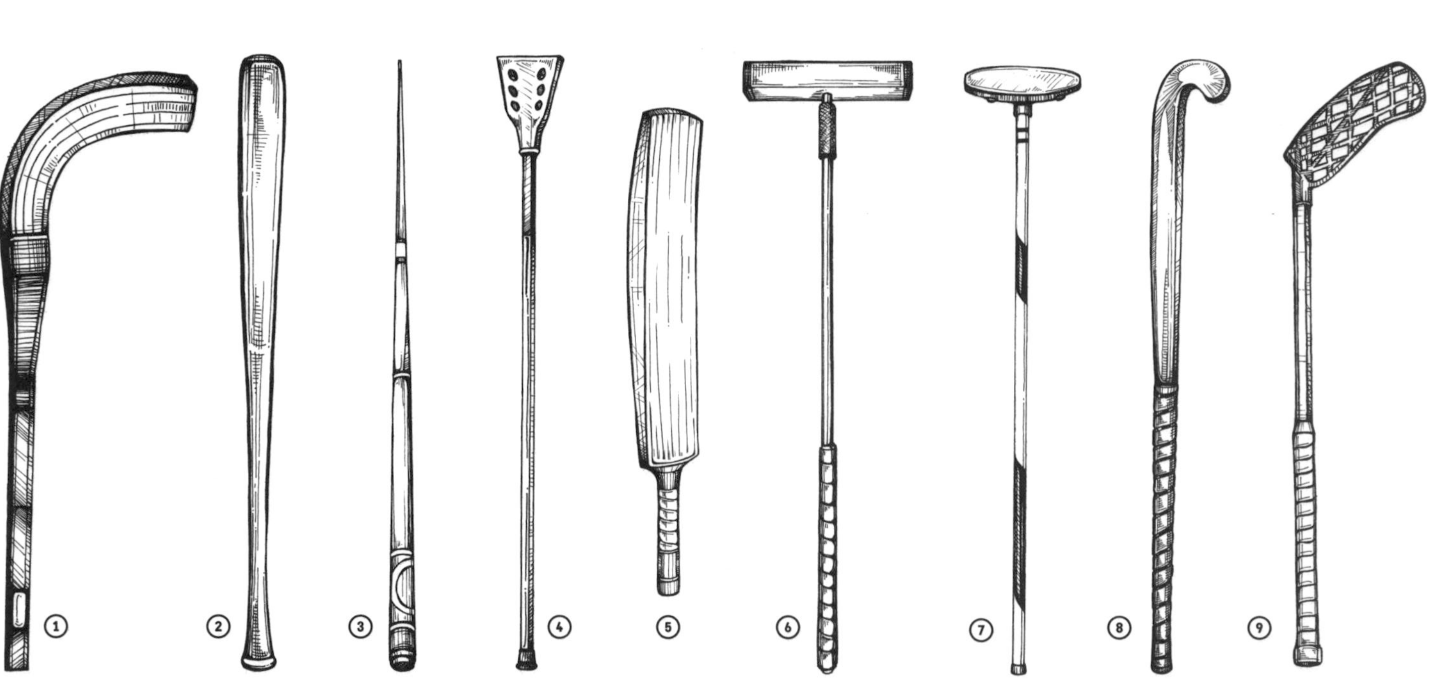

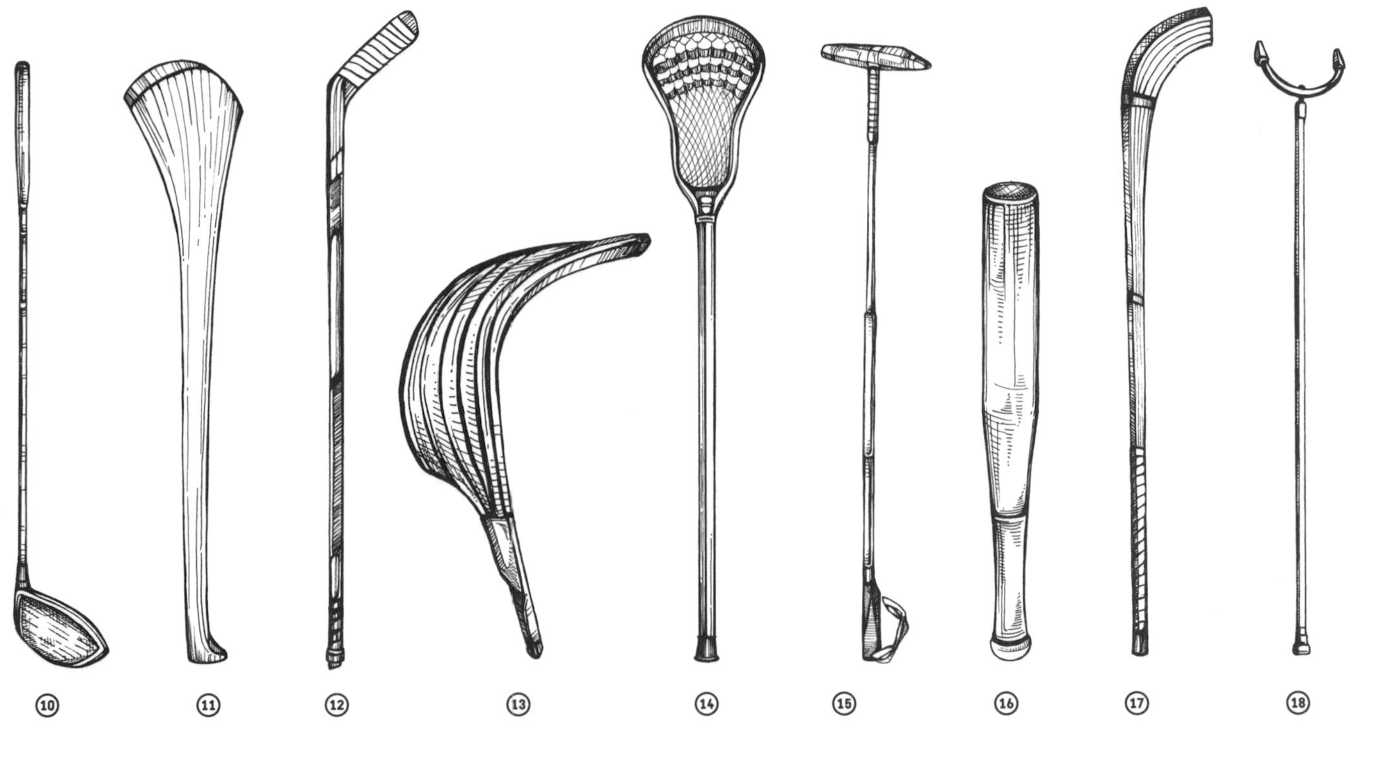

① BANDY STICK ② BASEBALL BAT ③ BILLIARDS CUE ④ BROOMBALL BROOM ⑤ CRICKET BAT ⑥ CROQUET MALLET ⑦ CURLING BROOM/BRUSH
⑧ FIELD HOCKEY STICK ⑨ FLOORBALL STICK ⑩ GOLF CLUB ⑪ HURLING HURLEY ⑫ ICE HOCKEY STICK ⑬ JAI ALAI CESTA
⑭ LACROSSE STICK ⑮ POLO MALLET ⑯ ROUNDERS BAT ⑰ SHINTY CAMAN ⑱ SHUFFLEBOARD CUE

WRESTLING

WRESTLING IS ALMOST CERTAINLY THE OLDEST OF THE martial arts—perhaps it predates *all* art. It is literally prehistoric, existing before humans began to chronicle their lives in writing of any kind: cave drawings in Asia from at least nine thousand years ago show a crowd of people watching two men wrestling. In fact, wrestling is older than Homo sapiens. Our evolutionary cousins—gorillas, orangutans, and chimpanzees—engage in "mock combat," or aggressive behavior absent the intent to do harm. (In other words, sport.)

Almost as soon as humans began to transcribe their goings-on for posterity, they were describing wrestling in one form or another, in various places: northern Africa and eastern India, most of China, Europe. The *Epic of Gilgamesh,* a Sumerian fable-like poem written in cuneiform more than four thousand years ago, includes references to officiated competitions that foreshadow modern pro wrestling extravaganzas, not least because they were accompanied by music. (And just so everyone is on the same page: pro wrestling—with its spandexed, soaring combatants and over-the-head chair whacks—is not the subject here.) In an Egyptian burial site called Beni Hasan, tombs from around the same time depict more than four hundred pairs of men demonstrating techniques still used in modern freestyle wrestling.

But no ancient people are more closely associated with wrestling than the Greeks, for whom the activity was more than sport. To them, it was a path to manhood—equal parts strength training, artistic expression, and test of will. The Greeks saw wrestling as elemental, which likely explains why most ancient forms involved naked combatants who were doused in olive oil and often covered with a thin layer of sand to protect their skin from summer's sun and winter's cold.

Wrestling was the final and most important competition in the pentathlon, the only crowned event of the ancient Olympics. The Greeks prized individual athletic achievement more than team success, which reflects how important heroism, bravery, and personal identity were to them. (Read Homer to find out.) Wrestling was so central to the Greeks that accounts and depictions of it can be found in most remnants of their culture: in words, from poetry to civil documentation; in art, from sculpture to pottery; in architecture, from government buildings to religious temples. And yet no complete (or even incomplete) set of wrestling rules exists from that period.

But Christopher Miller, a student of ancient Greek sports, has produced a tour de force of wrestling scholarship: "Submission Fighting and the Rules of Ancient Greek Wrestling," an eighteen-thousand-word research paper first published on JudoInfo.com in 2004 and later included in the *Ancient History Encyclopedia,* a not-for-profit educational website. Miller combed through dozens of primary sources as well as secondary texts that included digressions and asides about wrestling in works concerned with other matters. The authors make up a virtual who's who of world-changing brains: Aristophanes, Aristotle, Galen, Homer, Plato, Plutarch. Through impressive dot connecting and theorizing, Miller "found" fifteen rules of ancient Greek wrestling. Unlike the other sets of rules in *On the Origins of Sports,* they were not written at the time the game was blooming, but they are no less a reflection of the provenance of wrestling.

CHRISTOPHER MILLER'S "RULES OF ANCIENT GREEK WRESTLING" (c. 300 BC/AD 2004)

RULES	NOTES
1st **No intentional hitting or kicking is permitted.[1]**	*1. Two forms of wrestling are practiced today: freestyle and Greco-Roman. Both are Olympic sports—for now—but the one more common in the United States is freestyle. Neither permits "intentional hitting or kicking." Then there's is a third form of "wrestling" that wouldn't be anything at all if hitting and kicking weren't allowed—pro wrestling.*
2nd **No gouging the eyes or biting is permitted, since even the Pankration[2] does not allow these.**	*2. Pankration was a fairly lawless version of ancient grappling; in fact, eye gouging and biting were virtually the only acts competitors couldn't commit. (Killing an opponent was one way to victory!) Pankration and gladiator combat were both abolished around AD 400.*
3rd **It is at the discretion of the holders of the games whether or not twisting the fingers with the intention of forcing the opponent to concede defeat is permitted.**	
4th **Grasping the genitals is not permitted.**	
5th **All other holds intended to persuade the opponent to concede defeat through pain or fear are permitted[3] and are an integral part of the contest.**	*3. Other holds barred today: choke holds, joint locks, and the full nelson (whereby a wrestler slides his arms under a foe's armpits from behind then locks his hands together against the back of the other guy's head).*

RULES	NOTES
∞ *6th* ∞ **Infractions shall be punished by immediate whipping by the referee[4] until the undesirable behaviour is stopped.**	*4. It was a very different time. Penalties today can result in the deduction of a point or two and disqualification for serious or recurring violations.*
∞ *7th* ∞ **Three points[5] must be scored to win the match.**	*5. Modern matches are timed. For freestyle, that's two three-minute periods. The wrestler with the most points when the clock runs out wins.*
∞ *8th* ∞ **A point can be scored in any of three ways:[6]** **a) by the opponent's back touching the ground at any time** **b) by the opponent tapping or in some other way making clear that s/he[7] concedes defeat through pain or fear** **c) by the opponent making contact with ground outside the allocated wrestling-match ground with any part of his/her body**	*6. A point is also awarded for a reversal—that is, when a wrestler manages to switch from a defensive position to a controlling one. And in some team (high school, college, etc.) competitions, a takedown can be worth up to five points, depending on its impressiveness. Conversely, points can be deducted for stalling.* *7. Seems like the ancient Greeks were a bit more enlightened than we are in matters of gender equality. Women's freestyle wrestling didn't become an Olympic sport until 2004.*
∞ *9th* ∞ **After scoring a point, the opponent must be given time to rise on his/her feet and a few moments more before the wrestling may continue.**	
∞ *10th* ∞ **The match is both started and ended at the signal of the referee.**	

RULES	NOTES
∞ *11th* ∞ **The referee can at any time stop the match if s/he believes a point has been scored but the contestants have continued to wrestle unaware of the point having been scored.**	
∞ *12th* ∞ **The referee or other officials in charge of the contest, if other officials are presiding, shall resolve any dispute the contestants have over scoring, and their decision shall be final.**	
∞ *13th* ∞ **The wrestling-ground shall be a large square, 28.5 by 28.5 Metres, or any other size determined by the holders of the games, and it shall be all of sand or earth.**[8]	*8. The standard wrestling area today—42 feet by 42 feet for college events—is roughly half the size of the described arena. And mats of polyethylene foam have replaced the "sand or earth."*
∞ *14th* ∞ **The contestants shall begin the match at the center of the wrestling-ground outside of each other's touching-range,**[9] **the precise distance being at the discretion of the referee.**	*9. This "no touch" start to the match is reminiscent of the opening stance of a Greco-Roman contest, in which only above the waist holds are legal. Freestyle matches begin with one wrestler on all fours and the other behind him, grabbing his waist and an arm.*
∞ *15th* ∞ **All other more specific details are at the discretion of the officials presiding over the games.**	

WAR GAMES
COMBAT ROOTS OF SPORTS

Describing athletes as warriors may seem hyperbolic, but games have long served as a proxy for actual hostilities, from the man-to-man combat of wrestling to the territorial acquisition of football.

ARCHERY

Archery was the foremost tool of warfare from prehistoric times until the invention and spread of firearms resulted in its slow transformation to a recreational activity. One of the earliest recorded archery matches took place in Finsbury (now central London) in 1583.

FENCING
Fencing began as a training exercise for soldiers and elites, then evolved into a form of staged entertainment in Europe during the sixteenth and seventeenth centuries. The modern stylized sport we recognize took root in Italy and France in the 1800s.

JAVELIN
Roughly 5 million years ago, Senegalese chimps were already sharpening sticks for prehistoric combat and showing early humans how to do the same. Another 4,997,500 years (give or take) would pass until throwing a light spear—a javelin—the farthest distance became a sport in the Olympics.

LONG JUMP

A long jump has been useful on the battlefield since the world had puddles, but Greek armies formalized it as a method of training. Mounting competition among soldiers prompted the addition of the long jump to the Olympics as one of the five pentathlon challenges. It was considered to be one of the most difficult events because of a particular wrinkle: competitors jumped while carrying weights.

POLE VAULT

Vaulting poles were commonly used in ancient societies to conquer the daily challenge of navigating marshy areas or crossing narrow bodies of water. The Greeks used similar implements to hurdle enemy walls or mount animals. The first known competition was held in the Irish Tailteann Games, though, which began in 1829 BC.

SHOOTING SPORTS

Invented in ninth-century China, gunpowder would be around for three hundred years before it was used to power the first firearm: a bamboo tube that shot small tile pieces a few feet. Not long after, these weapons of war were repurposed for sport, and shooting matches were organized in Germany during the thirteenth century.

SHOT PUT

From none other than the most legendary of battlefields do we get our first glimpse of what would morph into the modern shot put: during the Siege of Troy, Homer tells us, Greek soldiers tried their hand at rock-throwing contests. In the eleventh century, at the Scottish Highland Games, the farthest throw signaled the strongest man and the mightiest warrior. European soldiers of the Middle Ages routinely staged cannonball-throwing contests. And so it has continued through the centuries.

SOURCES

The primary and secondary sources listed below represent what was for us an unusual process of research and synthesis. Populating this book led our team to hundreds of websites and publications, the majority having to do with sports but more than a few dealing with seemingly unrelated topics. But any broad history of sports is also an accounting of many other arcs of human endeavor—including commerce, culture, politics, religion, science, warfare—over time and across continents.

BOOKS

Belsky, Gary, and Neil Fine. *23 Ways to Get to First Base: The ESPN Uncyclopedia.* New York: ESPN Books, 2007.

Bodleian Library. *The Original Laws of Cricket.* Oxford: Bodleian Library, 2008.

———. *The Original Rules of Golf.* Oxford: Bodleian Library, 2009.

———. *The Original Rules of Rugby.* Oxford: Bodleian Library, 2007.

———. *The Original Rules of Tennis.* Oxford: Bodleian Library, 2010.

———. *The Rules of Association Football, 1863.* Oxford: Bodleian Library, 2006.

Bohn, Henry G., et al, eds. *Bohn's New Hand-Book of Games: Comprising Whist, Draughts, and Billiards.* Philadelphia: Henry F. Anners, 1856.

Camp, Walter, ed. *Spalding's Official Foot Ball Guide for 1906.* Carlisle, Penn.: Tuxedo Press, 2011.

Diamond, Dan, et al. *Total Hockey: The Official Encyclopedia of the National Hockey League.* Kingston, N.Y.: Total Sports, 2000.

Egan, Pierce. *Grose's Classical Dictionary of the Vulgar Tongue, Revised and Corrected, with the Addition of Numerous Slang Phrases Collected from Tried Authorities.* London: Grose, 1823.

Fielden, Greg, Bryan Hallman, and the auto editors of *Consumer Guide*. *NASCAR: The Complete History.* Lincolnwood, Ill.: Publications International Ltd., 2014.

Gross, Mary E., ed. *The Playground Book.* Cincinnati: Cincinnati Playgrounds, 1917.

Hotchkiss, John F. *500 Years of Golf Balls: History and Collector's Guide.* Dubuque, Iowa: Antique Trader Books, 1997.

Hult, Joan S., and Marianna Trekell, eds. *A Century of Women's Basketball: From Frailty to Final Four.* Reston, Va.: American Alliance for Health, Physical Education, Recreation, and Dance, 1991.

Kirchberg, Connie. *Hoop Lore: A History of the National Basketball Association.* Jefferson, N.C.: McFarland, 2007.

Liberman, Noah. *Glove Affairs: The Romance, History, and Tradition of the Baseball Glove.* Chicago: Triumph Books, 2003.

Noxon, Christopher. *Rejuvenile: Kickball, Cartoons, Cupcakes, and the Reinvention of the American Grown-up*. New York: Broadway Books, 2007.

O'Connor, Brendan, Neil Fine, and Gary Belsky. *Answer Guy: Extinguishing the Burning Questions of Sports with the Water Bucket of Truth.* New York: ESPN Books, Hyperion, 2002.

Thorn, John. *Baseball in the Garden of Eden: The Secret History of the Early Game.* New York: Simon & Schuster, 2012.

Thorn, John, Pete Palmer, and Michael Gershman. *Total Baseball: The Official Encyclopedia of Major League Baseball.* Kingston, N.Y.: Total Sports, 2001.

Waggoner, Glen, Kathleen Moloney, and Hugh Howard. *Baseball by the Rules: Pine Tar, Spitballs, and Midgets.* New York: Prentice Hall, 1990.

Walker, Douglas, and Graham Walker. *The Official Rock Paper Scissors Strategy Guide.* New York: Simon & Schuster, 2004.

WEBSITES

abcboxing.com
abcnews.go.com
about.com
americanprofile.com
americascup.com
amhistory.si.edu
ancient.eu
answers.yahoo.com
antiqueathlete.com
antiquehickorygolfclubs.com
athleticscholarships.net
augustasouthernnationals.org
baseball-almanac.com
baseball-reference.com
baseballglovecollector.com
basketballcoaching101.com
bbc.com
birthplaceofhockey.com
blackbeltmag.com
blackenterprise.com
bleacherreport.com
bloodyelbow.com
bloomberg.com
bowl.com
bowlingacademyinc.com
bowlingball.com
bowlingballs.us
bowlingmuseum.com
boxinghalloffame.com
britannica.com
businessinsider.com
cagepotato.com
candlepinbowling.com
cardschat.com
casinoarticles.com
cbsnews.com
cfbhall.com
cnn.com
coachup.com
collections.library.appstate.edu
cricket-rules.com
cs.purdue.edu
deadspin.com
dickssportinggoods.com
dictionary.reference.com
discovery.com
duckpins.com
ejmas.com
entertainment.howstuffworks.com
epicsports.com
espn.go.com
espncricinfo.com
f1h2o.com
facebook.com
factsaboutpoker.com
fantasyjudgment.com
fieldhockey.isport.com
fieldhockeybc.com
fifa.com
fih.ch
flowingdata.com
foxsports.com
fsta.org
funtrivia.com
getkempt.com
golf-information.info
golfing-scotland.com
golfball-guide.de
golfballmuseum.co.uk
golfeurope.com
hamptonroads.com
helpwithbowling.com
historical-pankration.com
history.co.uk
history.com
historyofsoccer.info
hooptactics.com
igfgolf.org
ikf.org
imgur.com

immaf.org
indianapolismotorspeedway.com
intotherough.co.uk
itftennis.com
japan-guide.com
judoinfo.com
kickassfacts.com
kickball.com
kickballstrategies.com
kshs.org
lastwordonsports.com
latimes.com
lawupdates.com
laxpower.com
majorleaguelacrosse.com
mastersgames.com
mentalfloss.com
mixedmartialsarts.com
mlb.com
mlive.com
mmafacts.com
mmafighting.com
mmaratings.net
motorsport.com
mrbaseball.com
myinterestingfacts.com
nascar.com
nationalgallery.org.uk
nba.com
ncaa.org
nfl.com
nhl.com
19cbaseball.com
nj.com
npr.org
nwcaonline.com
nytimes.com
oldbowling.com
oldlawnmowerclub.co.uk
olympic.org
pittsburghmma.com
planetseed.com
poker.com
pokerlistings.com
profootballhof.com
pubquizreference.co.uk
raiders.com
randa.org
rugbyfootballhistory.com
rugbynetwork.net
rugbyschool.net
samkass.com
scottishgolfhistory.org
sfia.org
shinty.com
shuffleboard.net
si.com
skittlealleysales.com
softschools.com
sports.yahoo.com
sports-information.org
sports-memorabilia-museum.com
sportsartifacts.com
sportycious.com
statista.com
tailteanngames.com
teamusa.org
theatlantic.com
thegamblersedge.com
thehockeynews.com
theopen.com
thepeoplehistory.com
thesportjournal.org
todayifoundout.com
topendsports.com
trackandfield.about.com
twoplustwo.com
ufc.com
ultimatefrisbee.com
underdognation.com
uni-watch.com
unitedworldwrestling.org
urbanoyster.com
usab.com

usabandy.com
usabaseball.com
usabasketball.org
usabroomball.com
usasoccer.com
usasumo.com
usatoday.com
usaultimate.org
usavolleyball.org
usga.org
uslacrosse.org
usta.org
volleyball.org
washingtonpost.com
wfdf.com
whatisultimate.com
wiffle.com
wikipedia.com
wimbledon.com
wisegeek.com
womenboxing.com
wordorigins.org
worldrps.com
worldsoccer.about.com
ymca.int

ACKNOWLEDGMENTS

The team at Artisan is as impressive as any we've encountered in publishing. Shoshana Gutmajer, our editor, pushed us to make the information in this volume as accessible and layered as it could and should be. For that, not to mention her enthusiasm for artful bookmaking, we will be forever grateful. Maureen Clark, copy editor and fact-checker extraordinaire, wowed us throughout this process with her careful attention and skill, as did Sibylle Kazeroid, our production editor. Sarah Rutherford's sublime illustrations bring this book alive in ways we never imagined, all of them beautiful. That her images and our words play so nicely together is a credit to the design team of Jacob Covey, Michelle Ishay-Cohen, and Renata Di Biase. Many thanks as well to Nancy Murray, production director; Allison McGeehon, director of publicity and marketing; and Mura Dominko, assistant editor. And, of course, none of this teamwork would have been possible without the vision of Artisan's publisher, Lia Ronnen, who thought to ask us for ideas in the first place. That was very kind of you, Lia.

Jane Dystel, our agent, is as fierce an advocate as any authors could want. And, in the end, she's in this business for all the right reasons, including a love of books that's in her DNA.

A handful of institutions and individuals were especially helpful to us in identifying and/or locating some of the rules we used, including The Hockey Museum, Woking, England (field hockey); The Wiffle Ball, Inc.; the Collegiate Football Hall of Fame (American football); the United States Bowling Congress; and Andrew Sam Mousalimas (GOPPPL).

We are especially grateful to the team at (and associates of) Elland Road Partners, our content and editorial consultancy, through which we undertook this project: Brendan O'Connor, a one-of-a-kind chronicler of popular sports history; Glen Waggoner, who writes with flair and enthusiasm; Deanna Cioppa, who writes with flair and ferocity; Ryan Hockensmith and Ryan McGee, whose knowledge of mixed martial arts and stock car racing, respectively, was invaluable to our treatment of those sports; Morty Ain and Ezra Roberts, whose research into fantasy sports and basketball, respectively, was keen and crucial; Nick Harris, who has forgotten more about cricket than we could ever hope to know; Isabelle Danforth Stillman and Samuel Franklin Tasch, whose research and prose can be found throughout; Haylin Belay, transcriber nonpareil; Carl Carccia, research whiz, who is as patient as he is dogged; and, of course, our valued friends and former colleagues Craig Winston, Milkov Gueorgui and Dale Brauner, of whom—if you knew what they can do and how gracious they are when doing it—you too would seek assistance and guidance as often as we have.

INDEX

ABOUT THE AUTHORS

Gary Belsky and Neil Fine are the former editor in chief and executive editor, respectively, of *ESPN The Magazine*, with more than three decades of combined experience in sports media. Founding partners of the editorial consulting firm Elland Road Partners, they have written several books together, including *23 Ways to Get to First Base: The ESPN Uncyclopedia* and *Answer Guy: Extinguishing the Burning Questions of Sports with the Water Bucket of Truth*.